B¢
$20.00
May '79

KEYNES, CAMBRIDGE AND *THE GENERAL THEORY*

Keynes, Cambridge and *The General Theory*

The process of criticism and discussion
connected with the development of
The General Theory

Proceedings of a conference held at the
University of Western Ontario

Sponsored by
The University of Western Ontario
The Hebrew University of Jerusalem
The Canada Council

Edited by
DON PATINKIN and J. CLARK LEITH

University of Toronto Press
Toronto and Buffalo

© Don Patinkin and J. Clark Leith 1978

All rights reserved. No part of this publication may be reproduced or transmitted, in any form or by any means, without permission

Published in the United Kingdom 1978 by
THE MACMILLAN PRESS LTD

First published 1978 in Canada and the United States of America by
UNIVERSITY OF TORONTO PRESS
Toronto and Buffalo

ISBN 0–8020–2296–0

Printed in Great Britain

Contents

	Preface	vii
	Programme Participants	x
1	Introductory Remarks *Grant Reuber*	1
2	The Process of Writing *The General Theory*: A Critical Survey *Don Patinkin*	3
3	Keynes and his Cambridge Colleagues *Austin Robinson*	25
4	Keynes as Seen by his Students in the 1930s (i) *Robert B. Bryce*; (ii) *Walter S. Salant*; (iii) *Lorie Tarshis*	39
5	Cambridge Discussion and Criticism Surrounding the Writing of *The General Theory*: A Chronicler's View *Donald E. Moggridge*	64
	Discussion	72
6	Keynes as a Literary Craftsman *Elizabeth Johnson*	90
7	Cambridge as an Academic Environment in the Early 1930s: A Reconstruction from the Late 1940s *Harry G. Johnson*	98
	Discussion	115

APPENDIXES

I	Robert B. Bryce's 1935 paper on 'An Introduction to a Monetary Theory of Employment' and related correspondence with Keynes	127
II	Correspondence between Richard F. Kahn and Don Patinkin on the 1931 multiplier article and the Cambridge 'Circus'	146
III	Some Comments on Keynesianism and the Swedish Theory of Expansion Before 1935 *Bertil Ohlin*	149
	Bibliography	166
	Index of names	175
	Index of subjects	181

Preface

In the history of modern economic ideas, Keynes's *General Theory* is famous not only for the revolution which it wrought in macroeconomic theory, but also for the legendary process of criticism and discussion which accompanied its development. It was this creative process which was the subject of the Conference whose results are presented here.

Until recently, most of what we knew about the process was by way of oral tradition. But in the framework of the magnificent edition of *The Collected Writings of John Maynard Keynes* which the Royal Economic Society has been publishing under the general editorship of Sir Austin Robinson, we were provided in 1973 with Volume XIII (edited by Donald Moggridge), containing a wealth of fascinating and hitherto unpublished correspondence and documents relating to it. The purpose of the Conference (held in October 1975) was to shed more light on the nature of this creative process by generating a dialogue between the oral and written history of ideas: between some of the individuals who had actually participated in the process and others who had studied (and in some cases also edited) the new documentary evidence. It was hoped that from this dialogue would emerge a better understanding of the inner workings of the process; the stages through which it proceeded and its influence on the final form of the *General Theory*; the personalities involved in the different stages and the respective roles they played, and the role of the famed 'Cambridge Circus' in particular; and the social and institutional framework within which these personalities worked and interacted.

In order to increase the fruitfulness of the dialogue, the Conference was kept small and informal. Thus discussion took place not only during the periods formally assigned for that purpose, but frequently also in the wake of interjections which were made during the presentation of the papers themselves. In this connection we should note that this volume is not, strictly speaking, a proceedings volume. Thus for example, in preparing their papers for publication (and we should here note that not all the participants did so) the authors were encouraged to revise them so as to incorporate the material of the aforementioned interjections. Similarly, they were encouraged to add to or elaborate upon their original contributions in accordance with any further memories or thoughts that they had in the wake of the Conference: for, after all, one of the purposes of the Conference was to generate such thoughts. Despite such revisions, however, the papers as here published do not differ basically from their form as presented. And except for some minor deletions, the same is true of the record of the discussion. This discussion was recorded on tape, and the published record represents a slightly edited version of the resulting transcription.

Some relevant biographical information about the programme participants – and in particular about their respective relations to Keynes or 'Keynesiology' – is provided in the list which follows. In addition, the Conference was attended by one or two representatives from most of the major Canadian universities.

For a variety of reasons, we were not able to have all the individuals whom we would have wanted to participate in the programme of the Conference. We are, however, happy that Lord Kahn and Bertil Ohlin have agreed to supplement this volume: the former with some earlier correspondence of his that bears on his famous multiplier article (Appendix II); the latter with direct comments on the proceedings of our Conference which he has presented in the form of a detailed paper on the relationship between Keynes and the Swedish school (Appendix III). We find this paper particularly significant for bringing out the fact that such a relationship existed even before the publication of the *General Theory*. We are also indebted to Lord Kahn, who is Keynes's literary executor, for granting permission to reproduce unpublished materials from the Keynes Papers.

In preparing this volume for publication, we have not standardised the spelling of words which are rendered differently in the different English-speaking countries from which our participants came. We have, however, standardised the system of bibliographical references. In particular, all page references to those of Keynes's writings which have already been reproduced in the *Collected Writings*, are to that edition. Keynes's books, however, are referred to by their original titles, sometimes supplemented by their respective volume numbers in that edition. The other volumes of that edition are referred to as *JMK* XIII, *JMK* XIV, and so forth, as the case may be.

As Grant Reuber explains in his introductory remarks, this Conference was jointly sponsored by the University of Western Ontario, the Hebrew University of Jerusalem, and the Canada Council. Our thanks to all of these institutions for this help.

David Laidler shared in many of the burdens of organising the Conference. The efficient support of the administrative staff of the Department of Economics at the University of Western Ontario – and of Judy Collis, Lillian Everest, and Marg Grant, in particular – contributed immeasurably to the smooth running of the Conference. The proceedings were clearly taped by Peter Krickmire and then transcribed by Ms. Tony Griffiths. Subsequent typing was efficiently carried out by Gwendoline Cohen in Jerusalem. Gabrielle Brenner, also of Jerusalem, provided valuable technical assistance, particularly with respect to the preparation of the bibliography. Dale Knisely has helped with the index. To all of

Preface

these individuals we are greatly indebted.

The work of the first of the undersigned was in part supported by a research grant from the Ford Foundation. He would like to express his sincerest appreciation to the Foundation, as well as to the Maurice Falk Institute for Economic Research in Israel which is administering it.

The editorial work of Leith was completed while he was visiting the Institute for International Economic Studies, Stockholm. The use of the Institute's facilities in this work is gratefully acknowledged.

As a token of their recognition of the great contribution to scholarship which the Royal Economic Society is making by its publication of *The Collected Writings of John Maynard Keynes*, the participants in this volume have decided to contribute any proceeds resulting from it to the Society in order to provide further support for this all-important project.

Jerusalem Don Patinkin
London, Ontario J. Clark Leith

It was with a deep sense of sadness that we learned of the death of Harry Johnson in May 1977. He strove tirelessly to advance the cause of economic science in all its dimensions, and in virtually all parts of the world, never ceasing in his quest for deeper understanding of both economic theory and policy. His untimely death is a great loss to the profession.

D.P.
J.C.L.

Programme Participants

Haim Barkai.   Associate Professor of Economics, Hebrew University of Jerusalem. BA, Hebrew University, 1952; PhD, London School of Economics, 1958.

Robert B. Bryce. Canadian public official since 1938. BSc (Engineering), University of Toronto, 1932. Student, Cambridge University, 1932–5, BA 1934. Research student, Harvard University, 1935–7. Secretary to the Canadian Government Advisory Committee during World War II. Secretary to the Cabinet 1954–1963; Deputy Minister of Finance 1963–70. Executive Director, International Monetary Fund, 1971–5.

Elizabeth Johnson. Editor, *The Collected Writings of John Maynard Keynes*, Vols. XV–XVIII. BA, University of Toronto; MS, Columbia University.
Author: 'The Collected Writings of John Maynard Keynes: Some Visceral Reactions' (1972); 'John Maynard Keynes: Scientist or Politician?' (1972); (with Harry Johnson) 'The Social and Intellectual Origins of *The General Theory*' (1974).

Harry G. Johnson.   Until his death in May 1977, Charles F. Grey Distinguished Service Professor of Economics, University of Chicago. BA, University of Toronto, 1943; MA, Cambridge University, 1951; PhD, Harvard University, 1958; Assistant Lecturer, Cambridge University, 1949; Lecturer, Cambridge University and Fellow, King's College, Cambridge, 1950–6.
Author: '*The General Theory* After Twenty-Five Years' (1961); 'The Keynesian Revolution and the Monetarist Counter-Revolution' (1972); 'Keynes and British Economics' (1975); (with Elizabeth Johnson) 'The Social and Intellectual Origins of *The General Theory*' (1974).

J. Clark Leith.   Associate Professor and Chairman (1972–6), Department of Economics, University of Western Ontario. BA, University of Toronto, 1959; MS 1960, PhD 1967, University of Wisconsin.

Donald E. Moggridge.   Professor of Economics, Scarborough College, University of Toronto. Editor, *The Collected Writings of John Maynard*

Keynes, Vols. XIII and XIV, as well as Vols. XIX to XXIX (forthcoming). BA, University of Toronto, 1965; MA Cambridge University, 1968; PhD Cambridge University, 1970.
Author: 'From the *Treatise* to *The General Theory*: An Exercise in Chronology' (1973); (with Susan Howson) 'Keynes on Monetary Policy, 1910–46' (1974); 'Keynes: The Economist' (1974); *Keynes* (1976); editor, *Keynes: Aspects of the Man and his Work* (1974).

Don Patinkin. Professor of Economics, Hebrew University of Jerusalem, and Visiting Professor of Economics, University of Western Ontario. BA 1943, PhD 1947, University of Chicago.
Author: 'Keynesian Monetary Theory and the Cambridge School' (1974); 'The Collected Writings of John Maynard Keynes: From the *Tract* to *The General Theory*' (1975); *Keynes' Monetary Thought: A Study of Its Development* (1976); 'Keynes and Econometrics: On the Interaction Between the Macroeconomics Revolutions of the Interwar Period' (1976).

Grant Reuber. Professor of Economics; Vice-President (Academic) and Provost, University of Western Ontario. BA, University of Western Ontario, 1950; MA 1954, PhD 1957, Harvard.

Sir Austin Robinson. Professor emeritus, Cambridge University, and General Editor, *The Collected Writings of John Maynard Keynes*. BA, Cambridge University, 1920. Lecturer in Economics at Cambridge, 1923–6 and 1929–49, Reader 1949–50, Professor 1950–65. Secretary of the Faculty Board at Cambridge, 1930–4.
Author: 'John Maynard Keynes 1883–1946' (1947); 'Could there have been a *General Theory* without Keynes?' (1964); 'John Maynard Keynes: Economist, Author, Statesman' (1972); 'Keynes: A Personal View' (1975).

Walter S. Salant. Senior Fellow, Brookings Institution. BS 1933, MA 1937, PhD, 1962, Harvard; student at Cambridge University, 1933–4.
Author: 'A Note on the Effects of a Changing Deficit' (1939); 'The Demand for Money and the Concept of Income Velocity' (1941); 'Introduction to William A. Salant's "Taxes: the Multiplier and the Inflationary Gap"' (1975).

Paul A. Samuelson. Institute Professor, Massachusetts Institute of Technology. BA, University of Chicago, 1935; MA 1936, PhD 1941, Harvard.
Author: 'Interactions between the Multiplier Analysis and the Principle of Acceleration' (1939); 'A Statistical Analysis of the Consumption Function' (1941); 'Lord Keynes and *The General Theory*'

(1946); 'The Simple Mathematics of Income Determination' (1948); 'A Brief Survey of Post-Keynesian Developments' (1963); 'The Balanced-Budget Multiplier: A Case Study in the Sociology and Psychology of Scientific Discovery' (1975).

Lorie Tarshis. Professor of Economics, Scarborough College, University of Toronto. Emeritus Professor of Economics, Stanford University. BComm, University of Toronto, 1932. Student at Cambridge University, 1932–6; BA 1934, PhD 1939, Cambridge University.
Author: 'Changes in Real and Money Wages' (1939); 'An Exposition of Keynesian Economics' (1948); 'The Elasticity of the Marginal Efficiency Function' (1961).

Donald Winch. Professor of the History of Economics, University of Sussex. BSc(Econ.) London, 1956, PhD Princeton, 1960.
Author: 'The Keynesian Revolution in Sweden' (1966); *Economics and Policy: A Historical Study* (1969; revised ed., 1972); (with Susan Howson) *The Economic Advisory Council, 1930–9; A Study in Economic Advice During Depression and Recovery* (1977).

OTHER CONTRIBUTORS

Lord Kahn. Professor emeritus, Cambridge University. BA Cambridge University, 1927. Fellow of King's College from 1930 to present. Author: 'The Relation of Home Investment to Unemployment' (1931); 'The Financing of Public Works: A Note' (1932); *Selected Essays on Employment and Growth* (1972).

Bertil Ohlin. Professor emeritus, Stockholm School of Economics. Cand.phil. Lund, 1917; BEc Stockholm School of Economics, 1919; MA Harvard 1923; PhD University of Stockholm, 1924.
Author: 'Transfer Difficulties, Real and Imagined' (1929); 'Introduction' to Knut Wicksell, *Interest and Prices*, (1936); 'Some Notes on the Stockholm Theory of Saving and Investment' (1937); 'Alternative Theories of the Rate of Interest: A Rejoinder' (1937); *The Problem of Employment Stabilization* (1949): also relevant Swedish publications discussed by Steiger (1976).

1 Introductory Remarks

GRANT REUBER

It is a pleasure to welcome you to this University and a privilege for me to open this Conference on Keynes, Cambridge, and *The General Theory*. We are especially pleased to have as our co-sponsors of this Conference the Hebrew University of Jerusalem. Both universities accept the fact that for some purposes at least money does matter and we wish to acknowledge the financial assistance of the Canada Council which has made this Conference possible. I would also like to acknowledge at this point the hard work done by Professor Leith and others in the Department here in planning the Conference and in making the necessary arrangements.

As you may recall, Keynes concluded the *General Theory* by extolling the importance of the ideas of economists and political philosophers. As he put it, 'the world is ruled by little else.' And he went on to declare in the final sentence of the book that 'soon or late, it is ideas, not vested interests, which are dangerous for good or ill.' The theme of this conference is to consider the process of discussion and criticism at Cambridge associated with the writing of the *General Theory*. In pursuing this theme, we are engaged in a study of the history of ideas, ideas that have transformed our subject intellectually and have also transformed public policy throughout the world. In reexamining the development of Keynes's ideas we are paying tribute not only to the author of those ideas but also to the primacy of ideas and intellect.

During the past decade Keynes's views have been undergoing a reassessment. This process has of course been greatly stimulated in recent years by the appearance of *The Collected Writings of John Maynard Keynes* published under the auspices of the Royal Economic Society. Some fourteen volumes have now appeared and more are forthcoming.

I suppose that if Keynes is looking down upon us from some heavenly height today, he will not be particularly surprised to see an international conference devoted to an examination of the history of his ideas. He may, however, be puzzled to find the Conference sponsored by an Israeli and a Canadian university, and he is almost sure to be perplexed to find it taking place in the wrong London – a place of which he was probably totally unaware throughout his lifetime. However, as a probabilist he will recognise that the unlikely can happen, and he will undoubtedly agree that this Conference reflects an unusually happy combination of circumstances.

The speakers at this Conference may be classified into two groups. Some knew Keynes personally as a colleague or as a teacher at Cambridge. The other group has played a leading role over the years in refining and criticising Keynes's ideas as well as examining the historical development of his thought. This juxtaposition, in addition to affording a variety of perspectives, also provides some indication of how the development of Keynes's thought, as revealed by the public record, compares with the impressions recalled by those who observed the process at first hand, and in some cases participated in it. Moreover, as is evident from the discussion that follows, the impressions gained by those at Cambridge in the thirties are by no means uniform – which is scarcely surprising when one considers the complexity, imagination and flair of the genius who created them.

2 The process of writing *The General Theory:* A Critical Survey [1]

DON PATINKIN

The subject of this Conference is a drama which took place in Cambridge in the early 1930s – the drama connected with the writing of the *General Theory*. Details of the *dramatis personae* will shortly be presented to us by Austin Robinson. Let me here only note that this was a great drama not only in retrospect, but also in the eyes of its protagonists at the time. Indeed, the huge mass of written materials that has survived from this drama is itself testimony to the conviction of these protagonists that these materials would ultimately have significant historical value.

Let me also note that this was a great drama not only from the purely intellectual viewpoint, but also from the socio-political one. For the period was one of fear and darkness as the Western world struggled with the greatest depression that it had known. A depression that appeared as some mysterious evil force which paralysed economies and inflicted the sufferings of unemployment upon millions: an evil force which no one knew how to overcome. In desperation, some countries even succumbed to totalitarian governments in an attempt to deal with the evil. And in those that did not, there was a definite feeling that by attempting to achieve a scientific understanding of the phenomenon of mass unemployment, one was not only making an intellectual contribution, but was also dealing with a critical problem that endangered the very existence of Western civilisation.

Our drama opens in 1930, though its antecedents obviously go back several years earlier. Keynes in 1930 is 47. He has just published a major work entitled *A Treatise on Money*. In his preface to the *General Theory*, Keynes describes that book as a 'natural evolution' from the *Treatise*. This may have been true in retrospect, but it certainly does not reflect Keynes's feelings at the time he wrote the *Treatise*. For at that time Keynes's regarded the *Treatise* not as a step in an ongoing evolution of his thinking, but as the definitive work on monetary economics for years to come: the *magnum opus* which would bring him worldwide scientific fame to match the worldwide popular fame he had achieved some ten years before as a result of the overnight success of his *Economic Consequences of the Peace* (1919).

Indeed, as Elizabeth Johnson's contribution to this Conference helps us understand, in the decade following the publication of his *Economic Consequences*, Keynes was better known as a publicist than as a scientist. Indeed, even his *Tract on Monetary Reform* (1923) was largely a reproduction of articles which he had published the year before in the *Manchester Guardian Commercial* – which undoubtedly explains why it is such a pleasure to re-read this book even today! Furthermore, though during the 1920s Keynes did publish many book reviews, obituaries, and biographical memoirs in the *Economic Journal* (of which he was then the editor), he published relatively few scientific articles proper, and none of them of much note until his famous exchange with Bertil Ohlin in 1929 on the German transfer problem.[2]

That Keynes at the time viewed the *Treatise* as his *magnum opus* is clear from his preface to the book, which he begins with the declaration that he proposes in it 'a novel means of approach to the fundamental problems of monetary theory.' And since the equations by means of which Keynes developed this approach in the book were designated by him as 'fundamental equations,' there can be little doubt as to how he regarded them! Similarly, in March 1930, when Keynes as a leading member of the Macmillan Committee felt that he should provide future witnesses with some guidance as to the questions at issue, what better way of doing so could there be than to distribute proofs of his forthcoming book among them?[3] Needless to say, the *Treatise* also provided the theoretical framework for the 'private testimony' which Keynes himself gave before the Committee at roughly the same time. And it again provided the framework for his June 1931 Harris lecture – a lecture in which Keynes gave a verbal rendition of his fundamental equations and went on to proclaim: 'That is my secret, the clue to the scientific explanation of booms and slumps (and of much else, as I should claim) which I offer you' (*JMK* XIII, p. 354).

In retrospect, the approach of the *Treatise* was a fairly simple one. It claimed that business cycles, or (to use the term of Keynes and his contemporaries) credit cycles, are caused by the alternation of profits and losses. Now, profits are caused by the excess of the price of a product over its cost of production, and losses by a shortfall. And so Keynes's analysis of the business cycle evolved into an analysis of what determines the price per unit of output relative to the cost per unit. This is the subject and the purpose of the so-called fundamental equations. I will not bother you with the obscure notation, so strange to us today, with which Keynes presented these equations. But when you finish examining these equations carefully, when you get down to their essence, what they say is the following:

index of price = index of cost of production + index of profits

– all per unit of output. And that is the fundamental equation!

Keynes recognises that this is an identity, and indeed says so. But he also says that it is an identity which is useful for classifying causal relationships. However, if we read the *Treatise* carefully, we find that Keynes frequently shifts across the very thin and indefinite line that lies between repeating an identity and trying to endow it with more meaning than it really has. Thus by making use of a special definition of income (namely, defining it to exclude excess profits) Keynes showed that the excess of investment over saving was equal to excess profits – and then claimed that such an excess *caused* an increase in price relative to costs.

Similarly, Keynes supplemented his fundamental equations with a dynamic theory which stated that a decline in the rate of interest (more specifically, of the 'market rate' relative to the 'natural rate') generated an excess of investment over saving, hence *generated* excess profits, and hence led firms to expand their output; conversely, a rise in the interest rate would generate losses and hence a contraction of output. Correspondingly, the way to stabilise prices, hence avoid excess profits or losses, and hence cycles, is for the Central Bank to adopt a policy of varying the market rate of interest so as to keep it equal to the natural rate.

I have noted the great aspirations which Keynes had for his *Treatise*: but as we all know, these aspirations were not to be fulfilled. For immediately upon publication, the *Treatise* met with criticism – some of it quite devastating – from friend and foe alike.

Among such friends were Ralph Hawtrey, who even before the final publication of the *Treatise* – on the basis of the galleys which Keynes had sent him for his comments – pointed out the tautological nature of the fundamental equations (*JMK* XIII, p. 152, points 9–10). Hawtrey also argued that the 'formula only takes account of the reduction of prices in relation to costs, and does not recognise the possibility of a reduction of output being caused directly by a contraction of demand without an intervening fall of price' (*JMK* XIII, p. 152, point 7). But because he was busy with other things (and I shall come back to this point later) Keynes did not make any changes in the galleys to take account of these criticisms. Indeed, he did not even reply to them until several months later, after the *Treatise* had already been published.

Much more sharply-worded criticisms were forthcoming from Friedrich von Hayek, then a young (32) professor at the London School of Economics, newly arrived from Vienna for the purpose of bringing the teaching of Austrian and Wicksellian economics to England. Hayek was at the time Keynes's leading rival in the field of business cycle theory and published a two-part critique of the *Treatise* in the pages of *Economica* (1931, 1932). One of Hayek's major points was that despite the fact that the difference between the market and natural rates of interest played a central role in Keynes's analysis, he does not explain what determines this natural rate. Keynes, says Hayek, refers to the strong similarities between his analysis and that of Wicksell; but Keynes does not realise that Wicksell based his analysis on Böhm-Bawerk's productivity theory of interest – a subject which is not even referred to in the *Treatise* (Hayek (1931), pp. 279 ff.).

Another source of criticism was the legendary Cambridge 'Circus', of which we have a representative with us today in the person of Austin Robinson. The term 'circus' here denotes 'circle' or more specifically 'circle of discussants', and I guess that today we would call it 'the Cambridge Seminar' or 'Cambridge Colloquium'. In any event, the 'Circus' consisted of a group of younger economists at Cambridge – all of them between 25 and 35 in age – who immediately after the publication of the *Treatise* in the fall of 1930 formed a seminar to discuss it. Its main members were Richard Kahn, James Meade, Piero Sraffa, Joan Robinson, Austin Robinson, and others on occasion – with Richard Kahn constituting the channel of communication between the group and Keynes. Keynes himself never participated in these discussions, and this (as will become clear later) may simply have been due to the fact that he did not have the time. In any event, one of Donald Moggridge's most valuable contributions as editor of Volumes XIII and XIV of the *Collected Writings* is his attempted reconstruction, on the basis of the 'pooled memories' of the aforementioned participants, of the major discussions of the 'Circus' during the first half of 1931 (*JMK* XIII, pp. 337–43). Thus one of the outcomes of these discussions was the demonstration that the paradox of the 'widow's cruse' which had so delighted Keynes in the *Treatise* (I, p. 125) was simply the consequence of his tacit assumption – which contradicted the basic general assumption of the *Treatise* – that despite the existence of profits, output remained constant (*JMK* XIII, p. 339).

Let me now say that I think the received version of the transition from the *Treatise* to the *General Theory* assigns too large a role to the discussions of the Cambridge 'Circus', and correspondingly too small a one to the criticisms of such individuals as Hawtrey, Robertson, and even Hayek. Thus in his aforementioned reconstruction, Moggridge reports that 'James Meade, an active participant in the discussions [of the Cambridge 'Circus'], returned to Oxford in the autumn of 1931 at the end of his year's visit to Trinity, Cambridge. He is cautiously confident that he took with him back to Oxford most of the essential ingredients of the subsequent system of the *General Theory*' (*JMK* XIII, p. 342). But as I shall later demonstrate, Meade could not have taken back with him that most essential ingredient of all – the theory of effective demand – which was not really developed until 1933. Similarly, I have not found support in the materials of *JMK* XIII and XIV for Joan Robinson's recent contention that these volumes show 'that there were moments when we had some trouble in getting Maynard to see what the point of his revolution really was' (Joan Robinson (1973), p. 3).

Insofar as the contributions of Hawtrey, Hayek, and Robertson are concerned, I can well understand how the frequent and frustrating failure to achieve communication with Keynes — and in particular the frequent and futile debates about terminology — has generated the impression that they contributed little if anything to the development of the *General Theory*. At the same time it should not be forgotten that Hawtrey and Hayek played an important role in bringing about one fundamental element of this development — namely, the broadening of Keynes's view of the nature of monetary theory. In particular, in the *Treatise*, as in most of the classic works in the field at that time,[4] 'monetary theory' was first and foremost a theory that explained the determination of the price level. And Hawtrey was the first one to point out to Keynes (doing so, as we have seen, even before the publication of the *Treatise*) that it was incumbent upon him also to supply a theory of output. But in accordance with his original view in the *Treatise*, Keynes (in his delayed reply of November 1930 to Hawtrey) rejected this contention and claimed that 'the question *how much* reduction of output is caused, whether by a realised fall of price or an anticipated fall of price, is important, but not strictly a monetary problem.' At the same time he went on to say 'if I were to write the book again, I should probably attempt to probe further into the difficulties of [the theory of short-run output]' — as indeed he was to undertake as the major objective of his *General Theory* (*JMK* XIII, pp. 145–6, italics in original).

Another aspect of the narrow view of monetary theory in the *Treatise* is its complete failure to make use of marginal analysis, something which was presumably considered to belong to value theory. Thus despite the fact that both the wage rate and *a fortiori* the rate of interest play major roles in the analysis of the *Treatise*, neither the marginal productivity of labor nor that of capital is even mentioned. This, of course, was the basis of Hayek's aforementioned complaint about the absence of a theory of capital and interest in the *Treatise*. On this point Keynes conceded (in the reply to Hayek that he published in *Economica* in November 1931) that 'later on, I will endeavour to make good this deficiency' (*JMK* XIII, p. 253). And this too was one of his major objectives in the *General Theory*.

I have noted that Keynes failed to fulfill his aspirations for the *Treatise*, and I would like now to suggest two circumstances connected with the writing of the *Treatise* that to my mind must have contributed to this failure. The first was the simple but frequently overlooked fact that Keynes too was of flesh and blood, subject like all mortals to the inexorable restraint that there are only 24 hours in the day; and there can be little doubt that Keynes just did not have enough hours to devote to the writing of the book, and especially of its final version. In particular, in August 1929, Keynes informed his publisher that he felt he had to 'embark upon a somewhat drastic rewriting' of what was then a one-volume book, for the most part in galley and page proof (*JMK* XIII, pp. 117–18). But three months later Keynes was appointed to the famous Macmillan Committee and proceeded to play a leading role in its deliberations

(Harrod (1951), p. 423). Then at the beginning of 1930 Keynes became a member – and a most active one – of the newly appointed Economic Advisory Council (see Howson and Winch (1976)). All this makes it difficult to believe that Keynes could have had enough time during 1930 to devote to the aforementioned final revision of the *Treatise* that he deemed necessary.

And indeed there are other indications of this pressure of time. Thus I have already mentioned that though Hawtrey had provided Keynes with basic criticisms of the *Treatise* before its publication (specifically, in the spring and summer of 1930), Keynes did not take account of them and did not even answer Hawtrey until a month after the book was published in October 1930. Keynes apologised for this delay in replying by explaining that he was, as we can well believe, 'overwhelmed' with work of the Macmillan Committee, the Economic Advisory Council 'and a hundred other matters' (*JMK* XIII, p. 133). And I suspect that this was also the reason that in 1930 Keynes did not give the series of lectures on monetary economics that it was his custom to give every fall term at Cambridge, and that in fall 1931 he deferred his lectures to the following spring.[5]

The second, and possibly related, adverse factor connected with the writing of the *Treatise* was, I conjecture, Keynes's failure to subject the book to enough pre-publication criticism. I know that this view too runs counter to the received one, according to which (to quote from the dust-jacket of its new edition) the *Treatise* was 'the outcome of six years of intensive work and argument with D. H. Robertson, R. G. Hawtrey, and others'. But all I can say is that the materials reproduced in *JMK* XIII provide very little indication of such 'work and argument,' and that which they do provide relates largely to discussions which took place during the last year before publication and thus (as in the case of Hawtrey) at too late a stage to have affected the final result. I also find support for this conjecture in Austin Robinson's statement in his 1947 memoir on Keynes that 'the fundamental equations of the *Treatise* ... were still relatively new and relatively undigested even by the people in Cambridge in closest touch with his work when the *Treatise* appeared in 1930' (1947, p. 53).[6]

And though it may make this sound like a morality play – like a didactic reaffirmation of the victory of good scientific procedures over bad ones – I would like to point out that in the writing of the *General Theory* the first of these adverse circumstances was much less in evidence, and the second, not at all. In particular, after the completion of the Macmillan Report in June 1931, Keynes seems to have been much less occupied than before with activities on behalf of the government. Similarly, after 1933 there was a falling-off in the intensity of his journalistic activities.[7] Correspondingly, I would conjecture that in the last two years before their respective publication, Keynes was able to concentrate far more on the writing of the *General Theory* than he had been able to on the writing of the *Treatise*.⁸ And insofar as pre-publication criticism of the *General Theory* is concerned, the wealth of material in *JMK* XIII speaks for itself, as indeed does the very subject of the present Conference.

May I continue in the spirit of a 'scientific morality play' to make one further point. In the wonderful memoir on Keynes that I have already mentioned, Austin Robinson (1947, p. 55) writes that it was a fortunate 'coincidence' that there was in the early 1930s 'a remarkable younger generation in Cambridge' who could supply criticism to Keynes as he developed his *General Theory*. But I suspect that an equally important part of this fruitful 'coincidence' was the fact that – as a result of his unhappy experience with the *Treatise* – Keynes then had a demand for such criticism! Similarly, when Keynes wrote in the preface to the *General Theory* that 'it is astonishing what foolish things one can temporarily believe if one thinks too long alone, particularly in economics (along with the other moral sciences), where it is often impossible to bring one's ideas to conclusive test either formal or experimental,' I suspect that he was also thinking of his own experiences with the *Treatise*.

My discussion until now has dealt with what can be denoted as the first stage of the process of criticism and discussion that marked the transition from the *Treatise* to the *General Theory*, a stage of (to borrow Moggridge's term) 'arguing out the *Treatise*.' It was a stage that can be said to have been more or less completed by the end of 1931. For by then the Cambridge 'Circus' as such was no longer in existence, and the aforementioned discussions with Hawtrey and Hayek had largely come to an end (though that with Robertson did continue through the first half of 1932). This first stage merged into a second one – the crucial, formative stage of writing the *General Theory*. Correspondingly, a necessary condition for discussing this stage in a meaningful way is first of all to specify the nature of the distinctive intellectual characteristic of the *General Theory* whose formation we wish to trace.

Let me, then, emphasise at the outset that the distinctive contribution of the *General Theory* is not the advocacy of a policy of public works expenditure. The *General Theory* is, as its name indicates, a book concerned with theory. It contains practically no discussion of policy. And in particular it contains only brief, passing discussions of the policy of public works expenditures. Furthermore, Keynes could not have seen the novelty of his book as lying in its advocacy of such a policy; for already in 1929, in his influential election pamphlet with Hubert Henderson entitled *Can Lloyd George Do It*, Keynes had been an outstanding and outspoken proponent of this policy. Correspondingly, the advocacy per se of public works expenditure was not the purpose of the *General Theory*; rather it was to provide a theoretical underpinning for such a policy.

In this connection let me digress for a moment and say that the failure to specify properly the nature of the distinctive contribution of the *General Theory* is a basic fault of a whole genre of literature which has grown up in the last few years with regard to alleged predecessors of Keynes. In most cases, when you start reading this literature, it turns out that what it describes are people who believed in public works expenditure before the *General Theory*. Thus one recent article of this genre[9] lists several economists in Germany who in 1930 and 1931 advocated public works expenditures – and cites Keynes's failure to refer to these economists as evidence that Keynes neglected the earlier literature. Now, there can be little doubt that Keynes was generally guilty of such a neglect; but this instance cannot be cited as a case in point. For if Keynes of the *General Theory* had wanted to cite earlier advocates of public works expenditure, he could have cited himself in 1929 and even earlier. Clearly, then, there is no basis for criticising him for not citing someone who had written in 1930 or 1931.

The distinctive contribution of the *General Theory* is instead best specified in the way Keynes himself did so in a letter he wrote to Roy Harrod in August 1936, commenting on the latter's review of the *General Theory*:

> ... You don't mention *effective demand* or, more precisely, the demand schedule for output as a whole, except in so far as it is implicit in the multiplier. To me the most extraordinary thing, regarded historically, is the complete disappearance of the theory of demand and supply for output as a whole, i.e. the theory of employment, *after* it had been for a quarter of a century the most discussed thing in economics. One of the most important transitions for me, after my *Treatise on Money* had been published, was suddenly realising this. It only came after I had enunciated to myself the psychological law that, when income increases, the gap between income and consumption will increase, – a conclusion of vast importance to my own thinking but not apparently, expressed just like that, to anyone else's. Then, appreciably later, came the notion of interest being the measure of liquidity preference, which became quite clear in my mind the moment I thought of it. And last of all, after an immense amount of muddling and many drafts, the proper definition of the marginal efficiency of capital linked up one thing with another. [*General Theory*, p. xv, italics in original; see also *JMK* XIV, p. 85.]

Now, Keynes himself had attributed the notion of the marginal efficiency of capital to Fisher; he did this somewhat late in the process of writing the *General Theory*, but then he did so generously. Insofar as the theory of liquidity preference is concerned, this is clearly a contribution of Keynes, but it is one that he had already developed considerably in the *Treatise*. This leaves the theory of effective demand as the distinctive analytical contribution of the *General Theory*.

Let me explain what I mean by the theory of effective demand, making

FIGURE 1

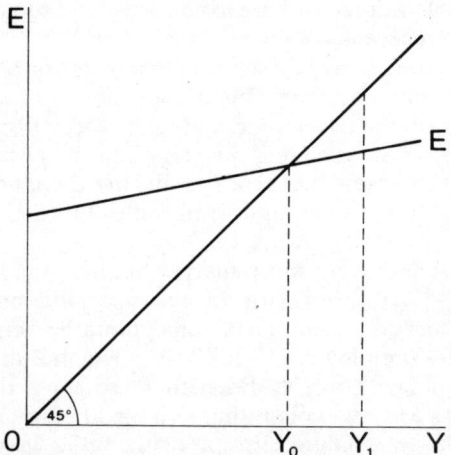

use (as Keynes unfortunately almost never did) of a diagram (figure 1). In particular, in terms of the familiar diagonal-cross diagram, it is not only that the intersection of the aggregate demand curve with the 45° line determines the equilibrium level of output Y_0, but even more so that changes in income themselves act as an equilibrating device. That is, if the economy is out of equilibrium at, say, Y_1, then the reduction in income itself will bring the economy to equilibrium by its influence on consumption or saving, depending on which language you wish to use. Correspondingly, as we have just seen, Keynes emphasises that a critical part of his analysis is the assumption that the marginal propensity to consume is less than unity. For if the marginal propensity to consume were equal to unity, you would not have any equilibrating device; for then as income would decrease, spending would decrease by exactly the same amount, so that any initial difference between aggregate demand and supply would remain unchanged. This is the crucial point of the *General Theory*: the theory of effective demand as a theory which equilibrates aggregate demand with supply by means of automatic changes in the level of output.

Now, you may feel that that is very obvious: it even appears on the front covers of some well known introductory textbooks. But we must be very careful. We have to put ourselves back forty-five years ago and even longer. The demand curve that the economist of that time had drilled into him was one based on the assumption of *ceteris paribus*. But how could you talk about a demand curve for output as a whole and keep other things constant? Thus the whole idea of transferring the concept of demand to aggregate demand was not as simple as one might think from the way we take it for granted today. Nor was it simple to conceive of a demand for aggregate output that was in some way different from aggregate income: as if national income expended could somehow differ from national income received.

That is part of the progress of science: that which once seemed difficult rapidly becomes commonplace. But on the other hand, when we come to study the history of the development of science, the history of the development of ideas, we have to put ourselves into the position of people of the time. And at that time the theory of effective demand was not at all a self-evident idea. It was a new and strange idea to which economists had to accustom themselves.

In order to bring this out more sharply, let me contrast Keynes's discussion in the *General Theory* with the corresponding one in the *Treatise* where Keynes considers a simple 'banana plantation' economy in an initial position of full-employment equilibrium which is disturbed because (in Keynes's words) 'into this Eden there enters a thrift campaign.' Keynes then proceeds to explain that as a result of the increased saving generated by this campaign, entrepreneurs suffer losses (for you will remember that in the *Treatise* the excess of savings over investment equals losses). Hence this will

> cause entrepreneurs to seek to protect themselves by throwing their employees out of work or reducing their wages. But even this will not improve their position, since the spending power of the public will be reduced by just as much as the aggregate costs of production. By however much entrepreneurs reduce wages and however many of their employees they throw out of work, they will continue to make losses so long as the community continues to save in excess of new investment. Thus there will be no position of equilibrium until either (a) all production ceases and the entire population starves to death; or (b) the thrift campaign is called off or peters out as a result of the growing poverty; or (c) investment is stimulated by some means or another so that its cost no longer lags behind the rate of saving [*Treatise* I, pp. 159–60].

In brief, it seems to me that Keynes is implicitly assuming here that the marginal propensity to spend is unity, so that a decline in output cannot reduce the excess of saving over investment and thus cannot act as an equilibrating force. Instead, the decline in output can come to an end either when it can decline no further: when 'all production ceases and the entire population starves to death' (and I cannot help but remark that the unhesitating way in which Keynes lists this coroner solution among the possible ones is yet another indication of his supreme confidence in the analysis of the *Treatise*). Alternatively, the decline might end as the result of some exogenous force that closes the gap between saving and investment: 'the thrift campaign is called off,' or 'investment is stimulated by some means or another.' And the very way in which Keynes also refers to the vague possibility that equilibrium might also be reestablished if 'the thrift campaign . . . peters out as a result of the growing poverty,' reveals how far he was then from seeing how changes in output – and hence income – act as a systematic influence on saving, and hence (via a marginal propensity to consume which is less than unity) as an endogenous, systematic equilibrating mechanism.[10]

Correspondingly, the question of when the formative stage of the *General Theory* had been completed is to me operationally defined as the question of when the theory of effective demand, inclusive of the foregoing equilibrating mechanism, was first formulated. Now it is true that there are some indications of such a mechanism in a letter which Keynes wrote to Kahn in September 1931 (*JMK* XIII, pp. 373–5); but the argument there is obscure and in any event does not seem to make use of the aforementioned systematic equilibrating mechanism.

A somewhat clearer indication of this mechanism is, however, to be found in a surviving fragment of a mid-1932 draft of the *General Theory* in which Keynes wrote:

> . . . it is natural to expect that, as the earnings of the public [E] decline, a point will eventually be reached at which the decline in total expenditure F, of both entrepreneurs and public taken together, will cease to be so great as the decline in E. For we can, I think, be sure that sooner or later the most virtuous intentions will break down before the pressure of increasing poverty, so that savings will fall off and negative saving will begin to appear in some quarter or another to offset the effect of losses on the expenditure of entrepreneurs. Sooner or later, for example, the determination of the government to pay for the dole out of additional taxation will break down; and even if it does not, the determination of the taxpayer to economise in his personal expenditure by the full amount of the additional taxes he must pay, will weaken. Indeed the mere law of survival must tend in this direction. . . .
>
> Indeed once we have reached the point at which spending decreases less than earnings decrease with investment stable, the attainment of equilibrium presents no problem. For provided that spending always increases less than earnings increase and decreases less than earnings decrease, i.e. provided ΔS and ΔE have the same sign, and that investment does not change, *any* level of output is a position of stable equilibrium. For any increase of output will bring in a retarding factor, since ΔS will be positive and consequently I being assumed constant, ΔQ will be negative; whilst equally any decrease of output will bring in a stimulating factor, since ΔS will be negative and consequently ΔQ positive. [*JMK* XIII, pp. 386–7, italics in original.]

The meaning of the symbols in the second paragraph of this passage is the same as in the *Treatise*; namely, S = saving, E = factor incomes (exclusive of abnormal profits), I = investment, and Q = profits, from which follows the crucial relation (again, as in the *Treatise*) $Q = I - S$. And this points up the most significant aspect of the mid-1932 draft: namely, that its analytical framework is basically still that of the *Treatise*. Indeed, the first paragraph of the foregoing passage – with its reference to the equilibrating effect of 'increasing poverty' – clearly echoes the second of the three alternatives in the passage from the *Treatise* which I have quoted earlier. Furthermore, and most important for our present purposes, the fact that the foregoing mid-1932 passage states that savings will begin to decline with declining output only after a certain 'pressure of poverty' is created, clearly shows that at that time Keynes had not yet fully recognised what he was later to designate as the 'conclusion of vast importance to [his] own thinking' about the 'psychological law that when income increases, the gap between income and consumption will increase' at all levels of income.[11]

It is also significant that the mid-1932 draft does not contain any explicit reference to the aggregate demand function or to its component consumption and investment functions. Nor do I think that this simply reflects a failure to state explicitly and formally what was implicitly understood. For Keynes's contention at the end of the foregoing passage that 'once we have reached the point at which spending decreases less than earnings . . . *any* level of output is a position of stable equilibrium' shows that he had not yet achieved a full understanding of the basic $C + I = Y$ equilibrium condition that was to constitute his theory of effective demand.

Further indication of the state of Keynes's thinking at the end of 1932 is provided by evidence which it is particularly appropriate to cite at this Conference: the unique 'archaeological' evidence on the chronology of the transition from the *Treatise* to the *General Theory* provided by Robert Bryce's notes on Keynes's lectures during the successive years 1932, 1933, and 1934 and Lorie Tarshis's notes for these years as well as 1935. These notes provide two independent observations on Keynes's thoughts on monetary economics in the fall of 1932, and like the mid-1932 draft of the *General Theory*, both of them show that at that time Keynes's thinking was still largely in the mold of the *Treatise*. The closest we find in these notes to what was to become the theory of effective demand was the following statement by Keynes, as recorded by Lorie Tarshis on 17 October, 1932:

> The decision of each individual re extent of disbursements will be affected by amount of income. If at a given level of distribution of income aggregate disbursement would add up to a different total (more) than amount of income – position untenable. Incomes will have to change until the total of income will add to

equal disbursement. Every individual disbursement alters individual incomes – I's and D's will change until amount of I's and D's are equal at a particular level.

Similarly, Bryce on that day recorded:

> If at a given level of income individual disbursement added up to more than income the position is untenable and change will be effected to position where aggregate community income equals disbursement. i.e. only rest is where aggregate income is equal to aggregate disbursements, due to effect of individual income on individual disbursements.

But like the mid-1932 draft, no further details are provided on the nature of the equilibrating process, and no explicit reference is made to the aggregate demand function and its component functions.[12]

And as a final bit of evidence on this point I would like to refer to the October 1933 article by Joan Robinson on 'The Theory of Money and the Analysis of Output' which (in her words eighteen years later) 'gives an outline of Keynes' theory as far as it had got in 1933' (Joan Robinson (1951), p. viii). In this article, Mrs. Robinson referred to the same revealing passage from the *Treatise* (I, pp. 159–60) that I have cited above and, implicitly making use of the analytical framework of the *Treatise*, quite correctly went on to say:

> [Keynes] points out that if savings exceed investment, consumption goods can only be sold at a loss. Their output will consequently decline until the real income of the population is reduced to such a low level that savings are perforce reduced to equality with investment. But [Keynes] completely overlooks the significance of this discovery, and throws it out in the most casual way without pausing to remark that he has proved that output may be in equilibrium at any number of different levels, and that while there is a natural tendency towards equilibrium between savings and investment (in a very long run), there is no natural tendency towards full employment of the factors of production. [Joan Robinson 1933, pp. 55–6.]

But the article did not refer explicitly to a consumption function, and *a fortiori* did not explain the crucial role that the less-than-unity marginal propensity to consume played in the equilibrating process. In brief, this article too did not contain the theory of effective demand.

When did Keynes first formulate the theory of effective demand? Our 'archaeological evidence' clearly indicates that this occurred during 1933. For in the lectures which Keynes gave in the fall of that year, we find him saying (according to Lorie Tarshis's notes for 20 November, 1933):

> We must assume this – relating peoples' consumption to their incomes. Not universally satisfactory but normally the psychological law is that the ΔC is $<$ the ΔY. The increment of consumption is less than increment of income. When their income increases they don't (over community as a whole) not whole of increase is spent on consumption. . . . This above law is not only necessary for the stability of the system but it also means that if propensity to spend is of such a character that $\Delta C < \Delta Y$ then ΔY can only be positive if ΔI is positive. There are two variables – the propensity to spend – the value of C corresponding to any value of Y – depending not only on Y now but expectations etc. Suppose that state of expectations is given – to every Y there corresponds a C and consequently one must choose that pair of values such that taking account of our given I, $Y = C + I$ holds. If we assume that as Y falls, C falls slower, and as Y rises, C rises at a different rate – there will be a set of values of C and Y to satisfy this.

And much the same thing is to be found in Bryce's corresponding notes. An even more explicit statement was presented by Keynes in a subsequent lecture when he said (according to Robert Bryce's notes[13] from 4 December, 1933):

> We have
> $$Y = C + I$$
> In a given state of the news
> In given w, C is a function of Y. $[C] = \phi_1(w,Y)$.
> I is a function of w [and the rate of interest, denoted by ρ] $= \phi_2(w,\rho)$
>   i.e. $Y = \phi_1(Y) + \phi_2(\rho)$ when w is given
> Hence it is largely ρ that is important.
> Assume given w.
> Suppose N total number of men employed
> N_1 producing for consumption
> N_2 producing for investment
> $N = N_1 + N_2$
> Assume propensity to spend and to consume given.
> Then $N_1 = f_1(N)$ $N_2 = f_2(\rho)$ (r[ate]. of i[nterest].)
> $N = f_1(N) + f_2(\rho)$.

So it is clear that by that time Keynes had achieved a full understanding of the theory of effective demand.

During the following months Keynes continued to work on his theory until he had developed it into the polished formulation which we find in the mid-1934 draft of the *General Theory*, the surviving fragments of which have been reproduced in *JMK* XIII (pp. 424–56). Indeed, this formulation of the theory of effective demand is in many ways more systematic and mathematically elegant than the one which finally appeared in the *General Theory*.[14]

Let me now relate all this to the central theme of our Conference – namely, the role of criticism and discussion in the development of the *General Theory*. And let me first of all observe that, like many lectures, Keynes's at Cambridge were also a form of dialogue: certainly implicitly so, and sometimes explicitly.[15] In any event, I feel that the challenge that confronted Keynes every fall to organise his thoughts so as to present in these lectures a report on 'work in progress' played an important and productive role in the development of the *General Theory*.

From the preceding account you will also understand my earlier contention that the discussions of the Cambridge 'Circus' could not have included the theory of effective demand. For the 'Circus' as such functioned only during 1930–1, whereas – as we have just seen – the theory of effective demand was developed only during 1933. On the other hand, during the formative period 1932–3, Keynes did carry on intensive discussions with two individuals who had been leading members of the 'Circus', namely, his two junior colleagues, Joan Robinson and, especially, Richard Kahn. But many of these discussions were oral, and even those that were written have for the most part been lost. So we are left in the unfortunate position of suffering from a paucity of material in *JMK* XIII for precisely that period which was the critical, formative one of the *General Theory*.

Before going on, let me discuss two pieces of counter evidence to my contention that Keynes first formulated his theory of effective demand in 1933. The first is the oft-cited statement in his June 1931 Harris Foundation lecture in which Keynes explained how an excess of savings generates a decline in output, and then went on to say:

> Now there is a reason for expecting an equilibrium point of decline to be reached. A given deficiency of investment causes a given decline of profit. A given decline of profit causes a given decline of output. Unless there is a constantly increasing deficiency of investment, there is eventually reached, therefore, a sufficiently low level of output which represents a kind of spurious equilibrium [*JMK* XIII, pp. 355–56].

At first sight, this would seem to be an adumbration of the unemployment-equilibrium notion of the *General Theory*. But closer examination of the context in which this paragraph appears indicates that this is not the case. For this context is one in which Keynes is analysing the forces which generate, not a continuing state of unemployment equilibrium, but the transitory stationary point at the trough of the business cycle. That is, what Keynes is analysing here is the causes of the eventual elimination of the excess of saving over investment which generates the slump, and its replacement at the turning point of the cycle by an opposite excess which then begins to generate the recovery.

What further distinguishes this discussion sharply from that of the *General Theory* is the fact that Keynes's primary explanation of why the economy reaches the aforementioned turning point is not in terms of variations in saving (which 'either varies in the wrong direction . . . or is substantially unchanged, or if it varies in the right direction, so as partly to compensate changes in investment, varies insufficiently,' *JMK* XIII, p. 354), but in terms of variations in investment. In particular, 'as soon as output begins to recover' (and Keynes does not really explain why this recovery occurs) 'the tide is turned and the decline in fixed investment is partly offset by increased investment in working capital' (ibid., p. 355). All this is far removed from the noncyclical analysis of the *General Theory* of the way in which an initial decline in investment generates a decrease in output which continues until the systematic downward influence such a decrease exerts on savings brings the economy to a new equilibrium position in which saving is once again equal to investment at the new, lower level of the latter – a level which remains unchanged throughout the adjustment process. In brief, all this is far removed from the systematic equilibrating role that changes in output – and consequent changes in saving – play in the *General Theory*.

The second item which is frequently cited as evidence of an early formulation of the theory of effective demand is Kahn's famous 1931 multiplier article.[16] The accompanying diagram (figure 2) presents the multiplier *as we teach it today*. An exogenous increase of ΔI in investment causes the aggregate demand curve to shift from E to E + ΔI, causing the equilibrium level of national income to increase to $Y_0 + \Delta Y$. Hence the multiplier is

$$\frac{\Delta Y}{\Delta I} = \frac{\Delta Y}{\Delta Y - \Delta C} = \frac{1}{1 - \frac{\Delta C}{\Delta Y}} = \frac{1}{1 - \text{MPC}},$$

where MPC is the marginal propensity to consume.

I said that this is the way we teach the multiplier today; and as such it clearly is a direct implication of the theory of effective demand. But this is *not* the way Richard Kahn first presented the multiplier in his 1931 article. And I am not simply saying that he did not present his analysis in terms of a diagram, but that (and this is the crucial point) he did not present it in the context of a comparative-statics equilibrium analysis of the level of national income. Instead, the multiplier of Kahn's article is the dynamic one, showing in terms of a declining geometric series the sequence of 'secondary employments' generated by a once-and-for-all increase in public works expenditures, and then deriving the multiplier by summing up this infinite series. Correspondingly, the notion of equilibrium is barely mentioned in Kahn's article; indeed it appears only once,

FIGURE 2

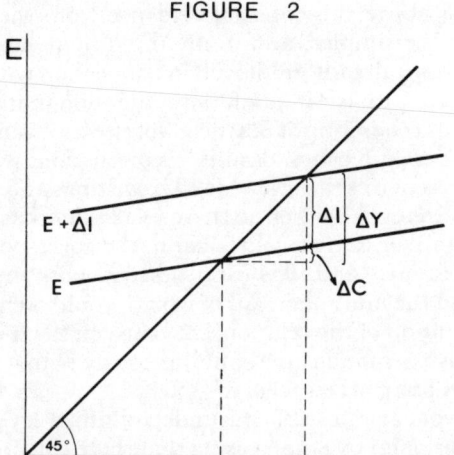

in a footnote (p. 12, n. 1) – and even then not with reference to the theory of effective demand.

There is another point that should be emphasised here. Kahn's article was written against the background of the already-mentioned Keynes–Henderson 1929 pamphlet on *Can Lloyd George Do It*; in that pamphlet Keynes not only advocates a policy of public-works expenditures, but also provides an explicit discussion of the 'primary' and 'secondary' employment which such expenditures generate – and (in a passage that is even more relevant for our purpose) goes on to say that 'the fact that many workpeople who are now unemployed would be receiving wages instead of unemployment pay would mean an increase in effective purchasing power which would give a general stimulus to trade' (*JMK* IX, pp. 103–7). Thus the idea that an initial public works expenditure would generate further increases in expenditure which in turn would generate further increases in employment was known before Kahn began his work on the multiplier. That was not what you needed Kahn for. Indeed, you needed him primarily for the opposite purpose. For the question was, if it is so good, why does it not go on to infinity? If you spend an additional pound, why does it not just keep on being spent by successive recipients until it employs everybody? Thus the real contribution of Kahn was less in demonstrating that the multiplier was greater than unity, than in defining and analysing the notion of leakages, and then demonstrating rigorously that as a result of these leakages the expansionary process converges to a finite limit. This is another reason why I do not consider the main thrust of Kahn's article to have been in the direction of the theory of effective demand.

But over and above this internal evidence from the text of Kahn's article, there is the simpler, and to my mind more conclusive, kind of evidence that I have already employed in connection with the discussion of the Cambridge 'Circus'. In brief, the contention that Kahn's 1931 article represented recognition of the theory of effective demand is inconsistent with the fact that Keynes, despite his discussions with Kahn at that time, did not present this theory in his 1932 writings and lectures.

Significantly enough, neither do these 1932 materials contain a reference to the multiplier. On the other hand, the corresponding materials for 1933 (lecture notes) and 1934 (draft) discuss both the theory of effective demand and the multiplier. All of which would seem to suggest that Keynes's recognition of the relationship between the multiplier and the theory of effective demand came simultaneously with – or perhaps even after – his formulation of this theory.[17]

In order to avoid any possible misunderstanding, let me conclude the discussion of this point by emphasising that there can be no doubt about the importance of Kahn's 1931 multiplier article in the history of the development of macroeconomic theory. Nor can there be any doubt that his multiplier formula can be derived directly from the theory of effective demand. But what I am saying is that this relationship was not seen by the protagonists of our drama at the time the article was first published. And though I am not sure it is relevant, I might add that – to the best of my knowledge – Richard Kahn has never claimed otherwise.[18]

Our story has now reached the middle of 1934. By the end of that year, galleys of the *General Theory* begin to flow – and with them begins what I would designate as the third and final stage of the writing of the *General Theory*, a stage devoted to obtaining criticisms of the successive galley-proofs of the book. And now Keynes for the first time exposes his work to criticism from people who are outside the intimate circle of his junior colleagues at Cambridge. Thus in January 1935 he sends galley-proofs to Dennis Robertson, whose originally close relations with Keynes had begun to weaken even before the publication of the *Treatise*.[19] Only a few months later, however, do galley-proofs begin to go to the 'outside world' – to Ralph Hawtrey in London (in March 1935) and to Roy Harrod in Oxford (in June 1935). Now from Cambridge to Oxford or London is not so 'outside' – but in Cambridge at that time it seemed that way.

A good deal of this correspondence has survived and has been reproduced in Volume XIII of Keynes's *Collected Writings*. It is a very intensive correspondence. Indeed, sometimes you have letters going back and forth the same day: such were the vanished glories of the British postal service!

This brings me to the final and most difficult question of all: what role in the development of the *General Theory* was actually played by the process of criticism and discussion that has been described in this paper? In order to answer this question let me once again make use of the distinction that I have drawn between the three stages of this development and express the opinion that the aforementioned criticism played an important role in the first stage, a much less important one in the last stage, and one whose importance it is difficult to judge in the second stage.

Let me elaborate on this cryptic evaluation. I think that there can be little doubt of the important role that was fulfilled in the first stage – especially by the criticisms of Hawtrey, Hayek, and the Cambridge 'Circus' – in jolting Keynes into realising the inadequacies of his then newly-published *Treatise* and in stimulating him accordingly to rethink the argument. On the other hand, judging from the materials (especially the successive galley-proofs themselves) that have been reproduced in *JMK* XIII, I think that though the detailed comments on the proofs that marked the third stage of the development of the *General Theory* were undoubtedly of great value in leading Keynes to clarify the exposition and tighten the argument at various points, they did not for the most part affect the book's basic conceptual framework. Indeed, a prime example of this distinction is afforded by the well-known instance in which Keynes accepted Harrod's suggestion to clarify his exposition by means of the savings-investment diagram which appears on page 180 of the *General Theory*, but adamantly rejected Harrod's attempt to persuade him to accept the general-equilibrium conceptual framework which lay behind the suggestion.[20]

As to the criticism received during the second stage of development – that most critical, formative stage of the *General Theory* during which Keynes was engaged in intensive discussions with Richard Kahn and Joan Robinson – the paucity of material that I have already noted makes it difficult to know what exactly transpired. But if we are to judge from the kind of criticisms that these two junior colleagues made in the third stage of the process, then in the second one too they were probably primarily concerned with points of detail and exposition, and not with the basic conceptual framework. In brief, it seems to me that during the formative stage too, it was Keynes who fulfilled the role of the intellectual innovator, continuously striving for better formulations of the theory of output, and then subjecting these successive formulations to the penetrating and fruitful criticisms of his younger colleagues.

Let me return for a moment to the third stage of the development of the *General Theory* and say that I do not think that Ralph Hawtrey and Dennis Robertson have received a fair hearing from history about their contribution, or rather potential contribution, to this stage. It is true that in part they did not get the message. Thus Volume XIII of the *Collected Writings* has now reproduced Keynes's letters to Richard Kahn and Joan Robinson complaining that Hawtrey just does not understand him and that there is also no point talking to Robertson. But I wish someone would sometime write a history of the development of the *General Theory* as seen by Hawtrey and Robertson, and tell us what these two were writing to their friends at that time! In any event, it is clear that they were right in some of the things that they were saying. Thus Hawtrey had some very relevant criticisms to make about Keynes's failure to distinguish adequately in his theory of effective demand between actual and anticipated quantities. And surely that most obscure Chapter 3 of the *General Theory* – the chapter which has provided raw materials for dozens of journal articles and PhD theses, each proclaiming that it and only it provides the true key to an understanding of 'what Keynes really meant' – surely that chapter could have been greatly improved if only Keynes had taken account of Hawtrey's criticisms.

Similarly, though we usually remember Keynes's already-mentioned footnote acknowledgment to Roy Harrod for his suggestion of the only analytical diagram that appears in the *General Theory*, we tend to forget that in this footnote Keynes also referred to the 'partly similar schematism' that Robertson had used in an article (1934) he published in the *Economic Journal* almost a year before the Keynes–Harrod correspondence on this point (*General Theory*, p. 180 n.; *JMK* XIII, pp. 544–61).

More generally, in his discussion with Keynes, Robertson had repeatedly asked (and I paraphrase), 'Why do you insist on saying that the rate of interest is determined by the quantity of money and only by the quantity of money? This is an article of religious faith with you' – as indeed it was. It reminds me of what Jacob Viner used to tell his students about the mercantilists: that it was difficult to believe that anyone had ever contended that gold was the only form of wealth – until you went and read the mercantilist literature and discovered that was precisely what some of them had said.[21] Similarly, Keynes repeatedly emphasised that the rate of interest was determined solely by the quantity of money. And when in connection with the discussion that I have already mentioned Harrod very timidly suggested that maybe other factors were involved, Keynes brusquely retorted (and again I paraphrase), 'If you do not accept this statement, then you do not accept my new teaching!' to which Harrod hastened to reply: 'No, no; you do me throughout great injustice. I have understood you much better than you think' (*JMK* XIII, p. 553). Anyway, one of Robertson's major criticisms of the proofs that Keynes sent him in February 1935 was that the rate of interest reflects the joint influences of the propensity to save, the productivity of capital, and liquidity preference – and not (as Keynes kept on insisting) of this last influence alone (*JMK* XIII, pp. 499 and 509). And in that debate, it was not Robertson who was the wrongheaded one.

*
* *

This, then, is the story of the *General Theory* as interpreted from the written documents by one who was not there, and indeed could not have been there. Let us now hear from some of those who were.

NOTES

1. This paper is based primarily upon Chapters 7–8 of my *Keynes' Monetary Thought* (1976a), whose respective penultimate drafts were circulated among the Conference participants. These chapters provide further documentation for the statements to be presented here. The paper also draws freely on the material in Patinkin (1975).

In preparing this paper for publication, I have taken account of some of the stimulating discussions which took place at the Conference, particularly with Paul Samuelson. I am also grateful to Elizabeth Johnson, Peter Howitt, David Laidler, and Donald Moggridge for subsequent comments. Needless to say, none of them is to be held responsible for the views here expressed.

The work on this paper has in part been supported by research grants from the Ford Foundation (received through the Israel Foundation Trustees), the Central Research Fund of the Hebrew University, the Israel Commission for Basic Research, and the Israel National Academy of Sciences and Humanities – to all of which I am most indebted.

2. See Keynes's publications during this period as listed in the A.E.A. *Index of Economic Journals*, vols. I–II. See also Elizabeth Johnson's stimulating article on 'Keynes: Scientist or Politician?' (1972).

I hope to discuss this point in greater detail on some future occasion.

3. See the 'Editorial Foreword' to the *Treatise* (I, p. xv).

4. As is evidenced by the very titles of such works as Irving Fisher's *Purchasing Power of Money: Its Determination and Relation to Credit Interest and Crises* (1911) and A. C. Pigou's 'Value of Money' (1917–18), as well as Knut Wicksell's *Interest and Prices: A Study of the Causes Regulating the Value of Money* (1898).

5. On these dates, see Moggridge (1973), p. 79.

6. For further documented discussion of this conjecture, see Patinkin (1976a, Chapter 3).

7. I hope to discuss this point further on some future occasion.

8. In his paper to this Conference, Donald Moggridge has referred to Keynes's appointment books. I think it would be very interesting to study them in order to see if they can provide any evidence with respect to the conjecture just presented in the text.

9. See Garvy (1975).

10. In the discussion which took place at this point, Paul Samuelson suggested that alternative (b) in the foregoing citation, with its reference to the 'result of the growing poverty,' might be interpreted as a systematic influence on saving. I do not think so, both because (as just noted) of the language used (namely, 'peters out') as well as the fact that if Keynes had conceived of alternative (b) as a systematic influence, then there would have been no reason for him to have listed two additional alternatives – not to speak of the fact that these alternatives are exogenous ones. Thus, it is significant that in a subsequent

(1932) allusion to the foregoing passage, Keynes does indeed describe alternative (b) as a systematic equilibrating mechanism — but then does not refer to any alternative ways in which equilibrium might be reached (see p. 14).

Paul Samuelson has asked me to say that he still maintains some doubts about the validity of my argument here.

11. These phrases are from Keynes's 1936 letter to Harrod cited above.

12. I am greatly indebted to both Robert Bryce and Lorie Tarshis for making their notes available to me.

Our third 'student representative', Walter Salant, has also preserved his notes for the single year (1934) that he attended Cambridge.

The citations from Tarshis's notes were added to this paper after the Conference, for it was only in the course of the Conference that I learned of their existence.

13. Lorie Tarshis was apparently absent on this occasion, for his lecture notes for that day carry the legend, 'Copied from Bryce's Notes.'

Professor T. K. Rymes of Carleton University (where Bryce's lecture notes are now deposited) has kindly informed me that the third line in the following citation was inserted in pencil between the second and third ones. This makes it clear that w (or the Greek ω, as it might actually be) denotes the 'state of the news.' I should also observe that in the original notes there is an arrow drawn between the parenthetical phrase '(r. of i.)' in the penultimate line and ρ in the equation which precedes it.

As a result of this more careful examination of the handwritten notes, the rendition presented here differs slightly — though not in any substantive way — from the one presented in my *Keynes' Monetary Thought* (1976a, p. 79, footnote 22).

14. For details, see Patinkin (1976a), pp. 73–6.

15. Thus in a letter from May 1932, Joan Robinson wrote to Keynes: 'Austin and Kahn and I were rather worried by some points in your last lecture, and we have written some remarks which perhaps you would like to see' (*JMK* XIII, p. 376).

16. Which appeared in the *Economic Journal* under the title 'The Relation of Home Investment to Unemployment'.

17. Note also how Keynes distinguishes between these two concepts at the beginning of the excerpt from his 1936 letter to Harrod cited on page 10 above.

18. Cf. Richard Kahn's letter reproduced in Appendix II, this volume.

19. See Patinkin (1976a), pp. 30–1.

20. *Ibid.*, p. 99.

21. See Viner (1937), pp. 26–7.

3 Keynes and his Cambridge Colleagues

AUSTIN ROBINSON

The assignment that I have been given today is to talk to you about Keynes's relations to his younger Cambridge colleagues. But I do not believe there is a useful distinction in this case between younger and older and I fear that I shall not attempt to make it. In trying to think how I can best do this and contribute to our discussions I have come to the conclusion that I must begin by giving you something of a picture of the set-up of Cambridge economics as it was at the beginning of the 1930s. It is very easy for those of us who live and work in the large faculties and vast graduate and research departments of today to forget that they are almost wholly creations of the post-World-War II epoch – to forget how minute were the economics faculties of 1930.

I am going to take the Cambridge set-up of 1930–1 because it was in October of 1930 that Keynes's *Treatise* was published, that its criticism and re-analysis was begun by the group of younger economists that we later nick-named the 'Circus,' and at the same time Keynes himself began to have second thoughts and to move on from the formulations of the *Treatise* towards the *General Theory*. At what precise moment the system of the *General Theory* was identified can, if you wish, be debated. Donald Moggridge will, I am sure, help, if you wish, to elucidate this. But there can be no possible question that it was during 1930–1 that the first re-examinations began. That is my reason for taking the Cambridge set-up of 1930–1 as my starting point.

At that moment the entire graduate staff of the Faculty of Economics and Politics in all capacities consisted of 13 persons. Pigou as the one professor, Dennis Robertson as the one reader, 10 lecturers, 1 assistant lecturer. Keynes himself never had in the technical sense any university post. But of these 13, two (Evans and Burn) were teaching economic history; two others (Alston and Thatcher) were wholly engaged in pass degree teaching and were (I hope I may be forgiven for saying) survivals, recognised by themselves as such, from the teaching of an earlier pass degree system. These apart, there were, in addition to Pigou and Robertson, only seven of us. One cannot discuss us realistically in terms of categories. One must, to make any sense, discuss in terms of individuals. Very bravely, very rashly, I propose to attempt to do that. But these were my friends. Some of them are still alive. I cannot hope to escape wholly from bias regarding them.

Let me then begin by listing them. Apart again from Pigou and Robertson, the economists involved were Claude Guillebaud and Gerald Shove from the pre-1914 generation; Maurice Dobb and myself from the earliest post-1919 generation of Cambridge economists; Humphrey Mynors – then assistant lecturer – from a slightly later Cambridge vintage of 1926; Piero Sraffa who had come to Cambridge from Italy in 1927 and Marjorie Hollond (Marjorie Tappan as she then was) who had come to Girton from America to do the college teaching of the women in 1923.[1]

Richard Kahn, who had taken the Tripos in 1928 was a very recently elected young Fellow of King's, still in his twenties. He had been invited to give his first few lectures that year on 'The Short Period' – the subject of his fellowship dissertation; but he held as yet no university post. Joan Robinson was a young economist, also still in her twenties, living and working in Cambridge, doing a little college teaching, but again as yet without any university post. (She gave her first short course in 1931–2.) We were (this is a point that Harry Johnson emphasises and I will not labour it more) scattered around the colleges and in most cases heavily occupied with college supervision (tutorials) as well as with university lecturing.

Let me just add, in case his name should be in the minds of any of you, that Frederick Lavington, who had lectured in Cambridge on economic fluctuations had died in 1927. He had been a very sick, but very brave man all the time that I knew him. He was little, if at all, involved in the argument going on around Keynes and Robertson. Two others, again, who had taught in the monetary field in Cambridge in earlier years, Walter Layton and Hubert Henderson, had left for other things. Keynes was in touch with both over practical issues, including Lloyd George's economic schemes. But Layton, by now editor of *The Economist*, was no longer interested in refinements of monetary theory. Henderson's thinking was well-known to Keynes through their joint work on the Economic Advisory Council and through Keynes's involvement in the *Nation* that Henderson had been editing.

May I come back, then, to the individuals in Cambridge and try to picture to you their various relations to Keynes?[2] But I think I shall only get this right if I remind you that the Cambridge of 1930–1 was by no means wholly concentrated on the arguments around Keynes and Robertson that led from the *Treatise* onward to the *General Theory*. When Joan Robinson and I came back from India and settled down again in Cambridge at the beginning of 1929, the most vigorous arguments of our younger friends were primarily concerned with Piero Sraffa's lectures and derived more remotely from his *Economic Journal* article in 1926, which led on to all the various articles by Sraffa himself, by Robertson, Shove and others that appeared in the *Economic Journal* early in 1930 and were familiar to us as the 'Symposium'. This earlier ferment (deriving from Sraffa) had successfully breached the complacency of the 1920s and the attitude, enshrined in Keynes's first preface to the *Cambridge Economic Handbooks*, that Marshall had done all the necessary thinking and it was for us just to apply it. Moreover for some of us this initial stimulus was greatly reinforced by the fact that Charles Gifford, a young undergraduate mathematician who had turned to economics and whom I was teaching, produced early in 1930 (I believe from something Yntema had written) what we subsequently called a marginal revenue curve on a day that Richard Kahn was lunching with us, so that I could retail it to them. Joan and he were quickly away on the lines that led up to *The Economics of Imperfect Competition* (1933) and the English contribution to all that rethinking.

I have digressed – if digression it is – to remind you of this because in 1930–1 we had not one but two revolutions in hand, and some of us were more involved in one and some of us in the other.

Let me come back then to the individuals and say a few words first about those who were less involved in the work around Keynes. Maurice Dobb was in those days rather much of a loner – a Marxist by conscience and conviction in a world in which Marxism was not yet fashionable – teaching orthodox economics conscientiously to pupils who had to acquire it, giving excellent lectures on labour and social conditions – not yet as much at the centre of Cambridge debate as he has been more recently, and not in the thick of the fray around Keynes and Keynes's theories.

Humphrey Mynors, later to become Deputy-Governor of the Bank of England, and I were both lecturing on industry and industrial organisation at a time when Cambridge still took detailed knowledge of particular industries very seriously. Both of us were more immediately concerned with the creation of a theory of the firm, with the application of the newly developing theories of oligopoly and imperfect competition and with trying to see how far some of these theories reconciled with the facts of industry. Neither of us was right in the thick of the *General Theory* arguments, though we were not outside it. In my own case it was going on all around me and I could not escape it had I wished (which I certainly did not). I was, like others, arguing it incessantly and absorbing it by continuing osmosis. But I was just finishing *The Structure of Competitive Industry*, which was published during 1931, and that was the centre of my own work.

Marjorie Hollond – Marjorie Tappan as she then was – had come to Girton in 1923. In 1930 she was lecturing on public finance and on economic fluctuations. She had a deep and intimate knowledge of the American banking systems, and I know that Keynes on more than one occasion was grateful for her help over such questions. But she was always somewhat diffident and retiring, too precise and scholarly to be an exciting, popular lecturer, not an aggressive propounder of new and exciting generalities.

May I come next to Gerald Shove and Claude Guillebaud? I have always hoped that someone would write a good account of Gerald Shove and his work. In the later 1930s and in the early post-1945 period he was one of the most interesting and effective of Cambridge lecturers. But this was, in a sense, a reincarnation. I was his pupil in 1921–2 and attended his inordinately dull lectures on trade union organisation. He had been a brilliant student in the 1910–14 period, whose conscience had made him a pacifist when war came. On the fringe of the Bloomsbury group, he had endured all the miseries of being a pacifist in a world that was war-mad. With my own generation of prematurely adult war veterans with a contempt for pacifists he found it difficult to establish an easy and relaxed intimacy. He and Fredegond, his poet wife, were infinitely kind. But I got at that stage very little from his teaching – he was then so painfully shy. It was in 1929–30 that he had a sabbatical year and came back a wholly different person. But even after that it is not, I think, wholly unfair to him to say that his gifts were critical rather than creative. In some ways he resembled Dennis Robertson in always wanting to insist that the world is not as simple as the simpler economic models of it – that nothing is wholly black or wholly white, but everything grey. His central interests were at that time in the rethinking of Marshallian value theory – the other of our two revolutions. With Keynes, as with all of us, Shove was an invaluable critic. But, as I say, his qualities as a critic were always greater than his qualities as a creator of models of what he would have regarded as oversimplifications. In relation to the *General Theory* work, there is no question that in the later stages Keynes was discussing with him his arguments with Pigou and getting from him valuable comments on that. But I do not think he played any major part in the first stages. There is certainly no written record of comments on drafts. He took no part that I can remember in the work of the 'Circus'.

I come now to Claude Guillebaud – Alfred Marshall's nephew and editor of the great Royal Economic Society edition of *The Principles* (1961). Like Shove, but for very different reasons, he too was a shy, unthrusting, person. He was, among the Cambridge economists, for many years one of my closest friends and I find it the more difficult for that reason to measure him. He would never have dreamed of claiming for himself that he was a great economist, measured by the standards of Marshall, Keynes, Pigou, Robertson. He was too modest, too self-effacing. And because this was the sort of person he was, he was a diffident and ineffectual lecturer. With his patience and his great gifts of friendship he was, on the other hand, one of the best tutors of Cambridge, prepared to take infinite trouble over his pupils. I can see him sitting there in Keynes's club on a Monday evening like a wise owl, saying rather little but, what it was, very much worth hearing. But he again played relatively little active part in what was going on around Keynes.

I am left then with Piero Sraffa, Dennis Robertson, Pigou, Richard Kahn, Joan Robinson and some of a still younger generation. It is this group that really played the major part with Keynes in the rethinking of the 1930s.

I find it almost impossible to describe Piero Sraffa to anyone who does not know him, and I do this with more difficulty because he is still alive and capable of expressing the strongest dissent from anything I may say. It was, as I have said earlier, his arrival in Cambridge in 1927 and his lectures in 1928 that gave Cambridge economics its second wind. As any economist will know, he has remained capable of demanding fundamental rethinking of whole branches of economics. It would be easy to imagine him as an iconoclastic human dynamo, constantly throwing out an endless stream of shocking ideas. In fact he could hardly be more different. His first lectures in Cambridge in 1928-9, devoted to analysing some of the ideas buried in Marshall's *Principles*, shocked him as much as, perhaps more than, they shocked his audience. He found the strain of lecturing almost intolerable (he would sit up all night before a lecture worrying about what he was going to say). In 1930, very soon after Pigou had made me secretary of the Faculty Board and responsible under the Board for organising the staffing and the lectures, Piero Sraffa came to me and begged to be allowed to resign his lectureship. He remained librarian of the Marshall Library and we managed a little later to get him made assistant director of research, with general responsibility for all research students, so that he could have a university post without the need any longer to lecture. He was in one sense always in the thick of the work going on around Keynes. As a member of King's College (he was not yet in those days a Fellow of Trinity) he saw more of Keynes than most of us did. But in all our discussions I remember him as much more like a kettle on a slow gas-ring. One waited hopefully for it to boil. When one had almost forgotten, it suddenly came to the boil. Piero Sraffa at full pressure, with a torrent of Italianate English, was something to remember, if only for its rarity. I find it extraordinarily difficult to guess his contribution. As a critic it was undeniably very considerable indeed. As an eliminator of mistakes and red-herrings and as a puncturer of other people's over-inflated bright ideas it was immense. I do not myself remember him as a major provider himself of bright new ideas. But that element in a collective operation may easily be overvalued. And of Piero Sraffa's creativity in everything that he himself set out to tackle there can be no possible question.

I come then to Pigou and Robertson. First Pigou. When I was an undergraduate doing economics in 1920-2 - and this was still true at the beginning of the 1930s - while Keynes dominated our thinking in political economy and our thinking about the economic issues of the day, it was Pigou, then still in his full vigour, who dominated the theoretical teaching. It was only in the middle thirties that the fibrillation of his heart reduced him to a shadow of himself. When I first knew him he was still the tall, powerfully built, athletic player of all ball-games – the former head of the school at Harrow who thought poorly of a small boy called Winston Churchill – the keen climber, with his cottage among the mountains in Cumberland where he led his friends up the climbs. Spending his summers in the Alps. In those days an excellent lecturer – very clear, very systematic, but at the same time very rooted in the Marshall tradition – 'it's all in Marshall'. In his undergraduate days he had been a great popular speaker, president of the union (the university debating society). He had stumped the country as a free trader during the tariff reform crusade. He had even – so Philip Noel Baker has told me – contemplated matrimony. But by the 1920s, and increasingly in his later years, he had developed a relationship with people curiously inconsistent with all of this – indeed its very antithesis. He was remote and aloof from us all. After a lecture on one or two occasions, when I was still an undergraduate, I took my courage into my hands and asked him a question about something. He gave me a careful and considered answer and then retreated into his shell. I myself got to know him a little better the year after I had taken the Tripos. He always set questions in his 'principles' lectures, following a tradition established by Marshall. Barbara Wootton,[3] who had corrected them when I wrote them, had left Cambridge – I was commanded to take on the job. Pigou, by then the complete misogynist, had never allowed Barbara Wootton into his room; she had to deliver the scripts with her comments to the King's porter's lodge. I, more privileged, was allowed to take them and give them to him in his room in King's and was spared five minutes of his time to talk to him about them. There was only one way to his heart – through climbing with him. In the early 1930s I stayed from time to time with him in the cottage at Buttermere. We talked climbing. We talked cricket. We talked about the latest Agatha Christie. On wet days we each worked at whatever each of us had in hand. But economics was taboo. I have never had a serious economic discussion with Pigou. If he liked something I had written he would, if I was lucky, send me a short and almost illegible note to say so. Of course, when in 1930 and later I was secretary of the Faculty Board, I discussed faculty business with him. But economics as economics never.

By the 1930s, Pigou who was then in his fifties had the writing of *The Economics of Welfare* behind him. As new ideas or new topics in economics came to the surface Pigou in a curious way digested them by writing a book about them himself,[4] and in an equally curious way it was through his books or articles rather than through discussion that most of us in Cambridge discovered what he was thinking. But because we could never discuss, we could misunderstand him and he could misunderstand us.

I think that this remoteness extended to his relations to Keynes. They were, of course, closer in two important ways. They were closer in age, and friends already by the 1930s of some twenty-five years. They were both Fellows of King's, dining together when Keynes was in Cambridge at the high table of the College. But I do not think that they often talked theoretical economics to each other. I think that most of Keynes's intellectual exchanges with Pigou were, like ours, on paper and are available to you in the pages of Don Moggridge's two volumes (*JMK* XIII and XIV).

But more generally I think the right picture to give you of Pigou is of a curiously aloof scholar, working away independently of all the rest of us on his own problems, sometimes ahead of the rest of us, more often slightly behind us in his choice of topics and rather isolated from Cambridge thinking that had not been published. And this isolation was at that moment the more serious because Cambridge was going through one of those recurring periods in which the oral tradition was far ahead of publication. Any final assessment of Pigou's relations to the development of 'Keynesian' economics must take account of the very interesting, and to those of us who heard them very moving, two lectures which he gave nearly twenty years later than the time with which I am concerned and after Keynes's death. Pigou, always the most scrupulously honest and just of men, said then, as those of you who know those lectures will remember, that 'in my original review-article on the *General Theory* I failed to grasp its significance and did not assign to Keynes the credit due for it'. And equally one must remember the ambivalence of Keynes's own attitude to Pigou – his strong desire, as in the case of Robertson, to persuade him if he could, and simultaneously a strong desire (which I encountered as his fellow editor of the *Economic Journal*) that Pigou, as professor and as a colleague at King's, should not be allowed, if it could be avoided, to make serious errors in what he published.

I come now to Dennis Robertson. I had known him when I was still a classic and not yet an economist. He taught me economics during part of my final year. You must picture him as a bachelor living in Trinity; as a very fine classical scholar – a splendid product of the Eton and Trinity classical traditions – one who in those traditions had become not only a master of the precise and exact use of words but also of the cautious, critical, analytical scholarship that belonged to Eton and Trinity and has now alas become defunct in economics, in a world that believes that only mathematics can be exact (I speak feelingly as one brought up in the classical tradition). In important ways Dennis Robertson was the best scholar of all of us. Pigou was conservative and could slip into mistakes. Keynes was the intuitive creator who could visualise a solution before he could formulate it. Robertson was less quick, less intuitive, less impulsive than Keynes. But in *Banking Policy and the Price Level* (1926) he was greatly original and creative and began much of our new thinking. Without him Keynes might never have got started on the *Treatise* and the *General Theory*.

Keynes had an immense respect for Robertson's scholarship, his thoroughness, his caution. He was happy only when Dennis had given his assent. Of course this meant argument backwards and forwards between them, and moments of strain when they disagreed, and each believed that he was right. But they had so much in common – their common background of Eton, of Cambridge economics, of interest in the theatre, and many other things – that until very late in the final working out of the *General Theory* the strain was never too great. But one must see this also through Robertson's eyes, and understand the sort of person he was. Where Keynes was a crusader, Dennis was an academic who had the right to sit on the fence. Where Keynes was always trying to secure agreement and action, Dennis was one of those who preferred to be right in a minority of one. It was for such a person a constant strain to be a brake on Keynes. And since Dennis, who was excessively modest regarding his own capacities, was constantly unsure whether he was right or wrong in being the brake, whether he was being over-cautious, the task of being Keynes's touchstone became increasingly burdensome. Keynes (and others of us also), right up to the publication of the *General Theory*, was convinced that Dennis was intellectually in agreement with him, and arguing only about presentation – that in the end he could and would agree. I am not going to discuss the subsequent tensions between them, which I am convinced have been greatly exaggerated. They have no bearing on the period that we are talking about today.

So I come to the younger generation and our relations to Keynes. To understand them one must first have a picture of Keynes himself. One must remember first that he was living two lives – a London life of Tuesday to Friday, a Cambridge life of Friday evening to Tuesday morning. Inside the busy Cambridge life had to be squeezed his bursaring of King's, his few pupils, the Keynes Club on Monday nights, college, faculty and university meetings, and from the time that I took over as assistant editor in 1934, any discussions of *Economic Journal* problems. He was a very busy man working unhurriedly on a very tight schedule. One could not drop in on him, as we constantly dropped in on each other, and argue till the argument was settled. At the same time he was the maestro. He was relaxed and easy to talk to. But one talked to him – or more strictly I found myself talking to him – not as the equal, as one as likely to be wrong as oneself – but as the authority, with much more experience, with much more thought given to the problem, than one had oneself. One needed to be very sure of one's ground before arguing with him vehemently. But if you did argue with him you never quite knew until later whether you had won the argument. You knew only if, the next time you got on to the subject, he retailed to you some of your own arguments. He never believed in private property in arguments, and was never very certain which were his own and which were other people's arguments.

If one remembers this it is easier to picture how it came about that the communications between the 'Circus' and Maynard Keynes took the curious form they did, with Richard Kahn serving, as James Meade has described it,[5] as a sort of 'angel-messenger' in a medieval morality play, carrying messages up and bringing them back from the deity. Richard Kahn was the inevitable angel-messenger for two reasons. He was a privileged recent pupil whose critical faculties Keynes greatly respected and constantly consulted. More important, he was a young Fellow of King's who dined with Keynes on the high table, met him constantly in his odd moments, and could thus seize the odd chance of talking to him.

If I think back now into those days the contrast with the Cambridge of today is not only that the graduate teaching staff was so tiny. It was also that we were so very much nearer to the undergraduates, and particularly the third year undergraduates. There was then no separate research department – that began only on a tiny scale in the late 1930s. There was virtually no graduate school – a few years earlier Bertil Ohlin, Gustav Cassel's daughter and I had represented the totality of it.[6] In the later 1930s Alec Cairncross, Walter Salant, and one or two others were working for the PhD. On the other hand, the vigorous thinking that was going on was shared continuously by the very able undergraduates of the day – Wynn Plumptre in 1930 and that astonishing vintage of 1934 which included Brian Reddaway, V. K. R. V. Rao and T. W. Hutchison as well as Bob Bryce and Lorie Tarshis. And the equally astonishing vintage of 1935 which included David Butt, David Champernowne, Stanley Dennison, Dick Stone. Throughout that period they, as well as visitors to Cambridge, were playing a very considerable part, and by no means a merely receptive part, in the furore of argument that was going on. And let me emphasise again that it is only by argument, by conflict if you like, that economics makes progress. It is painful, but it is inevitable, and never to be deprecated.

I come back then to the group of the younger generation of those years who, apart always from Keynes himself, were most involved in the argument that began in October 1930. In listing the purely Cambridge element in it I find myself constantly in danger of leaving out James Meade, who, following an example set by Harrod in 1922–3, was spending a year with us in 1930–1 before beginning to teach in Oxford. I remember him as more active than any of us, not only in the Keynesian arguments but also in those around the theory of value.

The *Treatise* was published on 31 October, 1930. Through the rest of 1930 and the Lent Term of 1931 we were busily reading it and digesting it. Even if we had absorbed some of the ideas over the previous years from the short courses of lectures that Keynes gave each year, and which all of us, faculty as well as undergraduates, had attended, this was our first opportunity to read them in their final form. Inevitably some of us – Richard Kahn, Joan Robinson, Piero Sraffa, James Meade and myself –

found ourselves arguing together about it. What came to be called the 'Circus' first emerged by accident rather than design. Three or four years back, in order to give more authentic substance to a necessary discussion in Don Moggridge's Vol. XIII of *The Collected Writings of John Maynard Keynes*, Richard Kahn, Piero Sraffa, James Meade, Joan and I lunched together, very appropriately in the restaurant of Keynes's Arts Theatre, with Don Moggridge there to question us and prod us. After lunch I sat down and wrote a first draft of our memories. We circulated my draft, others criticised and Don Moggridge revised it, corrected it and put it into final shape (see *JMK* XIII, pp. 337–43).

Re-reading it for my present purposes I feel that there are one or two things that have survived from my original draft that I should have made clearer. The 'Circus' is really a composite name for two essentially different operations. The first stage, wholly informal, was a series of arguments between the five of us in Richard Kahn's rooms in King's during the October term of 1930 and the Lent term of 1931. The second, rather more formal stage, was a series of seminars for a very rigidly selected group of undergraduates during the May term of 1931. But we would never have planned this second stage if we had not begun to find serious problems for discussion during the first – the November 1930 to March 1931 stage. My own memories of the first stage are very much clearer than those of the second stage. I am quite certain from what I can remember of my own minor contributions that what we came to call 'the widow's cruse fallacy' had been identified well before the end of March 1931 – that during those early discussions in Richard Kahn's room we had begun to ask ourselves how an initial increase of demand worked its way through into a given amount of expenditure and activity and finally exhausted its effects.

We had, as the note in *JMK* XIII (pp. 339–41) reminds you, very ready at hand the necessary tools, several of them evolved or first known to us in Cambridge during the previous few years. We had Richard Kahn's new work on the multiplier, giving greater precision to earlier ideas about the total extent of the effects of public works expenditure. We had his initial work, still unpublished, on short period pricing and other work was going on to refine and elaborate this. And remember the ultimate title of Keynes's book, the 'General Theory' – general in the sense that it was not uniquely true of a full-employment long period. We were scrupulously careful to distinguish between propositions in economics which were true in all times and circumstances and propositions which were true only in circumstances of full-employment equilibrium. It was the sin against the Holy Ghost in the Cambridge of 1931 to use arguments true only in full-employment equilibrium to solve problems of short-period equilibrium. In all this I firmly believe that Cambridge economics in the 1930s was ahead of very much that is being written and said in conferences today forty years later. And if one is not constantly aware of this, I think one can easily miss the full significance and meaning of many of the arguments that were going on during 1930–6.

But to go back to the tools available to us. Beside the multiplier and the short-period analysis, James Meade's fertile mind quickly provided other embroideries and improvements. I do not want to say that before the end of March 1931 we had all the essentials of the *General Theory*. But I do want to say that we had begun to ask ourselves the *questions* that the *General Theory* set out to answer. And inevitably in trying to see how the multiplier really worked out to finality we were beginning to see that savings and investment must in some way and at every stage reach equality.

But this seems to me to raise the fundamental question of what constitutes a theoretical break-through in economics. To my mind it has three stages. The first is the identification of a new question that clearly needs to be answered, but to which there is no ready-made answer in the existing corpus of economics. This stage not infrequently derives from the attempts of an applied economist (and Keynes was always basically an applied economist) trying to analyse some new economic trend or problem. The second stage is identification of the essential framework and operation of the model that will solve the problem. The third is the precise formulation of the model. My own belief is that, by the spring of 1931 those of us who composed the 'Circus' had begun to identify the new questions. We had begun to see some of the essential framework and operation of the necessary model. We had not of course, as yet, made serious progress towards final formulation. Which is the critical stage in a break-through? On this, may I commend you to what Keynes himself wrote in his *Essays in Biography* (1933) about the intuitive insights of Marshall and of Newton. He would, I feel certain, have regarded the first two stages as the creative stages and the third stage as a necessary, but less creative, formality.

Now all of this was being carried back to Keynes by Richard Kahn. Keynes, with what I have always regarded as quite extraordinary magnanimity, welcomed it, took it, improved it, and went dashing ahead with it. Perhaps this was the easier for him because his own thinking was already moving on. But in working out the various threads and repercussions and timings, one must remember that some of this thinking was reaching him before the end of 1930 and in the early months of 1931. Don Patinkin, in the chapters of his forthcoming monograph on Keynes that he has circulated among us,[7] has questioned a phrase which has survived from my original draft about the 'Circus' in which I wrote 'there may have been (*as some members believe*) a short period when the 'Circus' was slightly further on towards the *General Theory* than was Keynes. But it was a very short time' (*JMK* XIII, p. 342). When I wrote the words in brackets (that I have now italicised) I did not think there was any real difference of opinion as to where the 'Circus' had got to. But it was, if you remember the channels of communication, very much more difficult to know at any moment just how far Keynes had got. Richard Kahn, as angel-messenger, could not always tell whether Keynes had or had not accepted some suggestion or criticism.

Through the rest of that academic year of 1930–1 both Keynes and the 'Circus' went on thinking and arguing separately but not independently. I remain completely convinced – as is James Meade – that by the end of that academic year of 1930–1 the essentials of the *General Theory* model were known in outline. An immensity of formulation, tightening up, criticism and revision remained to be done. But we were well on the road and Keynes was with us, perhaps ahead of us, even if not yet, on the occasion of formal lectures, publicly adopting new formulations.[8]

In the later stages others were brought in – Hawtrey and Roy Harrod in particular. And as one moved forward from the initial visualisation to the subsequent formulation, Robertson, who had preferred not to take part in the work of the 'Circus', came back into the centre of stage. But I think the important thing to stress is that, after that short period in 1930–1, there was never any question where the initiative and leadership was coming from – from Maynard Keynes himself.

I am not going to try to tell you what contributions came from whom, and I would warn you against trying to answer that question from the evidence of the notes to Keynes by different people. Where a small group is constantly arguing together, arguing with their pupils and arguing with others outside, one seldom knows exactly who was initially responsible for which elements in the collective thinking, and any one person may be transmitting collective rather than individual ideas. What seems to me clear is that a group made up of individuals with very different gifts of critical faculties, of energy and persistence, of intuitive perception, is immensely stronger than any one individual in it.

These were the people that Keynes consulted and who tried to help him. But there is one final thing that I feel impelled to say. Some writers in recent years have deplored the fact that he did not consult more widely or in all cases adopt other people's suggestions. This is, I think to miss the point. This was not a Royal Commission on monetary theory set up to provide a collective view of what was or should be the appropriate and permanent orthodoxy. We in Cambridge were helping Keynes to write Keynes's own book, departing as we knew, in very important ways from current orthodoxy. If it proved that certain individuals were out of sympathy with the book, or wanted it to say what they themselves thought and not what Keynes, after reflection, thought, then Keynes had every right to write his own book in his own way, working with those who understood and sympathised. It was far better by 1936 that the book should propound Keynes's own ideas and allow the criticism of subsequent generations to digest and improve them than that he should attempt first to achieve compromise with ideas that he believed to be outmoded. But where Keynes and others considered arguments and then discarded them, I hope it is not presumptuous to urge some of today's critics to read and consider impartially the arguments of the 1930s as they now appear in Don Moggridge's two volumes.

I am sure that the Cambridge of 1930–1 that I have tried to picture to you must seem a madhouse, with the extraordinary personalities of Keynes himself, of Pigou, of Robertson, of Sraffa and others whom I need not list. But to my mind what is fascinating is how much economics has owed to people who in some sense were very unusual, very abnormal – to the overflowing academic energies of the successful stock-broker Ricardo, to the accidental preoccupations with population growth of the self-effacing, hair-lipped parson Robert Malthus, to the precocious and over-educated John Stuart Mill, to the neurotic hypochondriac Walras, to the over-sensitive, over-perfectionist, would-be-omniscient Alfred Marshall, to mention only a few in addition to those who come into this story. The big advances have come not from the orthodox pedestrians like myself, who make the marginal improvements, but from the people with unusual, often intuitive, gifts of perception, harnessed and interpreted by the more orthodox, more cautious scholars. This is true not only for economics. Cambridge mathematics from Newton onwards, Cambridge physics in the persons of J. J. Thompson and Rutherford, Cambridge biology in recent years have all made their great leaps in similar fashion. It does not at all surprise me that the really creative work in economics has come from such people. For myself, to live among some of them has been its own reward.

NOTES

1. In 1931, Pigou was aged 54; Robertson, Guillebaud and Shove were all around 41; Dobb was aged 31; Sraffa, Mrs. Hollond and I were around 33; Mynors was 28; Kahn was 26 and Joan Robinson 28.

2. The individuals and their number had slightly changed before the actual publication of the *General Theory* in 1936. By then Humphrey Mynors had left to join the Bank of England. Richard Kahn had become a lecturer and Joan Robinson an assistant lecturer. J. W. F. Rowe had come as a lecturer, in effect replacing Mynors. Colin Clark had been appointed lecturer in statistics in 1931. And John Hicks had come as an additional lecturer in 1935; but by then the work on the *General Theory* was nearing completion, and Hicks was sufficiently detached from it to be reasonably asked to review the book in the *Economic Journal* (1936).

3. Now Baroness Wootton of Abinger.

4. For instance, *The Theory of Unemployment* (1933), *The Economics of Stationary States* (1935), *Employment and Equilibrium* (1941).

5. See *JMK* XIII, pp. 338–9.

[6. Cf. p. 161 of Ohlin's paper in Appendix III below. – Eds.]

7. See pp. 59–60 of the since-published monograph (1976a).
8. See, for example, the very interesting letter from Keynes to Richard Kahn of 20 September, 1931 (*JMK* XIII, pp. 373–5).

4 Keynes as Seen by his Students in the 1930s

(i) ROBERT BRYCE

I must say I'm not sure what an aging bureaucrat can contribute to this company of scholars. I don't remember much of what happened forty years ago. I haven't had time to read Volume XIII of Keynes's *Collected Writings*, although I've leafed through it and wondered how on earth people leave so much behind them. It was my good fortune to be at Cambridge from mid-1932 to mid-1935 although I'm not satisfied that that amounts to 'being there' as Don Patinkin was indicating before the coffee break. The geography has to be very 'micro' to really count. It was 'good fortune' too since it was only because my father was in the gold mining business in the midst of the depression that I was able to be there. However, I was also lucky to be a member of the Political Economy Club.[1] Indeed I attended my first meeting and had to get up and speak before the fireplace the first day that I was studying economics. It was a somewhat terrifying experience. However, I got more accustomed to it later.

It is now known that I attended Keynes's lectures in 1932–4 and took notes of them. I've not read those notes for twenty or thirty years. I participated as an undergraduate and research student in many discussions of his ideas. I guess I have to say 'notably with Joan Robinson' who was my supervisor of studies for a year or two. Lorie and I went to her together for part of that period. But I also had some contacts with Kahn and Austin Robinson and Shove. Like many others I greatly enjoyed Dennis Robertson's lectures and conversation. However, I can't claim to have had any influence on Keynes's thinking through this period. It was quite clear that the circle to whom he listened was a small one, even in Cambridge. However, I did claim to understand it. One had to understand it in those days, in order to get through the tripos. So I had a strong incentive. I also had to understand the *Treatise* which really took more understanding than the *General Theory*. I had the misfortune one night to be the only student ever to deliver a paper to the Political Economy Club in Keynes's absence. This was a night when he came down with the flu immediately before the meeting. And that was my magnum opus on Keynes's theory, applied to the US boom of the late 1920s, so that I lost my only chance to influence him.

I need not say that I was impressed with Keynes; far better critics than I have described his able and complex mind. I saw it in action not only there in Cambridge, but many years later in Ottawa when Keynes came to talk to ministers several times in 1944 about the financing of the second phase of the war and some of the post-war problems. He was such an eloquent expositor that after the first meeting the ministers decided that they would not take any decision in his presence. They had to get out of ear-shot before they would trust themselves with what he had said. Indeed, there were times in those negotiations, where I was acting as secretary of the meetings, when I'll swear that Keynes himself got infatuated with his arguments and carried them further than his case really required or made desirable. But such, anyway, was the kind of, shall I call it forensic ability that I saw him display in Cambridge. If I may say so, I was most impressed by his institutional knowledge, and to this day I am still criticising various professors, not only economists, but sociologists and others nowadays because of a lack of knowledge of the institutional framework and processes of which they're talking. This is one thing I always felt about Keynes. At least he appeared to have a very good knowledge of the kind of markets he was talking about.

Well, I was not just convinced, I was converted. Converted sufficiently that I went in the spring of 1935 down to the London School of Economics a day or two a week as a missionary. There I attended Von Hayek's seminar on monetary theory and cycle-theory matters. This was the nearest concentration of heathen available from Cambridge and I was encouraged to go and tell them about it, about what the true faith was. I wrote a paper for the purpose[2] about what I thought the *General Theory* was. I didn't want to attribute it to Keynes because I wasn't sure that I'd got him quite right and I didn't want to ask him about the paper before I delivered it. Hayek very courteously gave me several sessions of his seminar to expose this thing to his students. I must say it was an exciting experience and I found a lot of people quite prepared to give the paper serious attention. I didn't find in this case or at Harvard that it required all the tortuous argument that one sees in the accounts of what went on in Cambridge.

I will say this, and I'll refer to it again later, the definitions and particularly the change in definitions as compared with the *Treatise*, of savings and income and profit were a very serious obstacle, and people wanted to talk far more about that and talk too little about the process, the essential process that Don Patinkin has been talking about: the equilibrating process of the system. But, when I told Keynes later about the sessions we had there at LSE, he told me that he too found it terribly tiresome – all this definition business. But when I read over some of his pages I can quite see that he was as guilty as anyone else on the definition matter.

I had sufficient encouragement from my episode at LSE that several months later when I left Cambridge I went over to Harvard where for six months, I suppose, I used the same notes that I had prepared for use in

Hayek's seminar to start the indoctrination of Harvard, before the *General Theory* appeared. I hesitate to say that it gave them a running start on the *General Theory*, but at least I had softened things up a little by the time the book came out. While it really prevented me from doing any research work at Harvard, at least it gave me a lot of contacts and fun. I got into a certain amount of trouble later with a US Senate sub-committee because in return for having some of the leading graduate students attend my study group on Keynes, I agreed to attend their study group on Marx. This became known to the authorities and I had quite a time talking myself out of this, until I found the paper I'd given to the study group on Marx and offered it to the reporters to look at. It was a discussion of the application of Lenin's theory of American agriculture to the Agricultural Adjustment Act of the 1930s – and they lost interest after two pages.

I felt that it was possible to get across the central ideas of the *General Theory* in a lot less complicated form than that which had appeared in the book and that when one did so, one could get a better response than with all the provocation that Keynes had introduced in the *General Theory*, let alone all the complications that were inherited from the *Treatise*. So, I guess the main point that I would make out of this is that it seemed to me that the central ideas, in particular the variability of employment and output and income and their role in the maintenance of short period equilibrium could be put more persuasively than they were in his book. There was a lot of talk in Cambridge in those days about short term equilibrium and middle term equilibrium, in distinction to long term equilibrium. I don't find much of this reflected in the discussion over Keynes, but it had its place, I felt, because that was the kind of equilibrium we had to talk about in terms of income and employment and output.

What can I say about the evolution of the *General Theory* from the *Treatise*? Really very little. I have forgotten what little I knew at the time and I must confess that I haven't been able to go through Volume XIII in the way I would have liked to in order to be here today. A few comments though. When I talked about Keynes to some group twenty-five years ago, I remember saying that one day – I guess in his lectures, or it could have been one night in the Political Economy Club – he drew a distinction between the process of original thought in which one really relied on intuition and the process of scholastic thought in which one tidied up the mess and wrote out the results with some precision. I guess my interpretation of the transition from the *Treatise* to the *General Theory* was that he was trying to carry on these two processes simultaneously and this was what made him, I think, quite impatient with a lot of people who were not prepared to follow him into it intuitively (as some of us were), but who wanted to see the thing all written down precisely.

My recollection of the difficulties of precision were that, when you really got down to talking about the processes that were at work in maintaining the kind of short-term equilibrium that we were talking about and affecting the various aggregates, everything influenced everything else. And there were innumerable factors, for example, that played upon the foreign balance and foreign lending as well as upon domestic savings and domestic investment and if you tried to put this down precisely you got into a degree of complexity where you were apt to lose the main point. On the other hand, if you just talked in words, you were apt to end up with arguments about what the words were, what the words were really meant to mean. You'd get into a semantic argument rather than arguments on the substance of the system that was at issue. So it seems to me that there was that sort of difficulty. Part of the problem was really to try to cut through the semantics on one side and the complexity of the system on the other and isolate and treat, in a sense, the main issues that were at stake.

Secondly, I think it was harder for people like Keynes and those around him, to get to this than it was for others, because they had been through the *Treatise* and the defence of the *Treatise* and the working out of the *Treatise*, where the definitions were unusual, the definitions of savings in particular. Words were being used in special senses. For this, I guess part of the heritage was from Dennis Robertson whose *Banking Policy and the Price Level* (1926) was full of these special words for saving which did contain and to some extent conveyed some rather subtle thoughts, but by the time you tried to distinguish one kind of 'lacking' from another and various other elements of savings the complexity was more than you could make head-or-tail of. Part of this, I think, survived in the terminology of the *Treatise*.

Thirdly, in the *Treatise* as Don Patinkin was saying before the coffee break, the focus was on prices rather than on output and employment. That was natural, I suppose, since the *Treatise* was written in the late twenties. And while there was a lot of unemployment in the UK nevertheless, unemployment wasn't the main problem for those of us overseas in the twenties and I guess Keynes and others were looking at the US as a clearer type of a largely self-sufficient economy. But to make the transition from the system of the *Treatise* to a system in which the essence was the variability of effective demand and of income and of employment, rather than prices, I guess was harder to do by a good deal than to pick up the idea relatively fresh.

In my own case, I started with the *Treatise* but it was on a few bare rocks up in Georgian Bay in 1932 as I prepared to go over to Cambridge and I had to do it alone. I think I learned enough of it to get along, but I didn't really have any intellectual attachment to it and when the ideas of the *General Theory* came along, I grasped them and my friends grasped them quickly because we felt that this was some real clue to what in fact was going on in most of our countries where we were in the throes of the terrible depression. I assume now in your teaching that you do the *General Theory* first or a much more compact modern version of it, and that the *Treatise* is a historical document and there isn't this problem of transition.

Of the process going on at Cambridge, I can't speak about what was happening between Keynes and the 'Circus' or the circle in which he was getting advice. I was certainly engaged in a great deal of talk and debate with my fellow students including the two who are at the table today. We talked out walking, we talked over tea, we talked over drinks, we talked at all hours of the day and night and we had enough access to some of the young dons as well as some of us in the Political Economy Club, that we thought there was a connection between the junior faculty people and ourselves. But even the Political Economy Club, I remember as a rather more informal type of discussion than Harry Johnson mentions in his paper for tomorrow. That may only be because I became bumptious enough that I intervened occasionally when I was uninvited and a number of others followed suit, so for a while I felt that there was enough discussion, oh, I won't call it 'cut-and-thrust', it was nothing as dangerous as that – but at least there were questions and answers.

It was only a short time later that I joined the Canadian Treasury. I lost track of the debate on the intellectual plane at that time. I was much more interested in using the framework of analysis in the *General Theory* and what one could do with it for trying to work out ideas on policy and policy measures. I guess my first ideas appeared in the Canadian budgets of 1939, both the peace budget in the spring and the war budget in September. I won't say Keynes's thought has gone on uninterruptedly in Ottawa since that time, but it's become accepted as a routine part of the analysis and work. I also found it in the IMF of course during the past four years, when I spent most of my time down there, where it was applied by a huge expert staff there to the problems of many countries – even a lot of countries where the measurement and influences on effective demand seem to me of secondary importance to the business of trying to run a government or a society at all in many of these developing countries. However, I would say that the understanding that I picked up in Cambridge in the thirties and had usefully refined in argument at Harvard has stood me and others in good stead since that time. We don't find it terribly helpful now in trying to get us out of this inflation mess, but that's a different question and I won't try to go into it now.

(ii) WALTER S. SALANT

I was at Cambridge for only one year and during that year Keynes lectured in only one semester, so I attended only eight of his lectures. That semester was one of the three semesters that Bob Bryce attended and one of four that Lorie Tarshis attended, so I am clearly a third-string member of this panel.

To a considerable extent I also have to echo what Bob Bryce said: one can't remember much of what happened forty years ago. I was at Cambridge as a research student for one year and came on very short notice. That may account for my not having been a member of the Political Economy Club, but I have sometimes wondered whether there might have been an explanation that was more interesting from a sociological point of view. Could it have been because I came from a country that was not in the Empire? It may seem hard to imagine now that considerations of Empire would have had great significance but things were different then. I have been assured at this conference that that was certainly not the explanation. Still, it might be interesting to try to find out whether any non-Empire students were members. In any case, my acquaintance with the views Keynes held at that time was based only on going to his lectures in the autumn of 1933 and on discussions with fellow students who did attend the meetings of the Political Economy Club.

Having come fresh from undergraduate economics at Harvard, I soon realised when I got to Cambridge how much I had not learned. My impression of what was important and welcome in Keynes's lectures was that here at last was a theory of output. That is the thing that Don Patinkin, in the chapter he has circulated, has stressed as the important thing. I would like to reinforce his view by calling to your attention – I can't say reminding you, because most of those here are too young ever to have known – what was the state of thought at the time. There was no such thing as a theory of output. Economics seemed to have two compartments between which there was no communication. There were the long-run principles, which you learned by studying the classical writers. Then there was something else, off in another corner, called Business Cycle Literature. It was hard to see what connection there was between these two compartments.

I have tried to think how one who has no acquaintance with the economics of that time could get a picture of what the subject was like and how little theory there was with which to approach problems of depression. It occurs to me that to get such an idea one should look first at such discussions of current economic situations as one would find in, say, the bulletins of the London and Cambridge Economic Service or in the *Review of Economic Statistics*, as it was then called, published by the Harvard Economics Department, with its attempts to forecast the business situation through use of A-curves, B-curves, and I can't remember what other apparatus, all of which bore no relation whatever to anything one would learn in Marshall or elsewhere. Another source that gives a view of the prevailing ability of theory to deal with macroeconomic problems is a book of essays published in 1934 by members of the Harvard Economics Department called *The Economics of the Recovery Program*, which contained essays by Schumpeter, the most senior author, Edward Chamberlin, Douglass Brown, Seymour Harris, Edward Mason, Wassily Leontief and Overton Taylor.

Paul Samuelson:
I think the Boston *Transcript* called it in a headline 'Harvard's second team strikes out.' Schumpeter was the only full professor among them; almost all the others were then only assistant professors or instructors.

Walter Salant (continuing):
That book is a collection of essays by people as up to date, presumably, in theory as you would have found at the time and it is interesting to see how they treated some of the problems. It is another world. That impression is partly the result of the book's being organised in a way that nobody would think of following now. The chapter titles are 'Depressions,' 'Purchasing Power,' 'Controlling Industry,' 'Helping Labor,' 'Higher Prices,' 'Helping the Farmer.' This might be explained by its addressing a specific set of programs but, still, we would now expect an organisation to include chapters on fiscal policy and monetary policy. Monetary policy is discussed in the chapter called 'Higher Prices' but fiscal policy receives only scattered attention.

More significant as indicators of difference in theory is the approach to specific problems. Savings is identified as a form of spending; money invested 'directly' in securities or mortgages or 'indirectly' in a savings account with a bank is 'spent as truly as money laid out upon sugar and clothing is spent' (page 30). Stimulating consumption expenditure directly 'raises the possibility . . . of the prices of food and clothing rising on account of an increase in *money* purchasing power in the hands of consumers before there can be a corresponding increase in production' (page 31). (Remember that this was written in late 1933, near the trough of the depression.) We read that, 'Relief costs money. Whether the immediate payment is made by public or by private agencies, the ultimate source of funds must be the money income of individuals' (page 68).

Flexibility of money wages to reflect the economic situation generally as well as in specific industries is referred to as necessary to avoid impeding necessary expansions or contractions and is followed by the observation that, 'In most cases, a very slight change in the rate of wages will be found to have a considerable effect upon the volume of employment. In this connection, the remarkable correlation between real wages and unemployment in Great Britain during the last decade is highly instructive' (page 84). There is no discussion or even apparent recognition that the relation between changes in the general levels of money and of real wages is a problem.

In short, the classical compartment was long-run and the business cycle introduced dynamics, but there was no concept of any long-run equilibrium of output. With classical principles, you couldn't explain how the world got into the mess that it was then in unless you made a major thing of frictions. That seemed to be the only way to establish any relationship. The point is that the state of affairs was totally unsatisfactory and that is what made so appealing to a young student just arriving the material that Keynes was presenting.

Now I'd like to turn to another point. Don Patinkin referred to the fact that the *General Theory* was a book about theory and not policy; before the *General Theory* many people, including Keynes himself, had advocated public works. Don referred to the article by George Garvy (1975) that was critical of Keynes for not having been acquainted with the German literature advocating public spending. What I would like to say about that issue is that, although Don is right in saying that the book was about theory and that the criticism about policy is to some degree misplaced, the book is also important for policy just *because* it is a book about theory. It is true, as one sees on reading Herbert Stein's book, *The Fiscal Revolution in America* (1969), that between 1929 and 1932 many economists understood the argument for deficit spending, whether on public works or on something else, and many noneconomists, as well as a few economists advocated such policies. Some economists did not because, although they understood the argument, they feared that if budget deficits were encouraged there would be a flight of capital from the United States that might inhibit revival of private investment, which involves more a question of judgment than one of theory. But there were many others who, despite the enormous and widespread unused capacity, simply associated budget deficits with domestic inflation and that view had wide conventional acceptance among the elite as being in accord with accepted theory. The reason the *General Theory* was important for policy was that it offered a countertheory.

Let me expand on that point. In 1971 I organised a session on Keynesians in Government for the annual meeting of the American Economic Association. I asked Alvin Hansen to be a discussant of one of the papers and I mentioned to him that I was also inviting Marriner Eccles, Chairman of the Federal Reserve Board during the Roosevelt and Truman Administrations, to be a discussant. (Eccles, although 82 at the time, was still going strong and was very active.) Hansen, responding in a letter dated 31 May, 1971, asked – and here I paraphrase – Why Eccles? He had a brilliant and original mind, and he strongly favored public spending in the deep depression but was by no stretch of the imagination a Keynesian. Ickes with his PWA favored government spending but he also was no Keynesian. Moulton favored a big public works program during the depression but he was anything but a Keynesian. Hansen then quoted a statement, (which he attributed to James Conant) that it takes a theory to kill a theory. 'Keynes killed neo-classical theory by showing that the economy is not self-sustaining, that unemployment is not just "*lapses*" from full employment.... People who in the old days supported public works as offsets to "lapses" from full employment were not Keynesians.'

The point is in the statement 'it takes a theory to kill a theory.' Facts are not sufficient, at least not until they become overwhelming. The proponents of established theory are skillful at ignoring facts that conflict with it. You need a theoretical refutation of established theory to make acceptable a policy that flies in its face.

Let me mention what I consider another illustration of this point. A few weeks ago Arthur Okun gave a paper presenting a model with a sector in which prices are set competitively and another sector in which sellers rationally make the prices and take whatever quantities of sales of output emerge. This was essentially a theoretical explanation of administered prices; it presented no new facts, only a theory. Gardiner Means and others have been talking about administered prices for about four decades and appear to have had very little impact on theorists, but Okun's paper, simply by giving a more satisfactory explanation of facts that had been observed for decades, seems to have advanced the subject.[3] And I would predict that, as a result, the facts will now be taken more seriously.

Similarly, I think the *General Theory* was important for public policy because it provided a countertheory with which to refute conventional theoretical objections to doing what, to the layman, was obviously necessary. Policies that were not acceptable before became acceptable, even though no facts had changed.

Finally, I would like to make a few observations about the theory of the rate of interest in relation to the *General Theory*. First, I want to mention something Don Patinkin may be interested in, although he may know of it already. Arthur Marget, who wrote an enormous two-volume work, *The Theory of Prices*, which seemed to be focused very largely on criticising Keynes, had written a PhD thesis at Harvard on a loan theory of the rate of interest. I have not read it but I remember having been told that this thesis expounded a monetary theory of the rate of interest. It may be worth looking at to see if it anticipated what is in the *General Theory*.

Second, in my lecture notes, which are probably not as full as those of Bob Bryce or Lorie Tarshis, there is a cryptic observation to the effect that 'This vitiates the real rate of interest doctrine.' Unfortunately, I shall have to go back to my notes to see what the antecedent of 'This' was. Since it is now the popular view that the nominal rate of interest reflects fully the expected rate of inflation, it would be worth going back to fuller lecture notes than mine to see whether Keynes had not already dealt with that point in his lectures. I may be reading something into them that wasn't there, but I think it worth looking into.[4]

Finally, there is an observation in your paper, Don, that you might want to reconsider in the light of a possible alternative interpretation. In connection with the argument between Keynes and Robertson on determination of the rate of interest, you noted Keynes's apparent failure to take into account the marginal productivity of capital and saving and you noted Robertson's insistence that these two things were important and that Keynes said that Robertson didn't get his point. You then commented that it was obvious who was being wrongheaded. It occurs to me that maybe what Keynes meant was that the marginal productivity of capital and saving were important but that they can't affect the nominal rate of interest unless they affect the demand for money. Maybe that is what he meant Robertson did not understand. In that case, it was a failure of communication and it would be a little hard to say that either party was wrongheaded. They may just have been going by each other, so to speak, and not making intellectual contact, rather than really disagreeing on a substantive point.

(iii) LORIE TARSHIS

First of all I'd like to add my bit to a couple of points that were raised earlier. It is certainly true that the *General Theory* is much more than an argument for public works. Don Patinkin mentioned this and Walter brought forward two names of non-Keynesians who favoured public works. Let me add one more name: Herbert Hoover was a firm advocate of public works and I can hardly believe that he thought of himself as a good Keynesian.

My second point has to do with a running debate between Don Patinkin and Paul Samuelson: in the *Treatise* and again in the Harris lectures Keynes makes the point that thrift declines, or at least it is likely to decline, as poverty increases, and if it does it may prove to be a stabilising force. The argument really has to do with the significance of Keynes's statement. A distinguished philosopher, formerly of the greater Cambridge and later of the lesser Cambridge, made I think the most appropriate statement about such a situation: 'that everything has been said before by somebody who did not discover it.' I suggest in this case that while Keynes certainly said it, I do not believe he was fully aware of its significance *at the time he said it*. It was only later, at least judging from my notes and my memory of discussions, that he fully realised the importance of such changes in output as a stabilising force. It seems to me that whilst Keynes here saw, though perhaps only dimly, the role that changes in output and income could perform in the equilibrating process, he neither allowed adequately for that role nor did he then see that the center of interest should be changes in the level of output, incomes and employment.

And now for my own 'contribution'. Occupying the third position on this panel, I am reminded of those days which Bob Bryce has mentioned and Walter Salant has rued – the days of the Political Economy Club. When we entered Keynes's rooms for a meeting we would be confronted at the door by Richard Kahn with slips of paper extending from his fist. As we came in, each undergraduate amongst us had to pick one of these slips of paper. If yours contained the number 1 you knew that your goose was cooked because you would be called on first, to discuss the paper that had just been read on a topic about which you probably knew nothing. If instead the slip was blank, it was real bliss because it meant you could just sit back and enjoy the whole evening without being called on to say anything. But if your number was 4 or 5 or 6 or 7, you knew that your goose was not only cooked but it was plucked too because those bright guys who had been assigned numbers 1, 2 and 3 would by then have said everything good including those great ideas you yourself had intended to set forth. And that is my position here, following on Bob and Walter. They have said it all.

Something has already been said about how it was to be a student at Cambridge in those glorious years 1932 to say 1935 or 1936. My background for Cambridge was to study at the same university as Bob, but I lacked his advantage of an education in mining engineering. Instead I had done economics. In a way that hurt, because in my third year I had had a very thorough drilling in the *Treatise on Money* and by the end of that year I must have been the *Treatise's* most devout believer. I really had managed to brainwash myself into regarding the *Treatise on Money* as the 'Final Truth'. Unfortunately, I lacked Hawtrey's genius in realising quickly that in fact it was deficient in several respects. So when I got to Cambridge and heard Keynes's first lectures in the autumn of 1932, along lines that seemed to differ from the *Treatise*, I wondered what he was talking about. What reconciled me to his new approach were the lectures of the following year. The year before the *Treatise*, when I was in my second year at Toronto, I had been assigned, for what was rather cruelly termed, 'An Introductory Course in Economics', a textbook which was not one of the products of our great multinationals, the Samuelson Corporation or the Lipsey Company Ltd., but a book which came right from the horse's mouth. It was Alfred Marshall's *Principles*. And so when I got to Cambridge, I already carried in my intellectual baggage − a rather pretentious term, I admit − some knowledge of Marshall's *Principles*: a reasonably deep and unreasonably sympathetic knowledge of the *Treatise*, together with a quite close acquaintance with *The Wealth of Nations* since Vincent Bladen was teaching economics then as he still is, and of course at least some of the interesting ideas that Harold Innis was developing. I quickly realised or at least I thought I had that Innis didn't cross the ocean very well. I suppose I thought that Adam Smith didn't cross the generations very well either so what I had as my primary buttress when I began in October 1932 to listen to Keynes's lectures on 'The Monetary Theory of Production' was Marshall's *Principles* and Keynes's *Treatise*. Naturally since I was already 21, I resisted the invasion of Keynes's new ideas because they appeared to threaten what I knew to be true from the *Treatise*. I resisted them really until I managed to see that what Keynes was doing, and he made this clear from early in the course – though I am not clear that I got it so early – was this: he was trying to bring together these two separate strands, the theory of value as presented in Marshall, and the theory of money of the *Treatise*. I don't pretend that I had been previously troubled by any inherent contradiction. Keynes, in the *Treatise*, had been concerned with the Theory of Money; Marshall, in the *Principles*, with the theory of value; and I was quite unconcerned that 'ne'er the twain did meet'.

I attended Keynes's lectures for four years and I seem to have missed only one, to judge from my notes. But as you may know, the demands on the lecturer were light; for him only seven in the Michaelmas term and no more for the rest of the year. The room was always full, with most or perhaps all of the Faculty present and a large number of students. As a very crude guess, based on a pretty misty memory, attendance was about 100; but it would be safer if I were to say 100 ± 100. I do remember that they were held on Mondays at 11.00 a.m. One very rare sight for lectures in economics at Cambridge: I recall proctors and their staff standing around, presumably to keep out interlopers. He talked quickly and clearly, with no bombast, and very much down to business. There was no 'small talk', and no effort to amuse the audience. The room was invariably hushed and it was clear that everyone was trying as hard as possible to follow him. You could almost feel the general sense that THIS WAS IT. Naturally, there was no discussion and there were no questions addressed to him during the lecture.

Apart from these lectures, my other main contact with him was at meetings of the Political Economy Club, which we all called the Keynes's Club. He and Kahn were invariably present with a sprinkling of other faculty – I remember Piero Sraffa, J. W. F. Rowe and Colin Clark as frequent attendants – Austin Robinson and Joan Robinson less often, and I cannot recall ever seeing D. H. Robertson or Pigou there. Sometimes academics from outside Cambridge attended too – I remember Paul Douglas and Henry Schultz from Chicago and Hubert Henderson. Keynes always occupied an easy chair which was to our right of the fireplace, usually sprawled out as though he were posing for the excellent caricature of him that David Low did. Finally, there was a contingent of students, a very few research students amongst them (Alec Cairncross and Ronald Walker were the two I remember best) and perhaps up to ten or twelve undergraduates. One meeting, held on an especially wet night with a paper on something to do with the East Indian Company in an especially critical, and for me an absolutely blank, decade in the eighteenth century managed to attract three students – the person who wrote the paper, Bob Bryce and me. There was no way in which the two of us could avoid being called upon to contribute what we knew to that discussion!

After the students had made their remarks, we all were served tea and fruit cake. Then Keynes asked each of the faculty members and distinguished visitors present whether he wished to speak. And after that Keynes stood up. It is a great pity that the tape recorder was not known at that time. He invariably managed to make that final part of the evening a glittering success. Sometimes – I guess usually – the paper and the discussion that followed it were merely the springboard from which after gentle criticism and encouragement for the students who had participated, he jumped into any or many related topics – with a wit, a grace and an imagination that were a joy to experience.

So far as I can remember, he was always gentle in criticism of students. He somehow managed to correct your errors and turn you around 180 degrees and still make you feel that you were pretty good. I gather that he was less patient with his colleagues and other contemporaries, who, I suppose he felt should know better.

Keynes's influence on students was striking. Most of us became zealots – probably some of you will feel that some of us have remained too zealous in his support for too long. In any event we were full of a missionary zeal. In part this was because we sensed that at last an economist was coming to grips with the most devastating economic disaster in centuries. Moreover it was exciting, once we realised what was happening, to see that economics could be a unified subject: – to see that the economics we learned at our 10 o'clock lectures on value theory was part and parcel of the economics we got in our 11 o'clock lectures on monetary economics. That at least was intellectually stimulating. But, in addition, and far more important was the realisation that the economist could now guide policy along sensible lines to bring about a restoration of prosperity and to solve unemployment. And best of all, it seemed reasonable to expect no opposition to such policies, except from bankruptcy lawyers, because almost everyone would gain from a restoration of prosperity. It was intoxicating, and doubly so because we felt we were a part of the revolution.

Naturally, many of us were attracted too, to Marx, although the students of economics at Cambridge seemed to have a much greater difficulty in accepting *Capital* than did the students in other fields. My own attitude on the matter was ambivalent; I looked to Keynes to validate the essence of Marx's theory of the breakdown of the capitalist economy and to Marx to enrichen Keynes's analysis. At the same time, I felt that Keynes could show us how to run a capitalist economy that was not subject to crisis.

In that connection, I remember a meeting of the Marshall Society – the large undergraduate economics club – at which John Strachey was the speaker; I believe the meeting was held in November 1935, or very early in 1936. John Strachey had written a few years earlier a most influential book, *The Coming Struggle for Power* (1932) which applied

Marx's insights to all the problems and issues that very naturally concerned students of that period. It was probably the most successful popularisation of Marx ever written in English. At the talk, and remember he appeared just a few months or weeks before the *General Theory*, he again argued, very persuasively I recall, that we would find the answers to such problems as why capitalism is doomed and the writers' and artists' roles in society, and so on, in Marx. After the discussion, I was asked to thank him, which of course I did. But in the course of my remarks I told him that there would appear very soon a book that would throw even more light on booms and slumps and capitalism's crisis than Marx's analysis could possibly do. I meant, of course, the *General Theory*. Well the combination of the *General Theory* and my attempt to sell it to him, created a situation of 'overkill'. A few years later – 1937 and 1938 I believe – two books by Strachey were published which showed a complete acceptance of Keynes and a rejection of substantial parts of Marx.

A second incident involving Marx, and this time Keynes rather than the *General Theory*, I can recall. Somehow, at a meeting of the Political Economy Club, which I expect you know was held in Keynes's rooms, several times a term on Monday evenings, the discussion briefly introduced the name of Karl Marx. Piero Sraffa was present that evening; he had a great reputation, at least among the students, as a Marx scholar, but I do not remember that he participated in that part of the discussion. At the close of the meeting, I found myself in line, as we walked to the door, directly behind Sraffa. Keynes was standing at the door to say good bye. As Sraffa approached, Keynes said – probably to tease him – 'I say there, Piero, is there anything to that Marx chap?'

After leaving for the US in June 1936, I started on my PhD dissertation for Cambridge University – writing it when I could find the time from a regular teaching position at Tufts University. The topic, begun under Colin Clark and later done without any help from a supervisor was 'The Determinants of Labour Income'. It was an attempt to create a macro-theory of distribution; a theory of the distribution of the total output of the economy. I believed – and still do – that conventional distribution theory was – despite its title – an exercise in *allocation theory* and it seemed to me that just as Keynes had extended conventional value (allocation) theory in such a way as to write a theory that explained how aggregate output was determined, I (or someone) could extend conventional distribution (allocation) theory in such a way as to explain how the distribution of the national income was determined.

Naturally, I was quickly drawn to Keynes's hunch in the *General Theory* (p. 10) about the inverse relation between changes in money and real wages. When I was finally able to get the data, I decided to check his views. I sent him my note, which of course raised a question about his hunch. I was overjoyed to receive a warm letter of acceptance very soon afterward and even more flattered to learn that he would have a comment on it (and Dunlop's article) in the same number of the *Economic Journal* (1939).

I never felt that my findings – even assuming they were valid – did anything to the essence of the *General Theory*. There were some pretty obvious ways of accounting for my results which raised no doubts at all about the substance of his work; but only minor points about the model he had chosen. I am inclined to think that many other criticisms of the *General Theory* which have become accepted have no more significance. But that is a study for another time.

This is all that I have to say in the way of memories of that period at Cambridge over thirty years ago. But I would like to take advantage of this opportunity to turn now to another subject related to Keynes, though one of a completely different nature. In particular, I would like now to present a brief discussion on the subject 'Keynes: The Neoclassical Base in the 1930s and today'.

Keynes in his preface to the *General Theory* refers to the 'difficulty' (of his work) 'which lies not in the new ideas, but in escaping from the old ones.' Now, the 'old ones' that caused me most of my troubles in his lectures were those I had absorbed from the *Treatise*. It was not difficult for me to give up Marshallian interest theory or even his version of Say's Law, set out in the words of John Stuart Mill and qualified in the *Principles*. But as I have noted above I had been so thoroughly convinced of the virtues of the *Treatise* that for a time I could see no point in any attempt to re-state it.

What persuaded me, I suppose, to welcome his new approach was some of the economics I had learned in Marshall and in its more modern formulation – in Joan Robinson's *Imperfect Competition* which I read upon publication in the summer of 1933, and Richard Kahn's lectures on 'The Short Period' which I attended in the autumn of 1932.

I only gradually became aware of the problem raised by the division of economics into the theory of value and the theory of money and eventually welcomed Keynes's efforts to bring them together. These efforts required in the final analysis dropping the price-output model of the *Treatise* in which when investment exceeded saving, it meant a rise in prices (relative to costs) which implied windfall profits which brought about an increase in output. Instead he focussed attention on the effects of changes in the demand for, or the costs of producing any output, upon prices and outputs simultaneously and thence upon prices in general and aggregate output. As a result of this change, Keynes was led to introduce the notion of effective demand – with its twin determinants, the aggregate demand function and the aggregate supply function. Apart from problems, to which Don Patinkin alludes, raised by the notion of the demand for (or supply of) output as a whole – to economists who had been brought up by Marshall to think always in terms of 'other things being equal' – this new approach of Keynes seemed to mark a forward step because in a way it meant a partial return to Marshall. And it did seem to give the proper response to that species of analysis – still current, I believe – in which we say: 'If we suppose that output does not change, prices must change by the full amount dictated by the change in demand (or supply). On the other hand, if we assume that firms make some output adjustment, the alteration in price will be smaller . . . and so on; – all as though the first option were random and the second then had merely to be consistent.

Unfortunately, in the years since the *General Theory* appeared, a spate of revisions, simplifications, and as I see a few of the changes, actual misunderstandings, have obscured some of the most valuable features of this part of Keynes's analysis. What I should like to do this morning is to present again these weary subjects, exegetical or Talmudic though the treatment will be, in trying to persuade you of two things:

(a)   that Keynes, despite his refusal to accept parts of Marshall derived a great deal of value from it which he employed in the *General Theory*, and
(b)   that Keynesians, to use Leijonhufvud's distinction, have, I suppose inadvertently, discarded a good deal that they should have felt called upon to defend – and by doing so have reduced our ability to understand how the economy works.

As I see it – and the view is certainly not very original – the most significant advance from the *Treatise* to the *General Theory* consisted, first, in formulating the problem – a concern with aggregate output or income – and then identifying the notion of effective demand as having the primary role in answering it. This meant dealing with the two aggregate functions – the aggregate demand (ADF) and the aggregate supply functions (ASF). Obviously, a good deal remains in modern Keynesian analysis of the aggregate demand function; by way of contrast, not much more remains of the aggregate supply function than the eerie grin of the disappeared cat which usually does not even rate mention in the index. Yet it is through the aggregate supply function that Keynes is most closely related to Marshall, and it is through it too that many of the bridges between micro- and macro-economics can be found, or to put this differently, where the micro-foundations of macro-economics are located.

The failure of economists after 1936 to give to the aggregate supply function the importance that Keynes judged it to deserve, is, I believe, unfortunate, though part of the blame belongs to Keynes himself and his collaborators because what Keynes meant can at times only be inferred by assuming that he was rational and then attempting to work out what he must have meant in order to arrive at the conclusions he did. It must be said that one of Britain's greatest writers did not quite cover himself with glory in Chapters 3 and 6 of the *General Theory*.

I hope this exercise will not be only a display of an antiquarian's folly, but that it will suggest that Keynes's analysis can even contribute something to our understanding of such nasty modern problems as 'stagflation.'

I shall say no more about the aggregate demand function here beyond making two points: first, since it is defined as the function that relates various levels of employment, or output to the proceeds expected from their sales, our first impulse would be to determine its precise form, ideally at least, by asking each producer how much he expected to receive from the sales of each and every level of output. After determining – God knows how! – the shares of each producer in each and every level of aggregate output, the total proceeds could be obtained by simple aggregation. Such an approach would however be subject to two criticisms at least. It would imply, for one, that every expectation of every producer, no matter how unrestrained or quixotic it might be, had to be taken as fully creditable. Obviously the aggregate demand function estimated in such a way would have little operational significance. Secondly, it would imply that a sensible estimate as to the prospective sales of one producer could be made without reference to the sales of all the others and hence without regard to the level of incomes generated. Keynes's way around these difficulties was simply to recognise the *constraints* upon the expectations of sellers – which experience itself would confirm – created by the need for consistency with the expected behaviour of buyers. Thus, we estimate what the sellers of consumer goods could expect from their sales, by directing attention to the purchasing plans of buyers, through the consumption function or the propensity to consume. In the same way, that component of total proceeds that comprises expectations about the sale of a certain amount of investment goods, is to be constrained by reference to the plans or intentions of the purchasers of output of that kind.

Thus the way in which the propensity to consume and the various functions that establish the spending plans of firms in respect to investment goods enter into the ADF is by establishing constraints that guide the economy's sellers as they set out their expectations of sales proceeds from various levels of output. Presumably, this guidance over their expectations is exercised through the experience of the recent and immediate past, and if this guidance is denied, a series of disappointed expectations will quickly drive those who have been holding them into bankruptcy, or at least confront them with profits smaller than they could have realised: – a relatively persuasive argument for accepting such guidance.

The other point I should like to make about the aggregate demand function is that whilst Keynes initially defined it as the function that relates 'various hypothetical quantities of *employment* to the proceeds which their outputs are expected to yield', he subsequently implied – or at least he did whilst discussing the propensity to consume in Chapter 6 –

that the independent variable, as a matter of convenience should be, not the various levels of employment but instead levels of income, measured in terms of wage units. There are problems that have to do with just which aggregate demand function should be used – that in which the independent variable is the level of employment or that in which it is the level of income, measured in wage units. It is clear or at least it should be that whatever the choice, it has to be consistent with the similar choice to be made amongst two or three versions of the aggregate supply function. There are problems here which I have not seen properly handled.

The aggregate supply function, like the aggregate demand function is concerned with the *whole* economy but this time the focus of our concern must be sellers or suppliers and their behaviour. In a capitalist economy we assume of course that the typical supplier is a profit-maximising firm. Such a firm, we assume, will choose the combination of price and output that promises the highest level of profit. It is, of course, confronted by a certain demand for its prospect and it knows its costs of producing the various levels of output.

Keynes defines the aggregate supply function with the 'output' variable being measured, as with the aggregate demand function, in terms of employment. Then the aggregate supply price of the output of a given level of *employment is that expectation of proceeds that will just* (and I will return to the meaning of this word) *make it worth the while of the producers to hire that many employees.* It will be useful, I believe, to look at this relation between any level of employment, and the proceeds required as the bait needed to justify it by examining, to begin with, this connection for a single firm.

Suppose we set as our independent variable a level of employment in one firm of N_1, and we determine that given its capital, technology and so on, that firm's output when its employees number N_1, would be O_1. Suppose too we have knowledge of its 'costs'. (For simplicity in Figure 1, I have set out only the marginal cost function.) The only other information we need is the elasticity of the demand for the product of the firm; call it e_1.

In order to determine the proceeds required we need to know the price it would charge, assuming it would choose the most profitable combination of price and output (already set at O_1). That can be found once we can discover the demand function it faces: we already 'know' its elasticity. So our problem comes down to this: what level of demand, given the marginal cost function and the demand elasticity, would lead the firm to produce O_1 units of output? (It would not contribute anything but unnecessary complexity to correct the level of sales receipts so as to convert it into the level of proceeds, but for those who worry, it is precisely the same problem that the modern statistician faces when he corrects the sales receipts of a firm so that he arrives at the value added.)

Referring to figure 1 we can see the answer. If the output O_1

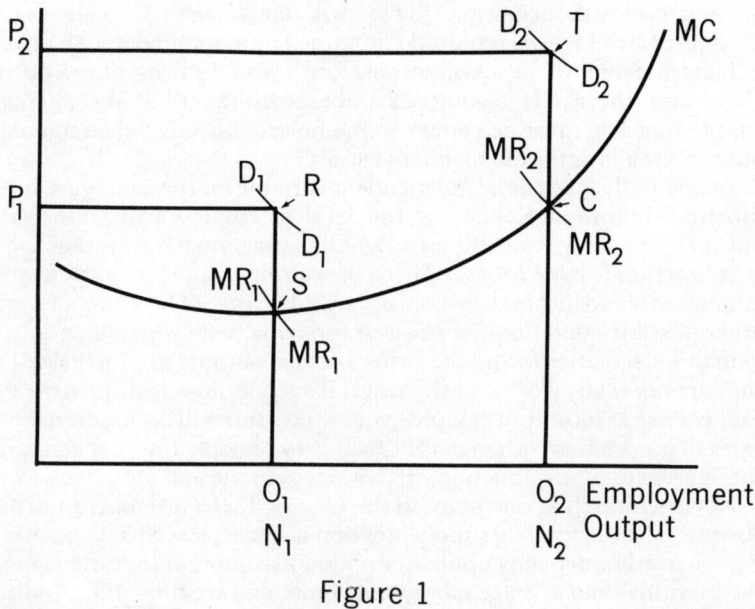

Figure 1

is to be the most profitable, its marginal cost, designated by S must be equal to the marginal revenue corresponding to that output. Since with an elasticity of demand equal to e, the demand curve must pass through a point vertically above O_1 and $e/(e-1)$ times the marginal revenue, it then follows that the price to be charged would be $e/(e-1)$ times S, the marginal cost. (In the diagram, in order to illustrate the procedure, I have assigned a specific value to the demand elasticity of 3. Then, the demand must pass through a point R which is 50% above the marginal cost.) The sales receipts required as an inducement to persuade the firm to produce O_1, the output corresponding to employment at N_1, would then be $P_1 \times O_1$.

The demand, assuming its elasticity is unchanged, would have to go through a point vertically above O_2 by the factor $e/(e-1)$ above C, the marginal cost of that output, if the firm is to choose to produce O_2 units of output. Again, referring to the diagram, it will be seen that if $e = 3$, the demand curve going through T would induce that output. *And note: assuming that the elasticity were 3, no demand curve other than D_2 could be found that would lead the firm to choose to produce O_2 units.* The price would then be P_2, and our expectation of sales receipts of $P_2 \times O_2$ would be the supply-price, in the sense in which Keynes uses the term, that would lead to such a level of production.

Imagine that this is done for all firms and for all outputs. Then for any aggregate output – in the sense of the economy's total output – the quota or contribution of each firm being known, though again God knows how, the aggregate proceeds required is obtained by summing over all firms.

If at least some of the marginal cost function of the firms have a positive slope over the range of outputs under consideration, the aggregate supply function must be convex to the horizontal axis, when aggregate output is taken as the independent variable.

Incidentally, even if the independent variable for the aggregate supply function, following Keynes, is the level of employment, rather than output, the ASF will only be a straight line function if the average labour cost function is itself *horizontal* over the relevant range of outputs and if labour costs constitute the whole of variable costs. (There are, of course, other possible conditions for this result having to do with changes in the demand elasticities facing the firms as their outputs are increased; but they are not really worth considering.) If average labour costs in the typical firm rise as its output expands, and surely this will occur, even if wage rates do not change, when output begins to press against capacity, then the aggregate supply function will be convex to the horizontal axis.

Keynes himself at one point in the *General Theory* attempts to demonstrate that the aggregate supply function is linear; it seems to me that his demonstration depends upon an implicit assumption that the slopes of the marginal and average labour cost functions are the same. And such an assumption is only realised when average labour costs remain unchanged over a range of output; and it is only over that range that the aggregate supply function would be linear, and incidentally with an elasticity of one.

Any point on the aggregate supply function represents an output or employment level that, in the given circumstances would yield the highest possible level of profit. If the economy's output is at a level at which the aggregate demand function is above the aggregate supply function, that output (made up of the outputs of all producers, will *not* be one which, given the demands for the product, the marginal cost functions for the various firms and the demand elasticities, is the most profitable. Instead, it will represent a situation in which the demands as actually realised exceed the demands on the expectations of which the individual firms have made their output decisions; alternatively it would represent a situation in which the firms are not trying to maximise their profits – even though, generally that is their aim. With the demand for the product of the typical firm higher than anticipated, the firm can do one of three things: it can draw down inventories in order to meet its customers' orders; or it can raise the price, keeping production constant; or instead it can move to a new output-price combination, which would provide a still higher level of profit. These possibilities can be seen in figures 2 and 3.

There, for the aggregate output O_2, the aggregate demand function exceeds the aggregate supply function. Looking at the situation of one firm (see figure 3) the demand as experienced (D_2) turns out to be above the demand required (D_1). (It is on the basis of D_1 that the firm chose an output of O_2 and set its price at P_1.) When the firm realises that it has underestimated the demand for its product, it can adjust by drawing down inventories, though presumably not for long. In the degree that firms in general were to do this, the aggregate demand function would be lowered. Or it could raise its price to P_2 but if the marginal cost is really MC as shown, while this would add to its profits, the firm could add even more by moving its output to O_3 and its price to P_3. Equilibrium, in the sense that all firms were optimising their positions given the determinants of the aggregate demand function and their marginal costs and demand elasticities, is only attained when the total output had risen to O_3, and the individual firm is in the situation pictured by figure 3.

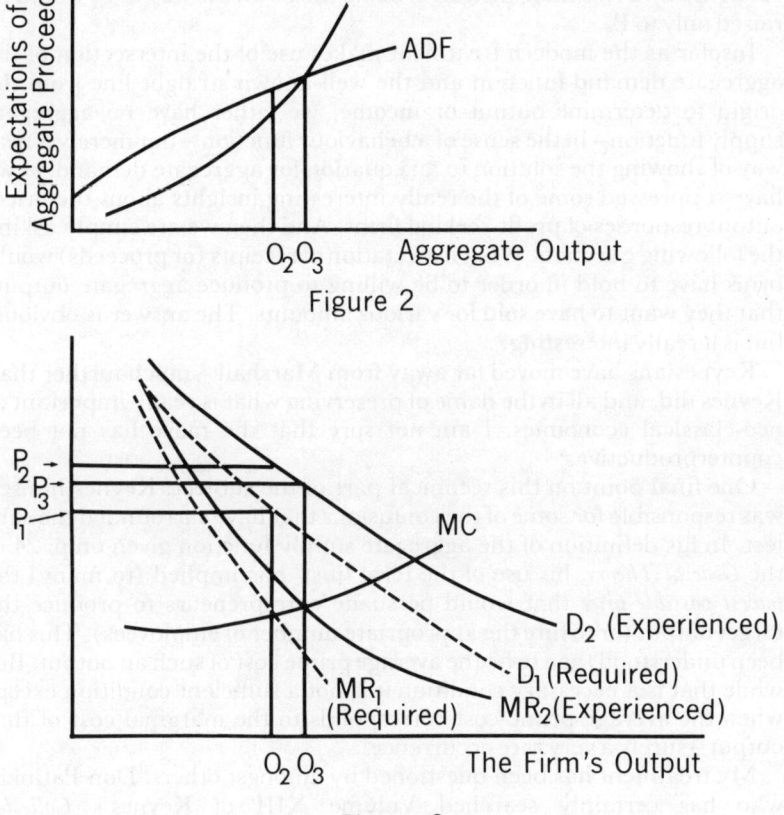

Figure 2

Figure 3

Hawtrey, we learn from the fascinating Volume XIII of Keynes's *Collected Writings*, edited by my colleague Don Moggridge, felt that the output for which the aggregate demand and supply functions were equal was one of zero profits. I believe Keynes was correct in rejecting this charge; that whilst an output like O_2 allows for a high level of *unanticipated* profits, O_3 provides for still higher profits. And surely, even though unanticipated profits are zero when the output is O_3, since it represents higher total profit than could be obtained with output at O_2, equilibrium obtains with output at O_3: not at O_2 or anything else. We need not consider this situation as one in which realisation differs from anticipation. It may be that D_2 (referring to figure 3) is expected and we merely want to determine whether an output price combination O_2 and P_1 represents a situation of equilibrium. The answer is surely in the negative because the individual firm(s) could raise its (their) profits by expanding their total output to O_3 (for the individual – see figure 3) or O_3 (for the economy – see figure 2). Price then, instead of being raised all the way to P_2 would be raised only to P_3.

Insofar as the modern treatment makes use of the intersection of the aggregate demand function and the well-known straight line from the origin to determine output or income, we either have no aggregate supply function – in the sense of a behaviour function – but merely a neat way of showing the solution to an equation for aggregate demand, *or* we have suppressed some of the really interesting insights about the price-output responses of profit-seeking firms. And then we are simply asking the following question: What expectation of receipts (or proceeds) would firms have to hold in order to be willing to produce aggregate outputs that they want to have sold for various amounts. The answer is obvious: but is it really interesting?

Keynesians have moved far away from Marshall – much further than Keynes did, and all in the name of preserving what is really important in neo-classical economics. I am not sure that the move has not been counterproductive.[5]

One final point on this technical part of the subject: Keynes himself was responsible for some of the confusions that have surrounded the subject. In his definition of the aggregate supply function given on p. 24 of the *General Theory*, his use of the term 'just' has implied (to many) the *lowest possible price* that would persuade entrepreneurs to produce the target output (or to hire the appropriate number of employees). This has been understood then to be the average prime cost of such an output. But while that is a necessary condition it is not a sufficient condition except when the average prime cost corresponds to the marginal cost of that output – surely a very rare occurrence!

My treatment has been questioned by amongst others, Don Patinkin who has certainly searched Volume XIII of Keynes's *Collected Writings* meticulously for evidence to support it. Well, one man's scribbling is, I suppose, another's prose. I believe that Keynes was quite conscious of what he wanted the aggregate supply function to represent. Thus, on 13 April, 1934 he wrote to R. F. Kahn as follows:

> I have been making rather extensive changes in the early chapters of my book, consequential on a simple and obvious, but beautiful and important (I think) precise definition of what is meant by effective demand:
>
> > Let W be the marginal prime cost of production when output is 0.
> > Let P be the expected selling price of this output.
> > Then OP is effective demand.
>
> On my theory OW = OP for all values of O, and entrepreneurs have to choose a value of O for which it is equal; otherwise the equality of price and marginal prime cost is infringed. This is the real starting point of everything. (JMK XIII, pp. 422–3).

Incidentally, this letter was written about two weeks after Keynes had been through what he referred to as 'a stiff week's supervision from RFK' (ibid.). Does this not mean that *equilibrium* for the suppliers, which was represented by various points on the aggregate supply function, were various maximum-profit combinations of price and output, each corresponding to demand at a particular level? Now, he assumed a situation of perfect competition in the various industries, and accordingly, since $e/(e-1)$ would then equal one, that price must equal the marginal cost for equilibrium to obtain. I interpret:

> Now, a firm's capital equipment being given, there is, each day, the question of the train of employment to be set going that day which will maximise the firm's quasi-rent. Under normal assumptions of competition etc. the condition of maximum quasi-rent will be satisfied by a volume of employment such that the prime cost of the marginal employment will be equal to the expected sale proceeds of the resulting increment of product. For the sake of simplicity and clearness of exposition, we shall, therefore, assume in what follows that we are dealing with this case; though a complete exposition (which would lead us beyond our present subject) must, of course, take account of, and adapt the argument to, the well-known exceptions to it. We shall assume, that is to say, that employment will be carried to a point at which $\varDelta D_w = \varDelta N$, ...

> Thus the innovation of the present theory is, at this stage, purely negative. Its significance will depend on our establishing our contention that there is, in general, only one level of output at which equality holds between marginal prime cost and the anticipated price, so that under competition the aim of maximising profit will cause entrepren-

eurs to choose that level of employment for which this equality holds [in this sense] (*JMK* XIII, pp. 426–7).

Further on this subject: I have located lecture notes I made whilst attending lectures on 'The Short Period' given by R. F. Kahn in the autumn of 1932. It is perfectly clear that even then, in November 1932, Richard Kahn with Joan Robinson, had gone as far as was needed to provide the basis for Keynes's aggregate supply function in the sense in which I have used the term. Let me quote from my notes of Kahn's lectures to substantiate this view: 'In a world where businessmen behave rationally . . .' [but do they? There may have to be a minor qualification.] (Summarised by L. T. August 1976). 'If A = average value and M = marginal value of quantity and e = elasticity of demand then $A = M \times e/(e-1)$. In equilibrium, MR = MC, and therefore price = marginal *cost* (in place of marginal revenue) multiplied by $e/(e-1)$. And when e is infinite, P = MC' (lecture notes from 23 November, 1932). 'Price (to get maximum returns) = $MC \times e/(e-1)$' (ibid., 30 November, 1932).

I suppose that one can argue till Doomsday about the significance of all of this. I see no way of doubting that Kahn and Joan Robinson had by then taken the subject as far as was needed; but how can we know that Keynes went along with them, or understood them? Perhaps it is correct, to quote from a letter that I have received on this point from Don Patinkin in which he says: '. . . it seems to me that your major argument is that my interpretation of Keynes could not be the right one for it makes Keynes appear "self-contradicting and wrong". And I say, that is precisely the case: on this point he was "self-contradicting and wrong". And, I say confused: witness his exposition in the 1934 draft. . . . Accordingly, I feel that if you contend that in the final published form of the *General Theory* Keynes had escaped from this confusion – and that, in particular, he interpreted the ASF as you are now doing – then it is incumbent upon you to cite chapter and verse from Keynes's writings . . . to support your contention. Insofar as your own interpretation and concern, I can only repeat that the precise and (for that time) complex MR = MC analysis that you present here seems to me to be quite foreign to Keynes' general analytical style.'

Of course, I cannot know how much communication there was between Kahn and Keynes between say, 1931 and 1935, but my impression is that there was a great deal and I would be very surprised if Kahn would have allowed Keynes to submit to the publisher a concept of the aggregate supply function that was notably deficient and primitive as compared to what Kahn (and some others in the 'Circus') had developed as early as November 1932!

In closing, I should like to commend those who have organised this Conference, and of course Austin Robinson, Donald Moggridge and

Elizabeth Johnson who have done so superb a job in editing Keynes' *Collected Writings*. I believe that Keynes still has an enormous amount to contribute to our understanding of the economy and trust that more economists, with so much material now available, will seek these insights directly rather than by the Rube Goldberg-like contrivances that have become fashionable; I mean by referring to X's critical comments on Y's contributions to Z's efforts to say what Keynes really meant.

NOTES

1. Keynes founded this club, of which he was always chairman, in 1909 and it continued, with a short interruption for the First World War, until 1937 (see Harrod (1951), pp. 149–53). It served the purpose of keeping Keynes in touch with a small select group of undergraduates (and research students) reading economics at Cambridge. During the period between the *Treatise* and the *General Theory*, it met on Monday evenings during term in Keynes's rooms at King's, and discussed a wide variety of subjects each normally introduced by a paper by one of the students.
2. [Reproduced in Appendix I below – Eds.]
3. The paper referred to is Arthur Okun's "Inflation: Its Mechanics and Welfare Costs" (1975).
4. On referring to my notes after the conference I found that this statement was in an early lecture in which Keynes was contrasting the classical view of the economy, which, he said, assumed that an entrepreneur will produce if he will thereby get 'larger production,' with his view that an entrepreneur will do so if he expects to get more money, whether it represents larger real output or not, and will not produce if he gets less money at the end, even if that represents more product. 'He would be better off by sitting on that money. . . . Future price changes which are unforeseen have no effect. Foreseen future prices affect present prices. . . . If rise of prices anticipated by market, owner of money cannot avoid loss. Idea of *real rate of interest* vitiated.' Quotations are from my notes on the lecture given 23 October, 1933.
5. In a longer paper written after the Conference, I have criticised the 45° straight-line-from-the-origin version of the aggregate supply function even more strongly. This paper is to appear in a volume honouring my close friend and former colleague Tibor Scitovsky.

5 Cambridge Discussion and Criticism Surrounding the Writing of *The General Theory*: A Chronicler's View

DONALD E. MOGGRIDGE

Although I have already had an opportunity to have my say on this topic, first in editing the evidence (*JMK* XIII and XIV), and second in a presentation to an earlier conference (Moggridge, 1973), I cannot really let this opportunity go by without a few remarks, if only because Don's stimulating work has raised somewhat different issues than I had considered before.

In an exercise such as this, even though we do have a considerable amount of evidence, we also face serious problems of weighting. I can best illustrate this if we look at the various types of materials in turn. First of all, we have memories. These are, for example, almost the only source of information on the 'Circus'. However, their reliability is variable, as I have often found in working on Keynes and in my earlier work on the 1920s. People are often not exact in their memories, especially when one is looking back over forty years, as we are in this case; they often need very detailed external stimuli to fit them in exactly.

Our second sort of evidence is correspondence, subject, of course, to the selectivity of what was and was not kept.[1] Even when the correspondence survives, it may leave problems. When there is, for example, a letter from Joan Robinson to Keynes, it may have been written as a summation of the collective opinion of several people. Of course, Joan may actually mention that it is, as she does on occasion in Volume XIII (e.g. p. 376), but on other occasions we must simply guess and be wary of attributing ideas.

Then, of course, we have drafts, which have relatively few problems beyond dating. Fortunately, as well, we have lecture notes. However, most of us are university teachers and, if we did compare what went down in our students' notebooks with what we thought we had said or intended to say, we wouldn't be completely sure of such a source again. For it all depends on the perceptions that are at the other end of the pen, not only on the lecturer. Thus we are in the hands of the reporter and we may have to decide, if we are lucky, among reporters. All lecture notes are not equal. But do we have any way of deciding which are better than others as guides to lectures where the lecturer's own notes, if they ever existed, have not survived?

Another possibility is publications. If nothing else they raise the problem of dating. Perhaps the classic case in our story is, of course, Joan Robinson's 1933 *Economica* article, which is a good example of the position reached in Cambridge eighteen months earlier, soon after the end of the 'Circus' but a bad example of where things stood in late 1932 or early 1933. Publications also raise the problem of how much outside evidence we use as indications of Keynes's evolving views. This is certainly a problem with the *Treatise*, where the final stages of re-writing coincided with Keynes's five spring 1930 days of 'private evidence' to the Macmillan Committee and the period of publication was almost coterminous with another three days of drafting 'evidence' to the Committee and Keynes's work for the Committee of Economists of the Economic Advisory Council. The problem remains during the years of the *General Theory*, given Keynes's extensive outside activities in areas related to the book. In the end, it is a matter of judgement on which people probably differ.

Finally, we have appointment books and diaries. The only problem is that they are far from complete. They tend to be fairly good during term time, but when Keynes went to Tilton during the vacations, when one suspects most of the more creative work took place, we have no indication from them as to whom he saw. So again there are problems.

And even with all of this evidence before us, we still have another problem to get over if we are fully to get inside the process of creation in 'Cambridge'. Austin Robinson has already mentioned it and Harry Johnson will raise it again tomorrow: the physical setting. For the small Cambridge faculty of the 1930s did not have a building. Thus we cannot equate Cambridge in the 1930s to the modern North American or English (outside of Oxford) departments that most of us know. There was not the opportunity for the casual discussion of problems in the coffee room or for colleagues casually dropping into each other's rooms saying, 'Look, I'm having problems with this argument. Can you see a way around it?'. Most of us have, at some time or other, exploited our colleagues in this way, but Cambridge economics in the 1930s could not operate in that manner. The faculty were dispersed among a number of colleges. If they were lucky enough to be in a college with more than one economist, members of the faculty might see colleagues over meals, although meals were not the place to do professional as opposed to college business. True, faculty members could visit each other in their college rooms for discussion, but at the loss of some spontaneity, for, given the way teaching and college meetings spread over the day, one would normally make an appointment. One did not casually drop in. True, such contacts as did occur might be important (see for example, *JMK* XIII, pp. 135 and 138), but they don't remove my point. That is that individual faculty members in the 1930s were, in many respects, more isolated in many senses than their successors in Cambridge or many of their contemporaries elsewhere. This is a matter of some importance.

Now given the available evidence, with all its problems, and the physical and social situation, what can we say about the process of discussion and criticism surrounding the writing of the *General Theory*? Perhaps the best way to go at it would be in stages, which for want of better words we might call dissatisfaction, creation and consolidation. First of all came the creation of active dissatisfaction on Keynes's part with the fomulations of the *Treatise*, itself the product of six years work. Then came the creation of an alternative vision and an alternative set of ideas. Finally came the consolidation of that vision and that set of ideas into a form suitable for the outside world, for publication. In each of these stages, the personnel varied somewhat, although throughout a certain important constancy remained – the core pair of Joan Robinson and, most important, Richard Kahn.

Although Keynes was not altogether satisfied with his *Treatise on Money* at the time he had finished it, he was certainly of the opinion that in it he had developed an improved theory of the credit cycle, which, despite its frequent necessity for qualitative judgements, was fit for application to affairs. True, he remarked, 'I could do it better and much shorter if I were to start over again' (*Treatise* I, pp. xvii–xviii), but he used the analysis of the book, with its 'special case' to allow for Britain's chronic unemployment problem of the 1920s, as the basis for his policy advice. Moreover, he used it fairly faithfully and consistently. Therefore, before he could turn to recasting his ideas, beyond minor adjustments in detail exposition or emphasis, he had to become convinced of the need for such a recasting: he had to become *actively dissatisfied* with the theory he had set out in the *Treatise*'s Book III.

This important first stage of the creation of dissatisfaction was not merely a product of 'Cambridge', and even within the 'Cambridge' context the individuals involved were more numerous than in the later stages of creation and consolidation. For over and above the members of the famous 'Circus' (Richard Kahn, James Meade, Joan Robinson, Austin Robinson, Piero Sraffa, and others) the inciters of discontent included Ralph Hawtrey,[2] Professor Pigou, Dennis Robertson and Professor Hayek. As a group (or, more correctly, a series of groups[3]) their comments, although diverse, tended to reinforce each other at crucial points. Thus, for example, both Robertson and Kahn picked up the dependence of the divergent behaviour of the price levels of investment and consumption goods in the fundamental equations on Keynes's peculiar savings assumptions and definitions (*JMK* XIII, pp. 212–13, 218, 237).[4] However, it seems clear that on this occasion, as so often later, Kahn's constant nagging was more important in getting Keynes to catch the point.[5] Similarly, Hawtrey's comments of June and July 1930 were resoundingly echoed by the 'Circus' in its discussion and christening of the 'widow's cruse fallacy' (*JMK* XIII, pp. 152, 339–40). Given these, and other, worries over definitions and detail, Hayek's own damaging extensive comments, plus his pointing out that Keynes's book lacked a developed theory of interest and capital, although perhaps somewhat discounted by Keynes on the ground that Hayek had not read the book 'with that measure of "good will" which an author is entitled to expect of a reader' (*JMK* XIII, p. 243), merely increased his difficulties.[6] Doubtless, the detailed discussions of the 'Circus', as relayed to Keynes by Richard Kahn, contemporaneous as they were with the fleshing out of the latter's 1931 article which provided a very strong hint of an alternative approach (the analysis of the supply and demand for output as a whole), were more effective, for they came from a group that was itself more thoroughly imbued with Keynes's own framework.[7] However, the increasing[8] public difficulties of Dennis Robertson and the stream of comment from outsiders less sympathetic to Keynes's approach doubtless played a part.

That these difficulties had affected Keynes is clear from his hints of an equilibrium at less than full employment in his 1931 Harris Foundation lectures in Chicago (*JMK* XIII, pp. 52–8) and his further discussion of the idea and of a relationship between consumption and income in September 1931 (*JMK* XIII, pp. 373–5). At this stage, however, the doubts and difficulties had not gone deep enough to affect his *Treatise*-based policy advice and prescriptions (Moggridge and Howson (1974), pp. 237–8). It was only at the end of 1931 that he began to mention 'endeavouring to express the whole thing over again more clearly *and from a different angle*' (*JMK* XIII, p. 243, italics added), a change in emphasis from the preface to the *Treatise*. At the time, he thought that the process might take two years: it actually took four.

In the process of 'working it out all over again' (*JMK* XIII, p. 172) the personnel involved in the discussions were much more 'Cambridge' than during the period of dissatisfaction creation. However, from the correspondence, it is clear that there were several forums for discussion or for the ventilation of ideas. The most important public forum in the early stages were Keynes's annual courses of eight lectures, which as in the 1920s dealt with work in progress. These lectures were attended by members of the Faculty, research students and advanced undergraduates. They provoked considerable discussion.[9] Robertson appears to have seen the lecture notes for the Easter term of 1932 in advance as the Keynes–Robertson terminological controversy continued, while at least Joan and Austin Robinson (and most probably Kahn) attended them. Joan Robinson and Richard Kahn certainly attended subsequent series, while Gerald Shove regretted he could not attend the Autumn 1933 series when he was playing a supportive role in Keynes's controversies on certain points with members of his own, older generation. Although we lack copies of students' lecture notes for the Easter term of 1932, we do have such notes for the rest of the pre-*General Theory* period and, despite the limitations of the genre as evidence, they have proved invaluable in charting Keynes's development. In addition to lectures, Keynes gave his ideas some public airing at his summing up of the discussions of the Political Economy Club on various occasions, with illustrative applications, where appropriate. In addition to lectures, there was probably discussion of points of detail in drafts (certainly the origin of the 1933 comment to Joan Robinson in *JMK* XIII, p. 419) and expositions (certainly in the 1933 discussions with Colin Clark on the size of the multiplier reported in *JMK* XIII, pp. 412–13). Naturally, the main burden during this period fell on Richard Kahn, who was formalising and constraining the product of Keynes's intuitive and impressionistic intellect – although Joan Robinson also had a role in the process. It was at this stage that the 'stiff supervisions' from Kahn had perhaps their greatest importance, as the truth, intuitively perceived in 1932, moved closer and closer to a proof fit for the outside world of economists, undergraduates and policy makers. By the end of the summer of 1934, events moved towards the final stage.

With the final period of consolidation Keynes moved outside 'Cambridge' in at least one sense, although in another sense neither Roy Harrod nor Ralph Hawtrey could really be considered rank outsiders. As before, Joan Robinson and Richard Kahn continued their strong supportive role, going over others' comments with Keynes (see, for example, *JMK* XIII, pp. 612, 634, 650–1) and improving Keynes's drafts with their own comments. They, and some research students, such as Bob Bryce, also became active emissaries and evangelists, carrying the new message to the wider world. Roy Harrod played a somewhat intermediate role. He was, it might be said, an initiate – as was James Meade – but he had been sufficiently detached from the act of creation to provide a different perspective, as shown by his attempts to moderate the book's tone and to take on puzzles which seem to have eluded the regular Cambridge critics. Ralph Hawtrey and Dennis Robertson were even further outside the inner circle. Although their comments may have been formally correct on occasion, they appear to have had little effect on the final product, except in cases where they either echoed points raised by others in closer sympathy with the whole exercise or where Kahn and Joan Robinson, who seem to have had access to some, if not all, of the comments of others, commended their criticisms to Keynes. Personalities also seem to have entered here in a significant way, for it is clear that Hawtrey's much more easy-going tolerance made more discussion possible than Robertson's pained conscience-keeping (Robinson (1975), p. 13). In just over a year, the book with all its faults was ready for publication.

Given this broad outline of what happened, what can we say about the whole process. Can we compare it with the evolution of the *Treatise* and perhaps see in the differences between the writing of the two books differences in the quality of parts of the final product. To put it briefly, I think we can, for the story outlined above differs considerably from that surrounding the *Treatise*, at least in detail.

Unlike the *General Theory*, the *Treatise* did not begin as an attempt to resolve difficulties in an earlier book, in this case the *Tract on Monetary Reform*. Rather, it began as an attempt at an expanded, more formal, more academic exposition of the principles of theory and policy embodied in the *Tract*. As in the case of the *General Theory*, the early stages in the composition of the *Treatise* saw Keynes in contact with new ideas, in this case ideas of the sort embodied in Dennis Robertson's *Banking Policy and Price Level* (1926). However, Robertson's work, although important in the final result, seems to have had a less fundamental impact than, say, Richard Kahn's work in 1930–1. The reasons for this are not clear, but they may have something to do with the fact that Keynes seems to have come onto the ideas to some extent independently (*JMK* XIII, pp. 16–29). Personalities may also have played a role, in that Robertson, an impeccable scholar always plagued by doubts about his own originality, was always unsure in discussions with Keynes, who treated his opinion very seriously, whether he was yielding to argument or friendship (E. A. G. Robinson (1975), pp. 12–14). With Richard Kahn on the other hand, this problem was not present and such exchanges as took place were less strained and, perhaps, therefore more productive.

In addition to Dennis Robertson, Keynes was also in contact with Piero Sraffa, A. C. Pigou and Hubert Henderson during the early stages of the *Treatise*. Although he maintained contact with Robertson and Sraffa through some of the middle period (Robertson was on leave in the Far East for eight months in 1926–7) and with Robertson and Pigou during the final stages, it is almost certainly true that the period surrounding the creation of the *Treatise* saw Keynes subject to less severe intellectual discipline than during the years of the *General Theory*. However well the individuals involved may have been attuned to each other on various other levels, however much some of them discussed, as they must have certainly done to some extent, the contents of Keynes's annual course of lectures dealing with his work in progress, they did not create the atmosphere of sustained, sympathetic, but tenacious argument that seems to have characterised Keynes's Cambridge of the early 1930s. (Perhaps they were too busy with that other revolution in Cambridge that came to fruition a few years before the *General Theory* – imperfect competition – but one suspects it was more than that.) Certainly, although the *Treatise*'s ideas did receive *some* outside airing during their creation, they were the product of much greater intellectual isolation than their successors. Moreover, this intellectual isolation appears to have resulted in many more intellectual doubts during the period of consolidation of the ideas of the *Treatise* than was the case with the *General Theory* with the consequence of more hurried recasting and rewriting, which, given Keynes's other activities,[10] inevitably affected the final product. Certainly after publishing the *General Theory*, perhaps reflecting on the experience of the two books, Keynes was more prepared to trust 'time and experience and the collaboration of a number of minds' (*JMK* XIV, p. 111) than he had been six years earlier, despite the more urgent evangelism in the book.

This brings us to the role of Keynes's younger colleagues in the act of creation. Although some of them may have overstated the extent to which they may have been leading and Keynes following, during the early stages of the creation of the ideas associated with the *General Theory* and although Schumpeter's near attribution of co-authorship to Richard Kahn (Schumpeter (1954), p. 1172) goes too far, their existence probably made much of the difference. Sympathetic to Keynes's whole exercise they were, as subsequent history has confirmed, certainly tenacious and untiring in argument. Moreover, they, and Richard Kahn in particular, were probably more attuned to formal economic argument than, say, Dennis Robertson or Hubert Henderson, more capable of the elegant, if occasionally Talmudic, formalisation necessary if the intuitive, impressionistic products of Keynes's mind were to convince the profession. In the event, they were remarkably successful, even if a more recent generation has begun to wonder whether the convincing occurred on exactly the appropriate points. But that is another story.

Thus I would certainly go along with many of Don Patinkin's suggestions as to the differences between the *Treatise* and the *General Theory*, at least in the round. However, I think we might both get a bit further on with more knowledge of the personalities involved and more appreciation of the quality of their interaction, not merely its quantity. For if the experience of a more recent period in Cambridge has taught me anything, sheer quantity, however measured, hardly does the trick.

NOTES

1. As an illustration of the problems that do exist in this area, we might note that after this Conference, a considerable additional volume of manuscript material concerning the composition and post-publication discussion of the *General Theory*, was discovered at Tilton in the spring of 1976. This material, which alters a few minor details but not the main lines of the story surrounding the book, will appear as a supplement to *JMK* XIII and XIV.

2. Although, following Eprime Eshag (1963) I have in the past included Hawtrey among the Cambridge School of monetary economists, it is clear from his background that, while he may have been influenced by Marshall's work, he was never formally taught by Marshall or his successors. Instead, he came to economics through his official interests and responsibilities.

3. The groups might be labelled the 'Circus', Robertson–Pigou–Sraffa, Hawtrey, Hayek.

4. Pigou was also troubled on this score (*JMK* XIII, pp. 214–18).

Discussion and Criticism of 'The General Theory'

5. As others in discussion agreed, Richard Kahn's style of controversy is both peculiar and probably important. Once Kahn gets onto a problem in someone's work, he nags. One got letters in the 1930s – one still gets letters in the 1970s – day after day. One may reply to letters, thinking that one can square Richard on a particular point, but more often than not he will come back on the same point from yet another angle until either you see his point or, more rarely, he sees his criticism was misapplied.

6. It is interesting to note Keynes's dependence on Richard Kahn and Piero Sraffa as the discussions with Hayek continued (*JMK* XIII, p. 265).

7. It was in Kahn's attempt to graft his multiplier onto Keynes's *Treatise* analysis, for example, that he made it clear that the book's analysis was of a limiting case (full employment) hardly relevant to the conditions of 1931 (Kahn (1931), pp. 9–10).

8. *JMK* XIII, p. 211. In his paper, Patinkin makes very little of this point – too little, in fact, given his hypothesis about the final stages in preparing the *Treatise*.

9. This discussion also occurred amongst undergraduates and research students, who carried it to their contemporaries elsewhere, particularly the London School of Economics where many of the contemporaries of the advanced overseas students in Cambridge were working in a different tradition. As the work in Cambridge became more fit for pervasion, these links became formalised in an Oxford–Cambridge–LSE research students' seminar which lasted until the 1970s, by which time the important news for oral transmission (or the interest in that news) had declined.

10. Interestingly enough, Keynes kept himself freer of other commitments during the last year of the *General Theory* period than he had done over the *Treatise*, but this to some extent reflected events beyond his control. After all, bodies such as the Macmillan Committee and the Economic Advisory Council do not arise in conformity with the demands of an economist's academic schedule.

Discussion

Patinkin: I would appreciate more information from the student panel about Keynes's performance as a teacher. How highly would you rank him in this respect? And another, more specific question: I have mentioned Keynes's puzzling failure to use diagrams in his presentation of the theory of effective demand in the *General Theory*. Did he use diagrams in his lectures?

Tarshis: I don't remember that he ever used diagrams in class.

Robinson: He certainly used diagrams in the supply curve of output as a whole.

Tarshis: He did? I don't remember that. I've got them in my notes, but I never knew whether I copied them from him, or whether I sketched them in on my own. He did however formulate such concepts as the Propensity to Consume or the Liquidity Preference Function on the blackboard.

Samuelson: Did he perpetrate the indiscretion of preparing a lecture?

Tarshis: He obviously had prepared them. Of course, in the last two years I attended the lectures – 1934 and 1935 – he was doing them from galley-proofs, though I don't think I ever saw him actually reading from the proofs. He was always fumbling with them. He was very clear. He was incredibly clear in lectures. He kept you in rapt attention for the 50 minutes of the lecture. He covered an enormous amount of ground in that time and everyone was completely silent. You had no trouble paying attention or hearing him. He was a fine lecturer. Those lectures were, I would say, the most popular lectures in economics. Weren't they, Austin?

Robinson: You had the whole of the younger faculty there, as well as all the others.

Tarshis: The faculty wasn't at all as big as the faculty at universities now.
 I would like to point out that none of the three of us here today were his

supervisees, but with those lucky people in King's College who were, I understand that he was enormously careful. He only picked the really top students at King's and then devoted a great deal of attention to them.

Samuelson: You should interview Sidney Alexander who must have been one of his last supervisees. Alexander graduated from Harvard in 1936 and was a Sheldon fellow in 1936–7. Keynes deigned to take him as a supervisee, probably on Taussig's recommendation. I didn't get the impression that it was all that exciting, but I don't want to report. I do know that he warned Sidney against the insidious disease of mathematics, that there was absolutely nothing in that sort of nonsense, and that he should not waste his time with it.

Tarshis: We have that in our lecture notes, too. He spent half a lecture once on it. He felt that the stuff of economics was not sharp or precise, and it was too easy to distort it and create for it the impression of an exactitude that it really lacked, and by subjecting it to mathematical manipulation also to wind up with a seriously distorted picture of the economy. That also comes out in the *General Theory* and even more clearly in Vol. XIII of the *Collected Writings*. He had little patience with the use – or should I say abuse? – of mathematics in economics.

At the Political Economy Club, Keynes was courtesy incarnate to students. I mean, you could make the greatest ass of yourself, as I did, I know, many times at that Club when you were called on to be No. 4 on the history of the East India Company in the decade 1770–80. You just had to talk, but he somehow made you feel that you had said something important. He wasn't as courteous to others, but that has only come out recently.

Robinson: He wasn't always as courteous to the faculty.

Tarshis: Yes, that was the impression one had. Even at the Political Economy Club he could be pretty sharp to the faculty, but the student who stood up there shivering, was always treated with decency, more than decency, with warmth and encouragement. In those respects I think that he was fantastic.

Bryce: I would say that at the Political Economy Club he was a very stimulating teacher in the way in which he could pick up all sorts of ideas and knit them together into a plausible whole on almost any damn subject. As Lorie says, 'If it's the East India Company – something emerges out of it.' I found this fascinating, but whether it was teaching or really just provocation, I really don't know.

Robinson: May I add, though, what I don't think that either of you brought out – the fact that the undergraduates talked first. The dons didn't draw a slip. If you wanted to, you could go onto the hearthrug and take part. Keynes spoke at the end. The astonishing thing was that in the winding up at the end of the whole discussion he would pick up the interesting points out of the paper and pat the paper writer on the head if he possibly could. But you found at the end, when you had already had three hours or more of discussion, that he was adding a great deal of fresh thinking that had never yet emerged in that discussion. That was what I remember of him in those meetings.

Tarshis: However much time remained, he always filled it with fascinating talk up to about ten minutes to 12 which had to be the closing time so those of us who didn't live in King's could get back to our colleges in time, by 12 o'clock.

Robinson: We would very often go on for $\frac{1}{2}$ hour or $\frac{3}{4}$ hour with Keynes on the hearthrug by himself.

Ben Higgins: (University of Ottawa): I think that what I can best contribute to this discussion is a few words on the Keynesian revolution as seen from London at that time. I was a student at the London School of Economics during 1933–5.

There was a joint London–Cambridge seminar which I attended on occasion, and once in a while the Master himself would turn up. But we in London, of course, regarded the strange things going on in Cambridge as nonsense, and very dangerous nonsense. Moreover, we could see that a man with such grace and wit and charm added to his brilliance might just possibly succeed in persuading some people that he was right. That was a frightening prospect indeed. It wasn't that there was a keen debate between London and Cambridge, because there was hardly any point of contact. We were very much under the influence of Hayek. He was our god. There were actually points of contact but we couldn't see them. The period of investment, for example, in Hayek's mind was an ex ante concept, not very different from the concept of liquidity preference. But all that was buried in the cumbersome three-dimensional diagrams with which Hayek presented his ideas and which made them seem like something, not psychological, but something in the field of engineering – the Structure of Capital.

But there is another element that hasn't been brought up yet. And that is the influence of the Stockholm School, because while we regarded Keynes as dangerous nonsense, for some reason the Stockholm School was perfectly respectable in London. Myrdal, Ohlin and Lindahl were all there from time to time. We read their publications and there were unpublished mimeographed documents that I remember, including discussions of what they thought was going on in Cambridge, which circulated among the students. This differential attitude towards Cambridge and Stockholm was curious in a way, because the ultimate policy views of the two were not different. Perhaps it was that the terminology of the Stockholm School was more familiar: the gap between savings and investment was still an important thing for them, instead of this crazy idea about savings and investment being an identity and so on. And also perhaps because in the Stockholm School the policy implications were not so clear. But what would interest me to know from the panel is how the Stockholm School was viewed from Cambridge at the time and whether the Swedes had any influence either directly or indirectly, either on Keynes or through Keynes or whatever.[1]

Bryce: I can't say much about the thinking in Cambridge about the Stockholm School frankly because I don't remember. We were aware that there were people out there saying some of these things, but we didn't spend all that much time on it because I guess we thought there was enough going on in Cambridge to occupy us. When I got to Harvard in 1935, I got involved, together with Wolfy [Wolfgang] Stolper, in a rather abortive translation of Myrdal's *Monetary Equilibrium* which had appeared in German in 1933, and I learned a lot about Myrdal's thinking from that, which I suppose was one of the most advanced treatments of the Stockholm School. I thought at least it was worth working on. By the time we had finished it, and somebody else had revised the translation (neither Stolper's English nor my German proved equal to the enterprise which we had undertaken at the invitation of someone on Wall Street whose name I have forgotten for the moment), I felt that it didn't contribute as directly and clearly as the *General Theory*.

Incidentally, Myrdal did a good deal of rewriting of the text when the Stolper–Bryce version was in galley-proof; this, of course, offended the publishers and resulted in none of us getting paid for any of the amount of work we did on it.

Robinson: I started to say that it was Keynes who put Richard Kahn down to translate Wicksell. When I was a research student at Cambridge, we had Ohlin living among us and we knew him pretty well. We had fairly close contacts at lower levels with Swedes. I don't want to say that the channels were as free as they would be today when we all travel about and attend world conferences, but there was no antipathy whatsoever to Swedes.

Salant: May I ask when Ohlin was there? I was wondering if one of the reasons that Bob couldn't remember much about it was that in Cambridge the Stockholm School was never mentioned.

Robinson: 1923–4, I think.

Winch: It is not necessary to rely on memory or deduction in these matters. There is, by now, a quite extensive body of literature dealing with the relationship between Keynes's theoretical and policy writings, the anti-depression policies of the Swedish Social Democrats, and the work of Swedish economists during the inter-war period. The debate on this matter was revived by Karl-Gustav Landgren in a book published in Swedish in 1960, which dealt with both the historical and theoretical background to the novel crisis policies introduced by the Social Democrats in the 1930s, and the respective parts played by Keynes's writings and those of the so-called Stockholm School in providing a basis for these policies. Since Landgren's main conclusions were that the programme of the Social Democrats owed more to the use made of British writings by the Swedish Finance Minister than to the work of Swedish economists, and that Ohlin's attempt to portray the Stockholm School as an autonomous native tradition was largely a post hoc fabrication, it will be clear why Landgren's book raised such a storm in Sweden. A whole issue of *Ekonomisk Tidskrift* (Volume LXII, No. 3, September 1960), was devoted to reviews of the book, and it has subsequently been the subject of a book-length critique by Otto Steiger (1971). There have been a number of attempts to convey the substance of this dispute to the English-speaking world,[2] but there is still a good case for having updated versions of the Landgren and Steiger books translated. A good deal of scholarly research on the history of Swedish economic policy and theory in the interwar period continues to be undertaken, largely, I believe, under the direction of Bo Gustaffson at the University of Uppsala. Some of the main Swedish protagonists are, of course, still with us, notably, Ohlin, Myrdal, and Lundberg. We are, therefore, in a position to juxtapose personal recollection and the evidence provided by letters, public documents, and other kinds of historical evidence.

Samuelson: Two remarks on the interaction between the Scandinavian and Keynesian traditions: First, I would like to introduce into the record an observation that George Halm once made to me about Richard Kahn's translation of Wicksell's *Interest and Prices*. Halm is Professor emeritus at Tufts University and now lives out on the West Coast. He once observed to me that Kahn's translation is better than the original German version of *Interest and Prices*. So you must be careful that the translator didn't commit the ultimate traitorous sin of value added. Value subtracted is one sin, and value added is another.

My second observation relates to Myrdal's *Monetary Equilibrium*, and let me simply assert my view about this book. I waited very anxiously for its translation because it was Ohlin who made these tremendous claims for the Stockholm School as a parallel scientific anticipator of Keynesian theory as well as policy. Naturally, when Bryce and Stolper didn't produce it quickly, we just waited with bated breath. I was disappointed with it. It turned out that output as the equilibrating variable, the root of a set of eqations in which it floats, is very much not present.

You must remember that the original Swedish version of Myrdal's book appeared earlier [1931] and then the German came somewhat later [1933]. Abba Lerner, who is a fairly unsparing character, wrote in the *Canadian Journal* of all places an article 'Some Swedish Stepping Stones in Economic Theory' (1940) and he examined the Swedish literature as available to him in English, and as I remember he found no merit: that it wasn't much of a stepping stone. I don't know whether the new data will bear that out.

Patinkin: May I amend and supplement Donald Winch's discussion in several ways. First of all, my impression from the articles that have appeared in English on the Landgren–Steiger debate is that it revolves mostly about the question of priority in certain policy views, and not about priority in theoretical contributions.[3] In particular, as I understand it, Landgren's main contention was that the Swedes got their public-works-expenditure policy from Keynes's *Can Lloyd George Do It?* Indeed, in a note which Ohlin has recently published in the *Journal of Economic Literature* (1974, p. 893), he admits that such an influence did exist.

Insofar as the Swedish theoretical contributions are concerned, if – as I have contended in my paper – the distinctive characteristic of the *General Theory* is its theory of effective demand and the equilibrating role which it assigns to changes in the level of output, then I am in complete agreement with Paul Samuelson that this is not to be found in Myrdal's *Monetary Equilibrium*. Nor is it to be found in Wicksell's *Interest and Prices*, whose main concern is indicated by its very title. It is true that Keynes's *Treatise* adds little to Wicksell's book, and it was in this context that Myrdal made his justified crack about the 'attractive Anglo-Saxon kind of unnecessary originality' (Myrdal [1933] 1939, pp. 8–9). But there is no justification for this crack with respect to the *General Theory*.

I would also like to say that I was in Stockholm last month for a Conference and took advantage of that opportunity to discuss this question with Myrdal and Ohlin, as well as with Erik Lundberg. My impression from these discussions – and it is only an impression, and certainly not something that should be attributed to any of the three foregoing individuals – is that there were no Swedish anticipations of the *General Theory* before 1931 – and that it is only in the Swedish literature of 1932–35 that we might find such anticipations, or, more accurately, simultaneous developments. But whether or not there were indeed such developments is a question which I am still studying.

Samuelson: In support of this view, I would like to note that Wicksell went out of his way to point out what was not always noticed, namely, that his theory of the business cycle was an innovation theory of the cycle. His theory of the cumulative process was a theory of the long trend of price levels. It was not the ups and downs of the business cycle. There are, however, many mansions in the Scandinavian house, and there is no doubt in my mind that Ragnar Frisch in his article on 'Circulation Planning' published in *Econometrica* in 1934 has a theory of output. I would, however, find it unbelievable that Maynard Keynes was influenced by them. Moreover, and if you want to keep the dates in mind, there was a Hungarian fellow, Edward Theiss, who published two articles in the pre-*General Theory* days — one in the *Journal of Political Economy* for 1933 and one in *Econometrica* for 1935. In the 1935 *Econometrica* article, which I remember in detail (my memory was stimulated on this because a Chinese who went over to mainland China, did a thesis, I think at Michigan State, on the discoverers of the acceleration principle and the multiplier), Theiss already has the multiplier and the accelerator, which is rather difficult to have unless you have an output which it reacted upon.

J. H. Hotson (University of Waterloo): I was delighted by Professor Tarshis's pointing to the aggregate supply function, the Z function of Chapter 3, as an extremely important part of Keynes's analysis which has been very neglected. As an old disciple of Sidney Weintraub, I feel very strongly on the point. I feel that when Paul Samuelson told us (and we are all his students) in his 1946 memorial essay on Keynes that the young and innocent should not read Chapter 3 and should hurry on to Books III, IV and VI, that he set up what Mrs. Robinson now calls the bastard Keynesian paradigm. And this is what has fallen apart on us; that the advice wasn't good. There are good things in Chapter 3; and Book V is Keynes's theory of the price level. We've wandered back to monetarism, and we've wandered back to a revised quantity theory, and never got straight what's in that supply function. It is not just a wage cost theory of prices, it is a theory of the cost unit. If we had read Book V of the *General Theory*, we wouldn't have got ourselves into the 'stagflation' dilemma that we got into in the 1960s when we thought we could raise taxes and not spend the money and that would depress demand — without looking at what it's going to do to the supply side. Businessmen treat their taxes and interest payments as costs and when these increase they raise their prices. We wouldn't have had to wait for the experience, and for myself and some others, like Robert Eisner, to point this out. We would have seen it ahead of time. I think that aggregate supply is very important and very neglected.

Samuelson: I don't wish to fail to accept any reproaches on this matter. I prefer to leave the point moot. But you remember that Miss Prism in Oscar Wilde's *Importance of Being Ernest* said that when you come to the section on the Indian rupee you may skip it as rather too sensational. I really didn't have in mind that Chapter 3 was too sensational, but I did have in mind what the old Baedeker used to say: Oxford and Cambridge, if time is short, skip Cambridge.

S. H. Ingerman (McGill University): I'm not happy to let the notion go by unchallenged that the keystone of Keynes's contribution is the output-equilibrating mechanism. I think there are two questions: One is the question, what is the main determinant of output? What is the mainspring determining output – and I understand Keynes to say it's investment. And secondly, what is this equilibrium we are talking about? Is it a very short-term equilibrium? How is that equilibrium defined? I have a feeling that that point has been fudged. I think that the position that the output-equilibrating mechanism is the main thing leads you to the sort of notion that Keynes's *General Theory* is really incidental to policy.

I think what Keynes was saying is that the expectations of entrepreneurs are important: that's what entrepreneurs will not guarantee you – full employment equilibrium. The notion of full employment, the notion of equilibrium, has got to be very much linked to some behavioral notions about what happens to expectations of entrepreneurs.

Tarshis: I'd like to ask Austin Robinson whether Keynes took an active part in the other revolution that was under way at Cambridge in the late 1920s and early 1930s – the one that had to do with the theory of value?

Robinson: I think a quick answer to that is almost none. He saw the manuscript of Joan's *Imperfect Competition* and told Macmillan that, though it might not a first glance look an exciting book to them, they certainly ought to publish it – a surprising but welcome decision. He may have read it with care; he may not have. He was editor of the *Economic Journal* of course, and published the 1930 'symposium' on 'Increasing Returns and the Representative Firm' – the Robertson, Sraffa, Shove exchanges. He was encouraging, he was interested, but he wasn't a partaker in that particular operation.

I wonder if I might make a very small point on Donald Moggridge's reference to Schumpeter's comments on the collaborative element in this. I think it is interesting to have in mind (Paul will probably be able to check for me) that Schumpeter in most of the summers through the 1930s, after finishing his year in Harvard, used to go back to Bonn or to Vienna, and on his way through came and stayed in Cambridge. He would nearly always ask Joan and myself, Richard Kahn, and occasionally Piero Sraffa, out to lunch and pump us about what had been going on in the past year. And, he would hear the developments of the past year through us, as we saw it. We may inadvertently have misled him as to the extent that it was ours and not Maynard's. It was certainly not our intention to do so, but he may have been more aware of the younger group around Keynes than was really appropriate to the truth of the balance between Keynes and the younger group.

Samuelson: I would like to press the discussion in an embarrassing direction, because I think that this is a priceless opportunity and we may not have the same opportunity again. Let me put to you a view which Schumpeter had some responsibility for but which went far beyond Schumpeter and at least one unreliable Cambridge person has encouraged that view. It has to do with the pivotal role of Richard Kahn and it goes to the effect that he's an elusive figure in the footnotes and acknowledgements of many Cambridge people but that no one will ever know the real truth, which is that his contribution is much greater than the apparent truth which people think they know. So let me put to you, just as the devil's advocate, the extreme view that the archangel who is going back and forth between the Cambridge 'Circus' and Keynes is actually the creator, letting all of you feel very contributive, supportive and so forth; giving Maynard the impression that he's on top of his form and that his role is an extremely important one. This has nothing to do with the logical minutia of Don Patinkin's discussion with me as to whether Kahn's 1931 multiplier article does have a pivotal role or doesn't have a pivotal role. I would like to get some reactions to this view.

Robinson: Richard Kahn's part in all this was tremendously large, and it has always seemed to me a crucial part in one sense. We, all of us in Cambridge at that time, when we had written something, submitted it to Richard Kahn to see if it was all right; and one always (if it was me) got it back with all my logical errors pointed out. I learnt the art of adding to the beginning of a sentence that I had wrongly drafted the words 'It is sometimes erroneously supposed that'. He did this for all of us, and he was involved in a great deal of the Cambridge work of that time. If you take the imperfect competition work, I have no doubt at all in my mind that this started as a joint game between Joan and Richard Kahn. They were trying to use the marginal revenue technique to solve problems which we had not been able to solve before, or which we in Cambridge had not solved before. His part in that was enormously large. But I think at the same time (and if you know Richard Kahn, I think you would agree with me) it was not equally easy to get constructive published work of his own out of him. The best way to use Richard Kahn's gifts was, I think, to take advantage of his meticulous criticisms which would turn an inadequate initial effort into something that was really satisfactory. Without Richard Kahn, in many cases, we could not have done what was done. How much did he contribute to the whole of the Keynes operation? I don't pretend to know. It was a large contribution. But, I feel absolutely and completely certain that Keynes was not a puppet, being played by ventriloquism by Richard Kahn.

Samuelson: That was intended as a joke. But what is there in the thesis that Keynes is God's midwife for Richard Kahn? It's quite obvious that Richard Kahn could not deliver out of himself for the reasons that you state well.

Robinson: I think it so often happens that two people who work together can produce much more than either of them could do individually. I think that a great deal of the *General Theory* would never have got to where it got without Richard Kahn. On the other hand I feel equally certain, in a different sort of way, that if we had left all the problems of moving on to the *General Theory* from the *Treatise* to Richard Kahn, he might have pondered them for years, and we might have been in the same situation as we are still in over the theory of the short period, where all that very important work that Kahn did was never in the end written up and published.

Samuelson: Don Patinkin is really moving towards an interpretation which lowers the estimate of the world of the importance of the 'Circus', leaving out the specific role of Richard. And if that's to be done, let's have it done on its merits with all the testing possible.

Robinson: I think Don Patinkin is wrong. I wish Donald Moggridge would add his feelings because he's worked with Richard Kahn most of his working life.

Moggridge: If I was going to sum it up on the basis of almost ten years of working with Richard Kahn, I would put it this way: Richard is very important. However, in many respects he is the perfect foil. Without Keynes's drive and Keynes's constant flow of new ideas it would not have happened. For Richard Kahn is fantastic if he has something to react to, but the impetus is coming from outside. If he has something to react to he is spurred on. If you have what you think is a good idea and want to see if it runs, Richard is superb, but it is less certain if one wants to work the process the other way around.

Winch: So far we have been talking as though we have to rely entirely on assessments of personality and 'style', whereas, of course, we have the famous 1931 article by Richard Kahn on the multiplier. The part played by this article in the process we are discussing is crucial. Perhaps the article is so famous that nobody reads it any more, or reads it through to the end. I have certainly always been perplexed by Lawrence Klein's patronising judgement on the significance of the article in his book on *The Keynesian Revolution* (1947, p. 36). All I'm doing at this point is simply saying that one mustn't forget that there is quite a lot of Kahn on paper there.

Robinson: Could we come back to what Don Patinkin was saying this morning about the multiplier article? The multiplier concept is there, as you were saying, in the 'Yellow Book' of 1928.[4] It was there, I think, long before that. I can remember, as an undergraduate taking another undergraduate, Jules Menken, for a walk in 1922 or thereabouts, and (I was no mathematician) asking why, if you put one person into employment and he spent his earnings, you did not put everybody into employment. This is a problem that we were aware of and trying to ask ourselves and Richard Kahn showed us how the series diminished and identified the leaks and all that. I think that was his contribution, a very important one. It is, as you were saying, true that some of the ingredients of the multiplier concept were there already in common circulation. But I still feel that that article represented a substantial advance.

Winch: This was one of several issues on which I was foolhardy enough to pass an opinion (Winch 1969, pp. 174–5) before all the new evidence was available. One of the things that struck me on re-reading Kahn's article in the later sixties was not so much the statement of the general multiplier relationship, but the thoroughness with which some of its applications to foreign trade, budgetary policy, and the debt burden were developed. The suggestions as to how the relationship could be applied to foreign trade seemed particularly interesting in view of the 'closed' character of the *General Theory*, and the fact that foreign trade multipliers were not worked out in detail until much later. My basic point is then that a reading of the whole article, bearing in mind its date, gives the impression of someone who may have begun with the public works problem of establishing the relationship between primary and secondary employment, but has rapidly moved on to consider its theoretical ramifications in a more ambitious way.

Robinson: May I just add that it was very relevant in the British situation in the early 1930s to ask what were the full consequences of public investment. We really did need to be able to estimate what the total effect of a public works policy might be expected to be. Even when much later I was in the Cabinet office in wartime, Sir John Anderson, who was then the Minister chiefly responsible for all our economic policies but had been involved in these things in the 1930s, was telling me that the multiplier simply represented how many extra people were put into employment by producing the inputs that were necessary for the outputs of the first man. It was, of course, necessary to estimate not only this but also and more important the additional consumption from the greater income. This was completely outside of the picture of many of the administrators who were discussing these problems.

The other point that I think has to be made is that even if we had known all the available literature, even if we could theoretically have found these things out from somebody else's writings, they had to be brought into Cambridge economics and into our own system of thinking by almost starting again from the beginning and then elaborating.

Samuelson: We believe you Austin.

Robinson: It was constantly necessary to do this. I am sorry, if we were undereducated at that stage.

Samuelson: I have a little handout which I would like to distribute at this point and which bears upon a small difference of emphasis between Don Patinkin and myself on the role of the multiplier article:

> Demonstration of 'Logical Equivalence' of finite-difference multiplier formula to (linear) output-determination model
>
> (1) $\dfrac{\Delta Y}{\Delta I} = \dfrac{1}{1-c} = 1 + c + c^2 + \ldots, \dfrac{\Delta C}{\Delta I} = \dfrac{1}{1-c}, 0 < c < 1$
>
> Rewrite (1) in *equivalent* notation.
>
> (2) $\dfrac{Y_1 - Y_0}{I_1 - I_0} = \dfrac{1}{1-c}$
>
> (3) $(1-c)(Y_1 - Y_0) = I_1 - I_0$
>
> (4) $Y_1 = (I_1 - I_0) + c(Y_1 - Y_0) + Y_0$
>
> Set $I_0 = 0$, which is admissible (as the "constant of integration" at the origin of the first-difference relation). Then we have, setting Y_1 notationally as Y, and I_1 as I,
>
> (5) $Y = \{I + Y_0 (1-c)\} + cY$
>
> Solve (5) for Y* root as function of 'multiplicand', which is $\{I + Y_0 (1-c)\}$,
>
> and so, we see, the *logical identity* of 'equation for output as a whole', and
>
> $\Delta Y = \dfrac{1}{1-c} \Delta I = (1 + c + c^2 + \ldots) \Delta I$

I would like, if I may, just briefly to set some considerations forward that I think have relevance to what the role of the 1931 Kahn article is, and many of them I think are in the direction of your thought, Don, and some of them, I think, only superficially away, but they represent the truth that you really have in mind. What we have to agree at the beginning is that it is only at a later stage that people had a full understanding of all the relationships between different parts of the theory. In fact, the science is at a decadent stage generally when it's embalmed and axiomatised and really all the implications are understood. So, I'm not arguing that the 1931 article of Kahn supercedes all the rest. But let's begin with the problem of public works. First, it is true that public works is an old staple in the policy world. Even in the Irish famine the absurdity was followed that you couldn't give people the small amount of grain that was brought in from America under laisser-faire Victorianism to the people outright. You had to make them pretend to work for it on the roads. You had the case of people dying and infecting each other as they tried to go through the charade of getting, what we would call, microeconomic relief by means of this well-established macroeconomic policy. However, it's by no means clear, and I agree with Don Patinkin completely that George Garvy has it all wrong, that this has any great bearing on what we are talking about: because you want to go back to that remark that some sage has made, that it takes a theory to kill a theory, that there has to be an understanding of the model before it's put in.

So there were a lot of people who were in favor of public works because they thought it was a good thing and they didn't think it necessary to explain why. But there was also a counter-literature claiming that public works did not add anything, even before the 1925 article on the 'Treasury View' that I suppose was written by Hawtrey. Is it known who wrote the later White Paper? Apparently the Chancellor went out of his way not to sign it even though he had it issued. Was it also Hawtrey?

Moggridge: Hawtrey wrote the article for *Economica* in 1925. It certainly proved influential in the Treasury. As far as I can tell, the notorious 1929 White Paper setting out the 'Treasury View'[5] (or at least the Treasury's contribution to it) came from Sir Richard Hopkins.

Samuelson: When I did research on this, I found in the 1920s articles on public works which stated two different things. One, that such works were simply a substitution for something else, and I would call this a form of Say's Law: that you weren't getting anything, but you were doing something re-distributive towards people who wouldn't get it otherwise. There were also other articles, I think one by Sir Arthur Bowley, in which it is very clearly indicated that there is no secondary multiplier.

Now, from this viewpoint what you need is a theoretical understanding of what the relationship is of this policy weapon. And, I quite agree that the big thing was, why is there a finite multiplier which is neither one nor infinity? A good way to approach this is the way J. M. Clark (1917) did, who himself independently discovered the theory of income determination and, what Don regards as a different thing, the multiplier. And he did this in the context of everything he did –

which was to do something to assignment: the Carnegie Foundation asked him to work out the economic effects of World War I on the United States. And when the belligerent countries gave us a favorable balance, Clark's problem was, not why that should be stimulating, because every business man knew that the Russian and the British munitions orders were stimulating, but why it was only finitely stimulating as against a view that was represented in Bagehot and to some degree in Pigou's *Industrial Fluctuations* (1927), that A causes B and that B causes C and there is no end to the process. So, it seems to me that although Richard is not the first to have this, his article is a big stepping stone on the way to the theory of the determination of output.

Now, to buttress that argument I have distributed this handout. I want to make the very simple logical point that if you have a differential equation, you also have its integral plus a constant of integration. The same thing is true of a finite difference equation: that is, up to a constant of integration the finite difference equation is logically isomorphic with its summation equation, as it is called. So, I have written out at length here the complete logical identity between the geometric-series formula and the familiar $1/(1 - MPC)$ formula: showing how, by use of nothing more than arithmetic, both have exactly the same content, no more and no less. If you just follow the steps, 1, 2, 3, 4, 5 you will get to the equation whose root floats to equate the two sides: a point, by the way, which all the Keynesians of that period of time were methodologically uncertain on, and this is true of Lerner and of Joan and of Keynes – what's an identity and what's a behavior equation, what's a virtual movement and what's a condition of equilibrium as against an identity? But just taking the vulgarisation of the Keynesian system, which is the one-equation linear theory of output as a whole, it is not logically something which adds an iota or subtracts an iota from the ΔY over ΔI equation at the beginning of my handout.

Now, this doesn't mean that what we in our infinite hindsight and great logical powers understand completely, was understood completely by the people involved – any more than when Schrödinger gave one version of the quantum theory and Heisenberg gave another, and it took six months to show their equivalence, each one of them did not see the other's point of view. But they are logically the same. And I think any tracing of influence must take this logical equivalence into account.

Patinkin: As Paul has indicated, this last question is one that the two of us have been discussing – both in person and by correspondence – for some time already, and I would like to come back to it again tomorrow morning in a broader framework after we hear Paul's talk. For the moment, let me only say – and in a sense, Paul agreed with this – that we are talking about the history of ideas, and I would say the history of ideas is in large part the history of how people became aware of latent isomorphisms;

therefore, to prove something is an isomorphism doesn't say anything about how the ideas actually developed. But I prefer to go into fuller detail on that tomorrow.

Right now, let me turn to the question Paul has raised about the role of Richard Kahn in the writing of the *General Theory*. It's a very interesting question, and also a very difficult question to answer. It also reminds me about that old joke about the perennial debate on the question of who wrote Shakespeare, to which one answer is that Shakespeare wasn't written by Shakespeare but by another man with the same name.

It's really very difficult to answer Paul's question. We must depend largely on personal impressions. Thus *JMK* XIII reproduces many of the comments that Kahn made in the course of the development of the *General Theory*. And then I ask, what kind of comments are they? What do they tell me about the man? And, then the picture I get is very much like what Donald Moggridge has described here. It is not one of a person who is getting out, initiating a large concept, or of a person who is working out and developing and seeing further implications of some theoretical construct which has already been started. It is instead of a person who is pointing out things which were important for precision, important for rigor, important for clarity and important for ensuring consistency; but I wouldn't say that there is an initiating of new ideas there. From the beginning of the discussions of the *General Theory*, this is the role that Kahn plays and this is the way he comes out in the comments he committed to paper. I would say that probably he was doing a similar thing in his personal discussions with Keynes, but my saying so doesn't prove it. You might say the opposite; that he was putting down in writing only his minor comments, whereas his major ones he transmitted in person. Also a possibility, but to my mind not a likely one.

Let me give another example. In his paper, Austin has mentioned the only document in Volume XIII – and in the chapters of my monograph that I have circulated here I have referred to it as such – which would indicate that already in 1931, Keynes was along the road to an understanding of the equilibrating role of changes in output – which, as I have emphasised, is the distinguishing feature of the *General Theory*. This document is Keynes's letter to Richard Kahn of 20 September, 1931 (*JMK* XIII, pp. 373–5). This is so much earlier than Keynes's first systematic presentation of this role in his lectures two years later that I often wanted to write Donald Moggridge about this letter and ask him if he was sure about that date. Maybe you can get a later date for that letter?

Moggridge: It's on the paper.

Patinkin: It's a pity.

Moggridge: It's not like a Pigou letter, which can be any date. Pigou has

only seven dates in his vocabulary: Monday, Tuesday, Wednesday. . . .
Other than that, he is completely timeless. In contrast, Keynes and
Kahn are very careful about dates.

Patinkin: But my point is that Kahn's response to that letter is very interesting. For what Kahn says is that he doesn't quite understand Keynes's argument! So that correspondence surely does not indicate that Kahn played a major role in the formulation of the *General Theory*.

Let me also add a comment on Schumpeter, because this bears on another question that I have discussed earlier with Paul as well as with Walter Salant. It is a delicate question. My feeling is that when Schumpeter in his *History of Economic Analysis* writes about Keynes, he should not be considered as a disinterested historian evaluating the contributions of different economists. Instead, he is an interested party: a contemporary who undoubtedly saw himself as a rival of Keynes in the field of business cycle theory. And so, when I read Schumpeter on Keynes, I note it, I register it, but I say to myself: here, Mr. Schumpeter, you are not a disinterested historian, so I have to take your opinion as just another one to be weighed against others.

Samuelson: Oh, naturally, right. He was jealous of Keynes and he was very jealous of the fact that all his best students went tearing after this fellow. He genuinely didn't see what there was that attracted them, so he blamed it on the Ricardian vice that he was giving policy. Schumpeter misunderstood the mind of a graduate student who doesn't really care a rip about policy but all he wants is an elegant model.

Patinkin: Another point with regard to Schumpeter is connected with Keynes's acknowledgment in the *General Theory* (p. 141) that his concept of the marginal efficiency of capital is identical with Irving Fisher's earlier concept of 'the rate of return over cost'. Now, one of Schumpeter's criticisms of Keynes was the valid one that he did not pay enough attention to the earlier literature. In this connection Schumpeter notes that Keynes arrived at the foregoing concept independently of Fisher, and then goes on to 'testify to the fact' that Keynes 'inserted the acknowledgment in question upon his attention's [sic] having been drawn to Fisher's formulation' (Schumpeter (1954), p. 1178, n. 15).

This naturally arouses one's curiosity about the identity of the mysterious personage whom Schumpeter had in mind. In our correspondence, Paul has suggested that this might have been Redvers Opie, who was at Oxford in the early 1930's, at which time (Paul tells me) he was also translating Schumpeter's *Theory of Economic Development* from the original German. On the other hand, Walter has suggested that it might have been Schumpeter himself. I wonder if any of the other people here can shed any further light on this.[6]

Salant: You remember in our correspondence you were claiming that there was no evidence that Schumpeter had been in a position to visit the UK. But here we have a statement by Austin Robinson that he was there in most of the summers in the 1930s and he pumped the members of the 'Circus' as to what was going on. I think what you want to be asking: did Schumpeter send any messages back to Keynes via the 'Circus'? Isn't that what you need?

Audience Member: There are a few people who feel that the *General Theory* is the surplus-value-of-labour theory of *Das Kapital*. I just wanted to ask Austin if there is any Karl Marx in the 'Circus'? Any string, any channel there, anything in the *General Theory*?

Robinson: I don't think so, not at that stage. Piero Sraffa, of course, was the best Marxian scholar among us. Joan in 1931 had not yet begun her interest in Marx. I don't think there is a Marxian influence into this at that stage.

Samuelson: Joan has written on this. She says that there was not, and that they could have saved themselves a lot of trouble and would have made the leap sooner than they did (she perhaps exaggerates the leap that they ever made in this regard) if they had known, and that Keynes himself had an opinion quite compatible with the one that was quoted here. He said 'Why would I bother with Karl Marx, the turbid rubbish of the cheap book stores. I know it to be an exploded doctrine'. And as he writes to Bernard Shaw in 1935, 'I'm Napoleon – and I'm about to come out with a new theory' (*JMK* XIV, pp. 492–3).

Ben Higgins (University of Ottawa): It is quite right that Schumpeter was very jealous of Keynes. I sat in Schumpeter's seminar at Harvard in the fall of 1938 and I remember it very well. It was a seminar on Keynes and the *General Theory*. The entrance to the room was at the back, and when Schumpeter came in he started talking as he walked up to the front, and he said, 'Well, I don't know how I'm going to present my seminar this year. I've never done it the same way twice.' By that time he had reached the front and was facing the students. Then he said, 'I'm sure of only one thing. I'm not going to defend my own theory. That will come out alright anyway.' So, in discussing Keynes and in discussing the *General Theory*, he didn't stoop to comparing Keynes with Schumpeter. Most of the seminar was devoted to the question, 'Is the *General Theory* any improvement over Irving Fisher?'

Samuelson: His jealousy of Keynes came about because of the *Treatise:* because Schumpeter had planned a great work on money, a full German tome, and Keynes uncharacteristically wrote such a thing: and I know from Schumpeter's student, Wolfie Stolper, that he felt that Keynes had got there before him.[7]

Discussion

Robinson: One small point about Schumpeter. I wouldn't like to give the impression that Schumpeter's relations were only with the younger group. They weren't. He came to Cambridge and gave three lectures for us in 1932. He knew Keynes, within limits, on the ordinary social level. I have a very vivid memory of this because I had been asked to dine with Keynes and Schumpeter at King's high table and I had had a message from Claude Guillebaud that our beloved Mary Marshall was believed to be dying. Keynes sat down to write her a brief note, telling her of our deep feelings and giving her the will to live. That memory of Schumpeter and Keynes together has always remained vivid in my mind. I have always been puzzled by the curious feeling of remoteness from Keynes that one finds in his essay in *Ten Great Economists*.

NOTES

1. [On this and the following discussion, see Ohlin's paper in Appendix III below. – Eds.]
2. See Winch (1966), Uhr (1973), and Gustafsson (1973).
3. [In the light of Steiger's recent article on 'Bertil Ohlin and the Origins of the Keynesian Revolution' (1976), I now see that this statement is incorrect – D.P.]
4. [The reference is to the yellow-covered report on *Britain's Industrial Future* (1928) in which the Liberal Party presented its economic program for the country, and its proposals for dealing with unemployment in particular. For further details, see Winch (1969), pp. 108–9 *et passim*. – Eds.]
5. *Memoranda on Certain Proposals Relating to Unemployment*, Cmd. 3331. London: HMSO, 1929.
6. [Since the Conference, Samuelson has discussed this question with Redvers Opie himself, who in reply provided him with a copy of a handwritten note (dated August 5, 1935) which R. F. Kahn sent to Opie at Oxford, and which in its entirety reads:

> Guillebaud tells me that you maintain that Fisher, in his *Theory of Interest* (1930), has a definition identical with Keynes' definition of the 'marginal efficiency of capital.' I wonder if you could let me have the reference.

A scribble at the bottom of this note indicates that Opie then referred Kahn to 'Fisher pp. 155, 168.'

This note together with the fact that the first record of Keynes' recognition of Fisher's priority in this matter is in a letter which Keynes wrote to Roy Harrod three weeks later, on August 27, 1935 (*JMK* XIII, p. 549; Patinkin 1976(a), pp. 80–1) constitute fairly conclusive confirmation of Samuelson's suggestion. Samuelson thinks that he himself may have learned of this incident from Schumpeter. – Eds.]

7. [Note Schumpeter's allusion to work in his October 1930 letter of congratulations to Keynes on the completion of the *Treatise* (*JMK* XIII, p. 176). As Moggridge notes, Schumpeter's work, entitled *Das Wesen des Geldes*, was not published until 1970 (ibid). We understand from Paul Samuelson that an English translation of this work is now being planned. – Eds.]

6 Keynes as a Literary Craftsman

ELIZABETH JOHNSON

It might seem to an economist that discussing Keynes as a literary practitioner is beside the point – like trying to dissect Shakespeare as an actor. I feel on the contrary that the subject is worth considering. 'The style is the man,' and Keynes's unmistakably recognisable style reveals and illuminates some fundamental attitudes; the characteristics and habits of the literary craftsman there displayed reflect on the characteristics and habits of the economist.

Economics as a discipline has at least its share of unclear, inelegant and pedestrian writers. I doubt that there is any other economist for whom a claim could be made as the author of works which can be read as literature in their own right. Not all of Keynes can be read this way – *The General Theory* is not what one settles down to in anticipation of a good read in bed – but *The Economic Consequences of the Peace* is compelling at even half a century's distance, *A Tract on Monetary Reform* serves as a model for its kind, and *Essays in Persuasion* and *Essays in Biography* are pure enjoyment.

The *Essays* and the posthumous *Two Memoirs* are literary Keynes at his very best. They also represent Keynes's own selection from the large body of his writing that was directed towards the non-economist but generally educated, intelligent reading public. With the passage of time many economists are unaware of the number (300 or so) and the scope of the articles he wrote for both the quality and the popular press. They may be more aware of the existence (but until all the Keynes Papers are published they will have no conception of the volume) of the scores of memoranda and reports that he wrote officially and unofficially for the advisers and would-be advisers of the British government.

The point is that besides being an economist, Keynes was a professional journalist and regarded himself as such. He was also a professional political propagandist for his own peculiar brand of personal politics. He wrote regularly and for money and during his earlier career at least he regarded the money part of it as important enough to bargain about.[1] One could argue indeed that all of his writing was journalism of one order or another – from his plan for a state bank for India, quickly put together for a Royal Commission's report, to the *Treatise on Money* and *The General Theory* which, though in academic guise, sought to produce instant cures for the economic ills of the body politic.

He wrote for the present moment, to the best of his ability at that moment, and with his notorious predilection for changing his mind in adaptation to changing circumstances, nothing was ever intended as his last word. He wrote (in 'Clissold,' *Essays in Persuasion*):

> ... this is not a good age for pure artists; nor is it a good one for classical perfections. Our most pregnant writers today are full of imperfections; they expose themselves to judgment; they do not look to be immortal.[2]

Human beings are often most discerning of the same qualities in others as they themselves possess. In praising the willingness of H. G. Wells to expose himself to judgment, he showed a fine appreciation of J. M. Keynes. He was not the man to be chagrined in the slightest to find his yesterday's winged words wrapping today's fish and chips.

Keynes said that he wrote 1000 words a day, a good professional average. Most of the time he must have been turning out something like an article a week. He wrote quickly in his rather crabbed handwriting, usually with little changing or crossing out, except perhaps when expressing an emotional piece of personal vituperation. I have the impression that he worked hard and intensely, but also that the performance would have appeared easy to the onlooker, and actually came to him easily. From his early days in the Treasury in World War I, and even earlier, he was able to draft quickly and clearly and to get something down on paper in response to a demand and a deadline. As an editor – and I am not thinking so much of the *Economic Journal* as his tour de force for the *Manchester Guardian* of the twelve *Reconstruction in Europe* supplements put together over 1921–3 – he was full of resource and endlessly adaptable.

Keynes wrote for money. *Economic Consequences* made him first comparatively and enjoyably rich, and then when he lost in speculating in the German mark, it paid his losses. Before this best seller his earnings from writing were the usual academic chicken feed, but after he had become a household name he regarded his writings as a regular source of income and bargained with the Government of India, who wanted him for another Royal Commission, to make up the loss of earnings his absence from England would entail.

He wrote, very successfully, for a world wide market; ironical, that – he was so insular a man. With the wildfire dissemination and translation of *Economic Consequences* his audience included the United States and Europe and even China and Japan. He employed a world wide clipping service for reviews, and he very soon had agents who would place his articles in the important newspapers of the major countries. He quickly learned to make sure of his copyright. He had a pretty good idea of the price he could ask and get in each quarter and acted accordingly.

But money was not what made Keynes a journalist. He was a crusader, a teacher and a preacher. It was his moral indignation at the Treaty of Versailles and the exorbitant demands for German reparation that first set him afire and kept him going from *The Economic Consequences of the Peace*, through *A Revision of the Treaty*, and article after article in the *Manchester Guardian*, *The Times* and the *Nation*, and its successor the *New Statesman*, from 1919 to 1932. It was moral indignation fused with intellectual indignation that inspired *The Economic Consequences of Mr. Churchill*. His mother's father was John Brown, a well-known Methodist minister; from his mother he inherited a strong reforming instinct. Awareness of his own intelligence and capabilities made him search for answers to the problems he saw, and his self-confidence gave him the courage of his convictions. He wanted to reform and convert, or as he put it, to *persuade* people, to persuade them to adopt the sensible and logical solutions that his inner eye perceived so clearly.

With his eyes 'turned towards,' as he put it, 'the possibilities of things,'[3] the world seemed infinitely remediable. All the world had to do was to adopt his prescriptions – offered with an air of energetic daring and cheerful optimism which added to their attractiveness.

If moral indignation and reforming zeal made Keynes a journalist, his own proficiency – the satisfaction of doing the job so well – kept him at it. He thought of himself as the intellectual persuader, but he also was a natural charmer, even a seducer – he had a syren's voice. He did it with words, words which represented logical ideas and precise thinking processes. But the words he used so logically and precisely also represented strong emotions and subtle shades of feeling. Words were his journeyman's tools – and he could use them as an artist. He took a natural pleasure in using his tools so well – in his performance, that is in the skill and the power of the persuader.

'Words,' Keynes said, 'ought to be a little wild – for they are the assault of thoughts upon the unthinking.'[4] From the very start he fancied himself in the role of the iconoclast, the enfant terrible. As a junior in the India Office he approached each new problem as a maladministered mess which he could set aright. 'If you at all agree . . . I could throw it into a minute,' he volunteered, deference to a superior only just masking his cockiness.[5] Most people lose this élan as the years pass, but a Treasury colleague of World War II, Dennis Proctor, recalled that his instinctive attitude to any new situation was to assume, first, that nobody was doing anything about it, and, secondly, that if they were, they were doing it wrong.[6] It was a lifetime habit of mind based on the conviction that he was armed with superior brains – which was undeniable – and, Cambridge Apostle that he was, gifted with superior sensibilities.

This assurance shows in some strikingly pithy opening sentences:

'The budget and the Economy Bill are replete with folly and injustice.'[7]

'One blames politicians, not for inconsistency, but for obstinacy.'[8]

Also in some dismissive sweeping statements:

'There are only three lines of policy to which it is worth the Cabinet's while to direct their minds. . . . All the rest is waste of time.'[9]

'In Great Britain our authorities have never talked such rubbish as their French colleagues or offended so grossly against all sound principles of finance.'[10]

He has the answer. Successive French finance ministers have done their utmost to revive the franc. 'What more could they have done?' asks Keynes. Simply: 'I will tell you.'[11] He can make a declaration into a good catch phrase: 'Whenever you save five shillings you put a man out of work for a day.'[12] Or use it to damn a whole group of people or a profession: 'There are limits to permissible misrepresentation, even at the hands of a lawyer.'[13]

Statements like these sometimes carry him overboard into his own variety of outrageous rudeness. I feel that describing an individual as 'endowed with more than a normal share of blindness and obstinacy'[14] is a bit much. The trouble is that it would not be so bad if it were not so strikingly well put. His most successful portraits – Woodrow Wilson and Lloyd George – balance a tight-rope eerily above the slough of bad taste or the jagged rocks of cruelty.

But Keynes in a didactic rather than a reforming frame of mind can take a more sober, measured tone. The beginning of *How to Pay for the War* is arresting without being combative: 'It is not easy for a free community to organise for war.'[15]

Sometimes the opening sentence is just very workmanlike: 'The report of the Economy Committee can be considered from several points of view.'[16] This article closes simply, with a summary of recommendations.

In the civil service he learned the customary technique of presenting an argument by numbered paragraphs or steps of reasoning. He uses itemisation very effectively for presentation of his own argument, demolition of his adversaries and the marshalling of his remedies. It makes it all seem very simple, rational and only commonsense.

Sometimes the matter to be simplified is very complicated, as in his 1930 article diagnosing 'The Great Slump.'[17] 'I doubt whether I can hope to bring what is in my mind into fully effective touch with the mind of the reader. I shall be saying too much for the layman, too little for the expert. . . .' He hits on a deliberately homely metaphor. 'We have magneto trouble.' (In another instance, it was the two drivers meeting in the middle of a highway, unable to pass each other without knowing the rule of the road.[18] There is something self-conscious about this; Keynes's own car was chauffeur-driven.)

He makes it a conversation with the reader, posing and answering questions, concluding 'If, then, I am right. . . .'[19] He was an adept at this expansive style of unbuttoned cosiness, especially in his radio talks, making the conversation so confiding that you almost forget that the dialogue is one-sided. The placing of his words, as in his writing, is faultless. If something is out of the usual order, it is for a purpose. Keynes can write 'Cold and lonely and futile it is,'[20] and never put a word wrong.

He had what was called an English classical education, which gave him a knowledge of the precise meanings of words and a respect for them. He was very particular that translations of his work should carry his exact meaning. He was a master of the brilliantly right use of the esoteric word. But his use of language only occasionally sends you to burrow in the dictionary; it is the appropriateness of his ordinary vocabulary that is noticeable.

Being conscious of the real meanings of words, he is also conscious of their overtones. 'Words ought to be a little wild,' that is, emotive – and he uses these overtones with great skill. A lovely example is his description of Russia – 'The beautiful and foolish youngest son of the European family, with hair on his head, nearer both to the earth and to heaven than his bald brothers in the West.'[21] It is East o' the Sun and West o' the Moon, but must have been beautifully evocative to the European inhabitants of the 1920s.

His announcement that the gold standard was a 'barbarous relic'[22] combines sense and emotion in a single memorable phrase. He took pleasure in words and in playing with them and his humour and fantasy are both very verbal. I like 'furtive Freudian cloak'[23] – gold again – and – still writing about gold – the detailed minutiae of 'the little household gods, who dwelt in purses and stockings and tin boxes'[24] – which reminds one very much of Virginia Woolf.

Like Virginia Woolf, he can freeze a figure in a single snapshot – young Alfred Marshall surreptitiously practising geometry on the way to school and 'standing still at intervals, with his toes turned in'.[25] Keynes much enjoyed writing his memoir of Marshall, which he said grew under his hand. His enjoyment soars into fantasy – the young Marshall 'would run away – to be a cabin-boy at Cambridge and climb the rigging of geometry and spy out the heavens'.[26]

Fantasy is never far from tumbling him into the absurd: he pictured the Russian communists of the 1920s as 'early Christians led by Attila . . . using the equipment of the Holy Inquisition and the Jesuit missions to enforce the literal economics of the New Testament'.[27]

A large element in his verbal humour is ridicule – generally a light-hearted rejoicing in human absurdity, usually with no bad aftertaste. He is fond of the *reductio ad absurdum* where ideas are piled impossibly like a house of cards until they are pushed too far and come sliding hilariously down. Such is the sudden descent of his mock lament for the 'old battle-cries' which 'are muffled or silent. The Church, the aristocracy, the landed interests, the rights of property, the glories of empire, the pride of the services, even beer and whisky – will never again be the guiding forces of British politics.'[28]

His keen eye for the absurd makes him a mordant satirist. Again the satire is expressed in a concrete physical image – the Americans erecting their sky-scraping Golden Calf,[29] the bank chairman chirruping among the bushes.[30]

The presence of irony pervades these word-pictures. I recall to you the Mitty-like scene of the average American graciously receiving the love and gratitude of his European debtors and overwhelming them with forgiveness.[31] The same irony, years later, leaves intuition for arithmetic and makes the calculation of the good works that could be done with the money represented by Britain's debt to America.[32]

The style of Keynes's early articles and letters to the editor is sober, no-nonsense, but effective. At that time he thought of himself as an academic whose excursions into the press were simply to put the record straight. The Treaty of Versailles with its attendant personal repercussions was the catalyst which converted him into a journalist by applying the emotional heat that was released in *The Economic Consequences of the Peace*. In writing it he learned that it didn't hurt to let go and pull out all the stops; and he grew comfortable with the magnificent organ voice he could produce. A purist might complain of flamboyance. Along with excesses of taste, it is possible to find, as his output swelled and he wrote in haste, an impatience leading to carelessness and to awkwardness in construction – but, considering the output, not often.

Economic Consequences combines two methods in a way which came to be his trademark. The process is somewhat like this: we are first presented with a sort of apocalyptic vision, clouded with foreboding and prophecy, riding the storm of a broad sweep through history lit up by flashes of insight and wit displayed in brilliant vignettes of individuals. Following this we are treated to a cold douche of statistics, a few figures to convince the hard-headed, number piled on number, the bombardment of heavy guns – it is very impressive.

In *Economic Consequences* Keynes has these two kinds of chapters combining appeal to heart and to head. In writing regularly for the *Nation* later on he would sometimes follow one week's emotional reasons with the facts and figures next week. So a con man typically snows his victim. And a Gemini, so the astrologers say – Keynes was born on the 5th of June – has a flair for making a little knowledge sound like a lot. Dennis Proctor said that his memoranda were full of factual inaccuracies.[33] He didn't stop for perfection before publication, thinking that publication was more important.

Was he a con man or do you prefer to look on him as a conjurer – a conjurer of words?

Pigou complained that he was too ready 'to hoist the flag of intellectual revolution,' stressing disagreements more than agreements – as he said,

> By defining common words in uncommon senses, as with savings and income in his earlier book, and 'full' employment – which was compatible with a large volume of unemployment – in his later one, he caused much confusion among persons less agile-minded than himself.[34]

That would be a paradox – a man so concerned with the precise meanings of words, so desirous of being properly understood, with such a facility for language and a firm command thereof. I am inclined to think Pigou was being rather inflexible.

However, I feel that you can draw some grain-of-salt conclusions from my observations – if you wish to – and I leave the drawing of them to you. Not being an economist myself, I am free to re-read the *Essays in Persuasion*, the *Essays in Biography* and the *Two Memoirs* with great pleasure, pleasure heightened by the delight one takes in watching the seemingly effortless, painstaking art of an old pro.

NOTES

1. Keynes's attitude later, when he had given up writing as a means of income, is the subject of an exchange of letters between himself and the editor of *The Listener*. 'A Delicate Question of Payment,' *Encounter*, November 1974 (Vol. 43, No. 5), pp. 24–8. To Keynes it was a matter of principle.
2. 'Clissold,' *Essays in Persuasion, JMK* IX, p. 320.
3. 'A Short View of Russia,' *ibid.*, p. 271.
4. 'National Self-Sufficiency,' pt. 5, *New Statesman and Nation*, July 15, 1933; reproduced in *JMK* XXI (forthcoming).
5. *JMK* XV, pp. 4–5.
6. P. D. Proctor, '[Keynes:] At the Treasury, 1940–46' (1949).
7. 'The Economy Bill,' *Essays in Persuasion, JMK* IX, p. 145.
8. 'The Stabilization of the Franc,' *ibid.*, p. 82.
9. 'The Economy Bill,' *ibid.*, pp. 148–9.
10. 'The Stabilization of the Franc,' *ibid.*, p. 85.
11. 'An Open Letter to the French Minister of Finance (Whoever He Is or May Be),' *ibid.*, p. 78.
12. 'Saving and Spending,' *ibid.*, p. 137.
13. Letter to the Editor of the *New York Times Book Review and Magazine*, April 23, 1922, reproduced in *JMK* XVII (forthcoming), p. 298.
14. Footnote referring to the Chancellor of the Exchequer, Philip Snowden, in 'Proposals for a Revenue Tariff,' *Essays in Persuasion, JMK* IX, p. 231.
15. 'How to Pay for the War,' *ibid.*, p. 372.
16. 'The Economy Report,' *ibid.*, p. 141.
17. 'The Great Slump of 1930,' *ibid.*, p. 126.
18. 'The Means to Prosperity,' *ibid.*, p. 335.

19. 'The Great Slump of 1930,' ibid., p. 131.
20. 'Am I a Liberal?' ibid., p. 296.
21. 'A Short View of Russia,' ibid., p. 257.
22. *A Tract on Monetary Reform, JMK* IV, p. 138.
23. *A Treatise on Money: Vol. 2, JMK* VI, Ch. 35, p. 259; also in 'Auri Sacra Fames,' *Essays in Persuasion, JMK* IX, p. 162.
24. Ibid., p. 163.
25. 'Alfred Marshall,' *Essays in Biography, JMK* X, p. 164.
26. Ibid., p. 164.
27. 'A Short View of Russia,' *Essays in Persuasion, JMK* IX, p. 257.
28. 'Am I a Liberal?' ibid., p. 298.
29. *A Revision of the Treaty, JMK* III, Ch. 6, p. 113; also in 'War Debts and the United States,' *Essays in Persuasion, JMK* IX, p. 41.
30. 'The Speeches of the Bank Chairmen,' ibid., p. 201.
31. *A Revision of the Treaty, JMK* III, Ch. 7, p. 126; also in 'War Debts and the United States,' *Essays in Persuasion, JMK* IX, pp. 43–4.
32. Ibid., pp. 50–1.
33. Proctor (1949).
34. A. C. Pigou, '[Keynes:] The Economist' (1949), p. 23.

7 Cambridge as an Academic Environment in the Early 1930s: A Reconstruction from the Late 1940s

HARRY G. JOHNSON

This paper owes its inspiration, and in part its justification, to a conversation with Don Patinkin in Jerusalem earlier this year, about the purpose and desired results of this Conference. Patinkin was anxious to talk about the relations between the (relatively few) economists with whom Keynes was personally and intellectually concerned during the transition from the *Treatise* to the *General Theory*, most of whom (especially if Hayek and Robbins at the London School of Economics are excluded as targets or butts representing 'orthodoxy') were Cambridge acquaintances, and most of those Cambridge colleagues. He was especially intrigued by the narrowness of the age differences among Keynes, Pigou, Robertson, and some others – a narrowness attributable to the appointment as Marshall's successor of the youthful Pigou over the much older Foxwell (whose many Cambridge supporters Marshall outgeneraled) and the interruption of the academic careers of Pigou's immediate juniors by the First World War – and he was anxious that this Conference should produce some understanding of what Cambridge was like in the period of writing of the *General Theory*, as an environment for economic discussion and research.

This interest struck a bell in my mind, since I have long been interested in the influence of the physical and social geography of economics departments on their character and their style of economic research. By physical geography here I mean what the terms imply – the spatial relationships and dimensions within which economists carry on their work. 'Social geography' is a more ambitious and far vaguer concept. I mean by it generally the social relationships among members of the same department, as influenced on the one hand by the hierarchy of tenure, remuneration, and power of decision or of influence over collective decision, and on the other hand by the activities and responsibilities of the department – especially teaching responsibilities, but sometimes also research responsibilities – and the cooperative efforts they may entail; also the social relationships of the department with its clientele – mainly its students; with its colleagues (peers) in departments in the rest of the university or similar institution in which it exists; with the professional academic community at large; and with the larger society of which the university is a constituent and into which most of its students graduate. All these relationships have an influence on both the style and content of economic discussion with colleagues in and close acquaintances outside the department, and the choice of audience and style of addressing it for oral (usually unpublished) and written (published) communication at the academic and professional level.

To illustrate briefly and casually the kind of influence I have in mind, my first teaching post was as a one-man replacement for a two-man department at Saint Francis Xavier University. I was very lonely, being a stranger in all relevant ways; and the effect was to press me strongly into reading, and writing lengthy, serious letters to distant friends. My predecessor, like my current colleagues in other fields, belonged to the community and was clearly exclusively a teacher of the young in the ways of the world as he understood them — I was shocked by his boast that he 'used the textbook only as a whipping-boy,' because I was too inexperienced to realise that what he had to whip it with was his (and the students' parents') social and economic experience. *His* quondam colleague, a very cultured German refugee, had like myself taken refuge in prodigious reading, and became a figure of student fun for his inappropriate scholarship. We were both misfits: the place demanded a concern with low-level teaching and the formation of adult character, and identification of economic and social interests with those of a generally poor community of farmers, fishermen, and coal miners, as against an exploiting class of shop keepers, equipment-suppliers, local bankers, and the coal and steel company.

My next teaching position was at the University of Toronto, as an instructor (below a lecturer, and therefore not a member of the voting department). The department was housed in an old building (formerly the McMaster University building) on the northern fringe of the campus between the football field and the Ontario Museum, so that one tended to eat in nearby cheap restaurants and not to consider oneself as part of a university community. Large offices and lecture rooms were on the ground floor, small offices on the fourth floor, with stairs and no elevator connecting them. Senior and much older staff members had the ground floor offices, junior untenured staff the fourth-floor cubbyholes. The vertical geographical distance between the two faculty groups corresponded to an age difference, a tenure and rank difference, and a social distance. Communication was difficult and almost nonexistent; one saw the Department Head briefly on appointment, to discuss teaching duties, and any difficulties one was foolish enough to voice, and once at one of two Sunday tea parties he offered to junior staff late in the year, one for sheep possibly on their way down from the fourth floor to the ground floor, and one for goats definitely on their way down from the fourth floor to the exit door. Apart from that, one saw him only by appointment under strain, usually for advice or a reference in connection with a possible job for next year; his stock response to an implicit request for reassurance was 'Well, we wouldn't want to stand in your way.' As a result, the ethos of the fourth floor was one of gossip, rumour, and sometimes panic; of needlessly hard and unfocused work, and of conviction that one was not good enough to be a scholar, that if one were one would not produce anything for hopeless years ahead, and that if one did produce something it would be read only by a handful of other scholars, all of whom would be devastatingly critical. No wonder so many used the exit!

As a final example before I return to my main theme, I would contrast briefly Harvard and Yale with Chicago in the 1960s, both I admit from a Chicago standpoint. Harvard and Yale were not (and are not now) Departments of Economics in the same sense as Chicago, in my objective judgment. They were congeries of small personal departments depending from individual senior professors, to whose seminars (their main activity) transient assistant professors attached themselves. The number and the transience of the assistant professors reflected the labour-intensive undergraduate teaching responsibilities of the departments. The relatively small quantity, and the policy orientation, of the published output of the tenured staff reflected the social position of the two Ivy League schools in the American society, and particularly the reliance of Democratic Party government on the advice and participation of established academic figures. Chicago's much larger published output, by contrast, represented the position of the social 'outsider' and, in a general way, the lesser role of the academic in the Republican Party's approach to government. Chicago, also, had no undergraduate teaching responsibilities, hence no need for numbers of transient assistant professors, and hence the ability to absorb a few transients into a much larger (but still numerically small) professional and social community. In addition, the Chicago academic community mostly lived within a mile of the campus, which both made encounters in the course of out of hours visits likely, and informal social gatherings at home easy to arrange – in contrast to the far-flung suburban living patterns of Harvard, MIT and Yale. Physical geography was also important: the Harvard and Yale economists were scattered among widely separated buildings, whereas the Chicago economists lived on one, the fourth, floor with a single elevator around and in which they automatically met frequently and informally.

I now turn to my theme, Cambridge as an academic environment for economics in the early 1930s. As my subtitle indicates, what I have to say is based on my own experience, as a student in 1945–6 and an assistant lecturer/lecturer from January 1949 to March 1956 (especially the first year or two, while Cambridge was still living the life and carrying on the fights of the 1930s). This was before the Department of Applied

Cambridge as an Academic Environment in the Early 1930s

Economics shifted from its temporary building on the courtyard of the Downing Street science buildings complex, and the Faculty of Economics and Politics and the Marshall Library shifted from the meagre facilities the Faculty had occupied in that complex since 1912 and the Library since 1925, respectively to the present reconditioned old house on West Road (the Department) and the modern buildings, complete with library, lecture rooms, auditorium, and most noticeably individual faculty offices and common room, they now occupy on Sidgwick Avenue, across the river near the University Library. For simplicity of writing, I shall describe Cambridge as it was prior to the geographical shift and concentration of location, and ignore the Department of Applied Economics, which was not in existence anyway in the early 1930s.

The dominant fact of Cambridge physical and social geography was the colleges, and the system of (predominately undergraduate) teaching based on them. Most of the serious teaching was done by supervision, usually by a Fellow of the college specialising in the relevant subject. This consisted of an hour a week per individual student (or for as small a group as could be managed, the numbers being vastly enlarged in the years of the postwar bulge), the supervision being based on an essay topic (either invented, or drawn from past examinations) assigned one week, and written, turned in, read, and discussed the next week. Holders of university assistant lectureships and higher posts were limited to twelve hours of supervision a week, except for professors, who were not allowed to supervise undergraduates. Fellows of colleges without university appointments, of whom there were some even in economics, such as Gerald Shove (long discriminated against as a conscientious objector in the First World War), were subject to no such restriction; and some, such as Shove, bore a very heavy teaching burden. Some colleges, notably King's, restricted their Fellows to teaching their own college's students only; other colleges were easier on this point. Colleges without Fellows relied on the services of university teachers without Fellowships, such as Maurice Dobb, my own undergraduate supervisor at Jesus (long denied a Fellowship because he was an avowed communist); and, in the postwar period at least, on graduate students and staff members of the Department of Applied Economics, though usually mainly for first-year-student supervision. University teachers without Fellowships had a lonely life; on the other hand, they were not obliged to take all the students admitted by the college tutor and his admission advisers (I remember a friend being shocked when Kahn told him that a certain first-year King's student he was supervising was certain to fail at the end of the year – but my friend had to teach him through the year anyway) and could instead, if good enough, 'shop around' for good students – as Joan Robinson did very shrewdly in my day.

A university appointment was not necessary to a successful Cambridge career. In some ways, indeed, a university position could be an inhibiting responsibility, since some of the college jobs were much better paid than university teaching posts but required either very long hours of extra work, or the sacrifice of ambition extending beyond the lectureship level, or too much effort to be consistent with a teaching post; on the other hand, a professorship involved resignation or abstention from any college post, as well as sacrifice of income from undergraduate supervision – a fact about which Richard Kahn protested bitterly when he became a professor and had to cease being bursar of King's. In addition, a university appointee was required to live not more than five miles from Great St. Mary's, and to be in residence a stipulated and fairly large minimum number of nights per term. By regulation, a university teacher who had a Fellowship received (in the early 1950s) only £100 a year of his Fellowship stipend above his university salary, though of course he also got a room or rooms, free dinners, and an entertainment allowance (and, if I remember, free postage). In the inflation of postwar II, however, and with the spreading tendency of Cambridge academics to marry young, the university gradually came to dominate the college as a source of income – one result being the initiation and subsequent improvement of social and catering facilities for non-college-Fellow teachers and researchers.

The university appointment, as such, was a very minor part of an individual's teaching responsibilities – that obligation Reddaway at one stage used to refer to as 'the forty-hour year'. One's forty hours, approximately, meant a two-lecture-a-week course in each of the two major teaching terms of eight weeks, and the same in the teaching part of the examination term (the first four weeks of the third eight-week term, the rest being for student reading, and examination week). It was, however, possible in some cases to take classes with less per-hour credit; for a few years, my load included eight classes in money for third year, shared by rotation over three groups with Joan Robinson and Richard Kahn (I had to make up the reading list, and explain to Kahn that once we decided the first person's first rotation we had fixed the whole programme, each year) and five lectures on the theory of the balance of payments. The lectures were mostly held in the Mill Lane lecture rooms (opened in 1928), though sometimes in other odd rooms in university buildings; and one of the classes was held in a room in King's. In other Faculties, lectures were frequently given in a room in the individual instructor's own college (or, when classes were small, in his own college study); and I suspect this was probably true of some of the lecture courses offered in the interwar period (the 'special lectures' offered in the early 1930s were presented in a university lecture hall). In any case, the fact that one gave so few formal lectures, and made a special trip away from one's own college or home to make them, in buildings intended for lecturing and not for loitering, meant that one had very little if any regular contact with other Faculty members outside of one's own college. There were, in fact, only four kinds of occasions on which one met non-college colleagues academically.

These were, first, if one were appointed to one of the Boards of Examiners. There were three of these: Tripos Part I, Preliminary Examination, and Tripos Part II. One was not allowed to examine in the subject on which one lectured for the year to which one taught it. The examinations were by papers, not by courses; all examiners (including two external examiners in Part II, usually Oxford or London dons but occasionally provincial professors) had to agree on the presence and the wording of all questions on all papers, each contributing some questions to other papers as well as the one for which he was primarily responsible; all papers had to be read by two examiners, and by one or more additional examiners in case of disagreement in marks or serious disparities between a candidate's performances on different papers; and the decisions on 'classes' (I, II(i), II(ii), III, and 'Special' – meaning failed this examination but would probably pass it on a re-trial, hence allowed a degree anyway) had to be agreed by all examiners and the list made out and signed, all within a couple of weeks' time. It was in the process of setting the questions, and even more in the grading of the candidates' performances, that doctrinal disputes and philosophical differences among Faculty members, and between them and non-Cambridge economics as represented by the external examiners, came into confrontation most seriously – elsewhere they could be studiously ignored, or steered on inconclusive non-collision courses. (The emphasis on the undergraduate final examinations and the marking and outcome of them, incidentally, explains the concentration of Joan Robinson and Nicholas Kaldor on criticism of what the undergraduate textbooks and the professors teach the young, and of 'orthodoxy' more generally.)

Secondly, one could get elected to the Faculty Board. To do so, however (for an economist, as distinct from an economic historian or politics specialist), required considerable seniority and/or, in my period, strong attachment to the left or the right political wing of the Department. The Faculty Board was a strongly political body, in the sense of both academic and party politics. It controlled the committees that selected new assistant lecturers and lecturers, and the Faculty representation and Faculty nominations for outside economist representation on the university committees that appointed professors (and, I believe, Readers). It also of course decided the day-to-day Faculty business.

Third, there was the Political Economy Club, founded by Keynes and continued by Robertson in my day. Student membership was by invitation, automatic for Part I Firsts and almost so for II(i)'s. Faculty were free to attend by implicit open invitation, visiting economists by explicit invitation only. Meetings were on Thursdays in my day; papers were written and read by students, mostly third year (sometimes second year students from the Commonwealth taking their second BA via the second and third (Part II) years of the Tripos). Students drew slips to determine the order in which they (six of them) were obliged to comment on the paper – a procedure derived from the Society of Apostles. Faculty were free to choose the point at which they spoke about the subject; visitors spoke by invitation. In Keynes's time, I was told, more than one visitor who chose to speak was told in no uncertain terms that he was a fool; Robertson was invariably gentle and polite. The proceedings were formal – set speeches rather than cut-and-thrust – but occasionally one found it worth while to carry on discussion with a colleague after the meeting formally ended.

Finally, in my day but I am fairly sure not before the war, early in each autumn term the Faculty put on a large sherry party, to which were invited all faculty and their wives, and all academic visitors to the Faculty and their wives. It says something for the lack of academic and social integration of the Cambridge Faculty that at one of these parties I met Claude Guillebaud (Marshall's nephew, and a life-long Cambridge man) who asked me, 'Who's that fellow over there?' I looked, and answered with surprise, 'Why, that's Andrew Roy. He's been a member of the Faculty for three years now!' Of course, Roy taught statistics ('applied economics') and was therefore somewhat out of the main stream, though he was regarded by the King's group as one of the Robertson-Guillebaud mob, and for that reason they tried unsuccessfully to refuse him tenure, in spite of the fact that he had already produced some first class articles and been co-author of a good book with Alan Prest.

With the exception of the few unlucky enough not to have won a college Fellowship, one's academic as well as social life lay within one's college (and in Keynes's case also in London), and not in the Faculty and among one's professional economist colleagues. There were of course some possibilities of social connections outside the college within the university community, such as D. H. Robertson's interest in acting, and Keynes's membership in the Society of Apostles. But the Society had in the postwar I period become largely a King's College group – there was a certain connection between the Society's homosexual orientation, veiledly disclosed in Keynes's *Two Memoirs* ('Dr. Melchior' and 'My Early Beliefs'), and King's College's reputation as the centre of homosexuality (before I became a Fellow of King's, I remember being shocked by a Cambridge Professor of Archaeology referring to King's College Chapel as 'The First Church of Christ, Sodomite' ; he was right – but the faithful did not proselytise their religion among mature adults). The connection was symbolised by E. M. Forster's posthumous novel *Maurice*, with its theme of the unthinkable transformation from intellectual to physical homosexuality.

The college was the centre of life, especially for the unmarried Fellows to whom college was home (with possibly a family or a devoted mother located elsewhere as a vacation home) and who did not participate much if at all in the home entertainments of the group of married dons; and bachelor Fellows were far commoner in the interwar period and early 1940s than they have since become.

Before I pursue this point, it is worth commenting on the fact that there was so little personal contact between economists in different colleges, even men of the same age group. One reason was presumably an indirect result of the long reign of the bachelor, and after the first war distinctly misogynist and misanthrope, Professor A. C. Pigou. Pigou, as his *Times* obituary (attributed to D. H. Robertson) rather acidly informs us, took little interest in Tripos reform and related teaching matters. Another reason was the very busy term timetable of a don – one bought a specially printed diary for the academic, not the calendar, year, already containing printed information on various university calendar events, and one quickly filled it with one's teaching and college fixtures and further crammed it with various kinds of meetings and appointments. A third reason was the emphasis on the privacy of one's college rooms; one opened them for one's pupils, and a few college familiars and cronies, but casual dropping in on or by colleagues was unwelcome on the one side and known to be presumptuous on the other. A final reason was the unfamiliarity and usually the inconvenience of the telephone, which so far as I can judge was generally installed in the Fellows' rooms only after the Second World War. In any case, the telephone was feared and shunned by the older generation – this is known to have been the case with Keynes, so far as casual contact with strangers and casual acquaintances was concerned, though he did we are told speak with the brokers every business morning by telephone. In place of the telephone and personal visits, communication with colleagues was carried on by handwritten notes. This was very efficient, in its way, since not only did the Cambridge post office make deliveries on the same day (at least three deliveries a day, I understand, in prewar II days) but the university had its own internal postal system, manned by the college porters. The college supervision and university lectures system was congenial to this system of communication. The lectures were very formal – Robertson and Dobb, to my personal knowledge, and in my generation Robin Matthews, wrote out their lectures in full and read them (in Robertson's case, it was a reading in a theatrical sense); and the students did not ask questions, but sat in respectful silence to the end – or did not come at all. The supervisions involved more personal contact and meeting of minds with the students, but they were basically a playing of the formal roles of instructor and instructed, and their essence was formal interpretation, criticism, and defense of a written document. It was natural enough – and incidentally a great boon subsequently to the editors of Keynes's papers – to request a written statement on a point of disagreement, and to give a written reply, among people who had little or no experience of open public argument, except perhaps in the artificial form of formal debates in the Cambridge Union.

I had two experiences, or more accurately one single experience and one sequence of them, of this system of academic communication in my early days at Cambridge, before it fell out of fashion with changing personalities and communication technology and habits. Just before I arrived in Cambridge, I had published a short note in *The Quarterly Journal of Economics* on 'An Error in Ricardo's Exposition of His Theory of Rent.' It was a typical case of over-generalising a particular arithmetical example into a general principle. On arrival in Cambridge I found Dobb and Sraffa much excited by my note, which they were sure was wrong; Sraffa even proposed to publish a criticism of my note, thereby breaking nineteen (I think) years of silence. They were then both Fellows of Trinity College, with rooms not too far apart. Nevertheless, I was shown a stack of notes that had passed between them, notes replete with such phrases as 'Johnson's fallacy is . . .'. I would have been overjoyed to have smoked Sraffa out of his long silence, especially as I knew for sure that my mathematics were correct. But unfortunately or fortunately Sraffa eventually looked up Edwin Cannan's history of thought (1929) and found the error already noted there, whereupon he dropped the subject. (That taught me two lessons: one about the scholarship of Cambridge, and the other about the scholarship of Joseph Schumpeter, who had got me to write up and publish the note. On balance I far prefer Schumpeter's style: if one does not know the literature, and a young man can prove an error one had not noticed, it is better to encourage him than to assume that he must be wrong; better still, of course, to check the literature to guard against unnecessary originality in the establishment of errors.) The other illustration concerns several attempts by Joan Robinson to engage me in economic discussion by return of post; the difficulty with her was that she proceeded directly to differences in conclusion, without exploration of the logical sequence by which she had reached hers and with obvious contempt for the processes of reasoning by which I had reached mine. Also, I never learned to fling the word 'fallacy' about with Cantabrigian abandon; and notes ending 'I challenge you to . . .' made me quail. But Joan Robinson was a natural public debater, not an ivory-tower academic correspondent.

Underlying the reasons just given for the isolation of Faculty members in their colleges, however, was a fundamental fact of physical geography, left implicit in the discussion so far. This was that the Faculty had effectively no geographic administrative and business centre. Geographically, it existed only as a staircase in the science building on Downing Street, just inside and to the right of the entrance archway. The location was about two blocks from the Mill Lane lecture rooms (themselves, as mentioned, no favourable venue for intra-Faculty encounters), and much more distant than that from any of the important economics teaching colleges – King's, Clare, Caius, Trinity, and St. John's. Most of the space was taken up by the Marshall Library, over the archway: while Faculty members met there occasionally *en passant*, while collecting or returning books (there were no limited borrowing periods for them, and most had substantial personal libraries and regularly bought the new books in the local bookshops) or browsing over the new journals displayed on the open shelves, the librarians naturally discouraged conversation in the Library's single large hall, and there was no place outside to congregate except the stairway and entrance hall. Above the Library was a large room used for the weekly meetings of the (general undergraduate) Marshall Society, and during daytime for a few classes and lectures, especially in statistics, the hand calculators being used at other times by a few hard working graduate students. Apart from that, there was the Royal Economic Society office on the first floor *en route* to the Marshall Library – a place swamped with new books received, RES publications awaiting sale, and stacks of manuscripts and galleys, presided over by Austin Robinson and his editorial assistant from time to time. On the ground floor, tucked under the stairs, was the Faculty office, a poky little room with one secretary in charge during my day. (I do not know whether there was even one, pre-war.) The secretary was theoretically – but not in practice – free to do Faculty member typing when not busy on Faculty business typing for the Faculty Secretary. In fact, those who had letters or (much more rarely) manuscripts to be typed used their college office or a famous Cambridge institution, Miss Pate's, which did typing and sent in girls to take dictation of letters. (I remember Kahn once telling me that he had a girl in one morning a week from Miss Pate's, because otherwise his correspondence would get out of hand.) I was unique at that time inasmuch as I could do my own typing. Fortunately, the prosperity of the Department of Applied Economics under Richard Stone's direction enabled one to wangle professional typing of statistical or mathematical papers free of charge from time to time.

There is one other relevant fact, so obvious that I forgot it in the first draft of this paper – the automobile was virtually unknown to the academic, even in the early 1950s. (The only car owners I recall were Ruth Cohen, who had been corrupted by a travelling fellowship in the United States prewar, and Nicholas Kaldor, who was independently very wealthy.) The automobile vastly encourages spatial mobility, partly by saving time, and partly by removing the boredom of slowly traversing space on foot. Without it (and without the convenient telephone), spatial movement requires calculation of the time-cost of movement of personal physical location, and estimation of the probability of a journey being fruitless. In short, the absence of the automobile, and the resulting need to go by foot or bicycle for short distances and by train for longer ones, powerfully reinforced the other incentives to make one's college rooms the focus of one's academic activities, and to communicate with colleagues by postal notes.

To return to the main theme, one's professional and social life was concentrated inside one's college. That meant that one was more or less entirely on one's own as an economist; and this was true even of the few large colleges, and not so large ones such as King's, which either needed more than one economist for teaching, or had one to spare as a by-product of some college administrative position. The reason was that, even though the Cambridge Economics Faculty (and other Faculties) made a great point of democratic equality, and everyone called everyone else by his first name (I remember Kahn being so distressed by my persistence in calling him 'Mr. Kahn' that he finally asked me point-blank to please call him Richard), there were both very definite age and generation differentials that were respected by great formality in people's behaviour to one another even if they were Fellows of the same College. Insistence on the outer forms of democratic equality is, to be sure, not unknown in North America – both at Harvard, when I was a graduate student there, and later at Chicago, I remember being struck by the habit of referring to colleagues as 'Mister ——' partly because it was the American equivalent of Cambridge first names, but also because in Cambridge, and in the United Kingdom generally, one was careful to describe colleagues in front of non-colleagues as 'Doctor' or 'Professor,' but only when they actually held the title; in the less eminent Departments in the United States, however, rank is noticed and described fairly punctiliously. The important difference, however, was that in Cambridge it was age group rather than rank that segregated Department members hierarchically; and this was related on the one hand to the fact that the archetypical Cambridge or Oxford don made his career from matriculation to retirement and ultimately death or senile incarceration in the same college, and on the other hand to the related fact that each succeeding year's crop of BA's made their subsequent careers and positions in British society on the basis of their relative competitive performance on that one year's examinations. Thus the peer-group and the rivals were defined once and for all, and naturally included only a few individuals close in age to oneself.

My own experience, in any case, was that I received no assistance whatsoever from my seniors in the Faculty, and especially those in my own college, in the way of comments on my early professional papers. In fact, though I continued to give them copies, I got used to having Kahn ask me, some six months later, whether the paper I had given him was going to be published, and when I said 'yes' he would express gratitude that he would now not have to read it. They, in their turn, occasionally remembered to give me a copy of something they had written, but I 'was not expected to reply' (to quote the standard King's College High Table rule when a guest's health was proposed); I remember once pointing out to Kaldor that in a paper on policy theory he had forgotten his own past demonstration that after a certain point increasing a tariff to improve a country's terms of trade would make the country worse and not better off; only slightly and momentarily embarrassed, he admitted that the paper had already been sold to the FAO, but would be published where no one would notice it.

Since the so-called 'Circus' played a significant role at one stage in the transition from *The Treatise* to *The General Theory*, it is worth recording perhaps that in 1949–50 or 1950–1 or so we junior Cambridge lecturers did run an informal seminar, for the purpose of reading Samuelson's *Foundations*. But it was always difficult to arrange a time at which we could all meet, and for us individually to manage to do our homework, and the effort eventually petered out. Instead, the Department of Applied Economics seminar, run by its full-time research staff, became the centre for mathematical-theoretical and econometrically inclined junior Faculty staff.

The isolation of a career centred on the individual's college, with contact with comparable professional economists being derived almost exclusively from the reading one chose to do, and with only a small number of such economists, almost exclusively located in Cambridge, Oxford, and London, being considered as worthy of attention or criticism, obviously had a number of conditioning effects on professional academic writing.

To begin with, apart from the reading of literature and the pursuit of controversy within Cambridge by note of hand, there were three main types of personal participation in everyday economic discussion. One, already discussed, was through the formal lecturing. Here there was essentially no feedback from the students – except through the dropping off of auditors, which was an institutionalised expectation attributable to a variety of reasons and not easily translatable into a judgment of professional competence in general, let alone a judgment on the validity of particular arguments or formulations of problems. (Where it might seem to be so, it could be explained away by political bias motivating supervisors to advise their supervisees against attending.)

A second, also not very useful professionally, was through conversation with other, non-economist, Fellows, especially at High Table (dinner). In this connection, college practices differed greatly in the extent to which regular dinners at High Table meant a random alternation of dinner conversationalists. In Jesus College, for example, where I was attached to High Table before I won my King's Fellowship, one assembled always in order of seniority, and could escape one's lifetime dinner companions only by bringing a guest to sit at the Master's right hand, or arriving apologetically too late for the procession and the grace, and sitting at the bottom of the table with the hope of having a neighbour outstanding enough to compensate the sodden drag of the ever-present College Chaplain. In King's, on the other hand (thanks partly to the geographical accident that Senior Common Room was not directly adjacent to the High Table end of the hall, but at the opposite end), one entered in a straggling mob after the Provost, and could with luck select one's table neighbours; it was also respectable, thanks to Pigou's example, to arrive consistently just after the grace for vaguely agnostic reasons, and thus be able to sit among kindred unreligious spirits. In any case, the rule was that one must not 'talk shop'. This meant, in practice, that one talked either about cultural events or about government social and economic policy, in either case relying for level and topics on careful reading of *The Times*. *The Times* was, and for that matter still is, the British economist's only really seriously required reading; and a steady diet of it has a profound influence in shaping British economists' concepts of both economic policy problems and feasible ('politically acceptable') solutions to them. This is, incidentally, an important point about British economic policy discussion both past and present. It has certainly been important (and dangerous) in recent years, when *The Times* leaders on economic policy have been written by bright young Oxford BAs in Politics, Philosophy and Economics, who believe in the standard Oxford panaceas of a higher price for gold (for the international monetary system), incomes policy (for inflation and the balance of payments) and international commodity agreements (for economic development and international justice). The influence of *The Times*, and for the early part of the period *The Manchester Guardian*, and perhaps also *The Telegraph*, on British economists' conceptions of Britain's economic problems in the interwar period has not so far as I know been seriously discussed: I would like to recommend it as a subject for serious study in British economic history and the recent history of the development of economic theory, one aspect of which would be the influence of the quality British press on Keynes's economic writings.

The third, and by far the most serious and important, personal exposure to economic discussion came through the supervisions. These, however, were only very rarely exacting in the sense that one had a pupil both able and argumentative to deal with. For this there were two main reasons, apart from the fact that one taught all three years and that the pupils naturally varied in quality. One was that the tutor or tutors, in deciding admissions, tended to be guided both by the desire for a representative sample of students likely to fill the various positions of social and economic success in British industry, government, landed estate agriculture, and so on, and by an ideal concept of the type of young man that should represent what the college stood for, an ideal which stressed all-roundness, good family, or sophistication rather than solid academic excellence. In my time, they were fighting a losing battle on behalf of the nonintellectual indifferent student; but in the interwar period, I understand, they were both short of revenue and students, and willing to stretch admission rules very far in favour of the progeny of previous undergraduate members of the College.

The other reason was that, because in contrast to other Triposes Economics had a one-year Part I and a two-year Part II, it tended to attract many more students for the Part I than continued into Part II, the students switching to a preferred Tripos for their Part II and their degree. In particular, intending Law students could avoid the horrors of Roman Law, compulsory in the Law Part I, by taking Part I Economics instead. Part I Economics was also used, sometimes, as a means of obtaining a BA for a really dim but blue-blooded student, in combination with Part I Agriculture (or Estate Management). In consequence, the preponderance of one's supervisory activities was occupied by Part I teaching of elementary principles. (The Faculty exploited this situation by minimising the lectures for Part I students by offering no optional lecture courses at that level, and using its Part I student numbers to justify appointments of lecturers who gave Part II optional courses; there was also some evidence of professional discrimination against Part I lecturing, which tended to be assigned to the weaker colleagues.) College Fellows with special administrative responsibilities in their colleges, or with special bargaining power, could however manage to confine their supervisory work to supervisions, or classes, with selected high quality students, as presumably Keynes did and as Kaldor managed to do in my time.

This kind of audience for one's everyday teaching and discussion of economics necessarily forms and distorts one's concept of the audience one is addressing through one's written work – if, that is, one does not, as many Oxford and Cambridge dons do, content oneself with oral communication through lectures, supervisions, and discussions with economist and non-economist academic cronies and colleagues. The most obvious example is actually a common Oxford style, related to the character of the Politics, Philosophy and Economics course and examination tradition, and best exemplified in the work of R. F. Harrod, J. R. Hicks, and many other lesser luminaries, which can best be described as a sort of conversation with oneself, a dramatic monologue performed for a somewhat dim audience of economic amateurs, in which one works one's way laboriously through a succession of false starts and red herrings, eventually winding up with the more or less obvious and correct approach and solution to the problem at hand. It is a style presumably effective for instruction of a captive audience of bashful undergraduates, whom one is committed to instruct for an hour on some basic principle that could be communicated in a few minutes to anyone with a logical mind and a distrust of the economic pronouncements of the socially powerful but academically illiterate; but it is tedious in the extreme for a professional economist to have to wade through. The Cambridge equivalent is a little less tedious but equally irritating to a professional. It posits a nameless horde of faceless orthodox nincompoops, among whom a few recognisable faces can be discerned, and proceeds to ridicule a travesty of their published, presumed, or imputed views in the process of revealing the unorthodox truth in a simple encapsulated form suitable for the average undergraduate to swallow without gagging. This is the extreme form of the modern post-Keynesian-Cambridge style, which unfortunately the *General Theory* did so much to implant. It has three major elements in it, traceable directly to salient characteristics of Cambridge as an academic environment: the belief that fundamental questions of social and economic policy are ultimately determined by debate among a handful of academic economists, in Cambridge and at most two other British universities; that policy failure is the result of bad – and bad means orthodox, or more generally pedestrian, tedious, and unimaginative – economics; and that the world is to be put right by instructing the undergraduate students at Cambridge and elsewhere in the complex fallacies committed by orthodox economics and the simple truth as derived by anti-orthodox economic theory. The older, pre-*General Theory* Cambridge style was much gentler and more sophisticated, though it had the same basic ingredients: concentration on criticism of the work of a few eminent British economists, often not identified directly by name and reference (a scathing and extremely unscholarly attack on Hayek in the *General Theory*, for example, is indexed, necessarily, under 'wild duck'); allusions to the economic views and pronouncements of leading contemporary political figures; digressions into speculations of a vaguely philosophical or historical nature, of a type appealing to cultured undergraduates; and the basic assumption that the principal aim is to instruct undergraduates and guide them through the literature. A further noteworthy characteristic is the tendency to eschew both mathematics, except for illustrative purposes, and statistical analysis going beyond the capacity of an intelligent layman. In this respect, the Cambridge style was heavily and lastingly imprinted by the views of Alfred Marshall on the writing of economics, though Marshall's desire to write for the instruction of the average intelligent businessman has long since been abandoned in favour of writing for the instruction of the ebullient undergraduate, the sole remaining exception being the efforts of James Meade (Oxford-trained) to write formal economic theory in a form relevant to the concerns of the economic policy maker.

In conclusion, I would like to raise briefly two subjects suggested to me by consideration of Cambridge as an environment for academic economists, but which I have not as yet had time to pursue further. First, I have mentioned that the examination framework of PPE at Oxford tends to produce a particular, philosophy-oriented, style of economic writing among its professional economist products. It seems to me that Cambridge philosophy had a similar influence on Cambridge economics thinking, discussion, and writing, despite the separation of economics from philosophy, and largely also from politics, in the structure of the Cambridge Tripos, an influence mediated through Keynes as a result of his membership in the Society of Apostles, his early work on probability, his interest in collecting old books, and his friendship with Frank Ramsey and other King's College philosophers. What I have in mind here specifically is Keynes's use, particularly in the early 1930s (e.g. his reply to Ohlin in the controversy over German reparations in June 1929, and his correspondence with Robertson and others just after the *Treatise* was published) of a particular philosophy discussion device, which can be paraphrased as 'I cannot answer your question until you explain to me what you mean by the words . . .' (or, 'I cannot be sure I have understood your question because I do not know what you mean by the words . . .') – a device which became discredited during the Second World War by the Brains Trust philosopher C. E. M. Joad's stock answer to a question, 'It all depends what you mean by . . .' (some crucial word in the question). I suspect that this device – which is of course a very attractive one for turning an undergraduate's awkward questions into an opportunity for teaching him what one knows and dismissing other peoples' analyses as unsatisfactory – and the philosophical approach underlying it – which stresses semantic analysis of statements to the neglect of the operational and scientific purpose of the logical analysis of which the statements are constituents – had a great deal to do with both the obvious logical inconsistencies in the *General Theory* (which can also be explained by a rather amateurish but on the whole commendable desire to provide empirically observable referents for the theoretical constructs) and the heated semantic debates that ensued on its publication (especially about the savings/investment identity/equality).

The second subject is the influence of the nature of the Cambridge and Oxford College as an economic institution on the ideas of academic economists resident therein. The colleges are, or largely were until the 'student troubles' of the late 1960s, fundamentally feudal institutions, based on landed property owned by the college, administered cooperatively by the Fellows collectively and specifically by a subgroup among them semi-self-selected by administrative interest and loosely controlled by a system of semi-egalitarian semi-gerontological personal-participation democracy, functioning to turn out qualified members of the elite or the establishment (including their own replacements) and dependent on the organised supporting services of the college servants, or porters and kitchen staff. Keynes, as Bursar of King's, was one of the pioneers in shifting the financial base of the college system from landed property to industrial stocks and bonds. (He was also the innovator of the shift by his college from dependence on land rents to direct farm management, a story not relevant here but which ultimately proved a very expensive mistake for the college.) This shift involved, in Keynes's hands, an emphasis on speculation and capital gains, which had an obvious influence on his professional work: Robertson indeed criticised the theory of liquidity preference as 'a college bursar's theory of interest,' referring particularly to

Keynes's neglect of interest as the productive return on capital. More generally, it is possible to relate Keynes's social philosophy to the nature of the College as an economic institution, in two major ways. One concerns the working class and its welfare: if one thinks of the attitude of a college governing body towards its college servants, it seems natural to think of guaranteed employment as the main obligation of the employer towards its employees, together with the payment of wages just competitive with going market wage rates or slightly below, and with gratitude and loyalty assured by the conferment of extensive fringe benefits (notably sports facilities, subsidised housing, and free food and drink). The other concerns attitudes to the entrepreneurial class: it would be natural for college Fellows who had trained the business executive class, usually at the lower end of the spectrum of academic capacity and performance, to regard businessmen as a class as rather inferior to college Fellows, people for whom some reputable nonacademic nongovernmental employment should be found, but who should not be rewarded on an inordinate scale for success in their second-rate activities. It would also be natural for such men to believe that the messes into which the practical world of business and politics got itself resulted from the defect of inferior intelligence or the lack of a system of corporate decision-taking comparable to that of a college Fellowship body and its Council, and to look to intelligent academic discussion by dispassionate and public-spirited people as the obvious means by which to create a better world. (For a modern version of this point of view, see Robin L. Marris, *Economic Theory of Managerial Capitalism* (1964).)

Discussion

Cliff Lloyd (Simon Fraser University):[1] One of the things that comes down through all the discussion here has been a search for the smoking gun – the day that the light dawned. I think most of us who have experienced any kind of making-something-up process, may feel that there may not have been such a day. You may have had in the back of your mind all along a vague view of how something works, but you were never called upon to really make it explicit and work it out. I don't know enough of the existing documentary evidence to know: is there evidence that there was such a thing as the day the light dawned? That is, isn't it possible that Keynes, or perhaps Kahn, always sort of had vaguely this kind of view in his head, but that he was never moved to have to actually say it explicitly? So that the search for the day that the light dawned may be misleading.

H. Johnson: I see Cliff's point. Most of us have in the back of our minds ideas involving a lot more conjecture than we have actual proof: and often we just go on and never do prove something. Sometimes we decide we had better prove it: and this is not a 'light-dawning' process. A light-dawning process is a problem which you are grappling with and you have to solve it somehow and the light dawns and you see how to solve it. That's a different type of problem and I think the point is that it may be that Keynes didn't have such a day of sudden revelation which then dictated the path of future writing. But I wouldn't know. Even those who were there usually don't know that that's the day the light dawned.

Samuelson: I think that we can all go to biography, and that includes autobiography, and discuss cases. I would have thought – in fact, I used it in my 1946 piece, the language of 'Keynes on the road to Damascus' – that faith comes if I start out on the road named Saul, and then suddenly in a blinding motion, I become Paul. But you lose faith without even knowing it. You just wake up one day and discover that you haven't had it for a long time and you haven't missed it. Sometimes, we know, an idea comes suddenly: for example, it can even come in the bathtub, and you run through the street shouting 'eureka'. Shackle has told us that he was doing the dishes, looking out the window, I think, when suddenly he thought, by God, they've got it wrong, they've got it upside down: it's not probability, it's surprise.

Robinson: I agree entirely with that view that there is a moment when the light dawns and you begin to move in a certain direction, and I think it's important when you are working out the timing of a whole series of different stages.

I come back to something Paul was talking about earlier. Whatever view one takes of the *Treatise* (perhaps I don't take quite as gloomy view of it as Paul does), I ask myself whether Keynes could have written and published the *Treatise* in its present form if the light had already dawned on the road to the *General Theory*. I don't believe he could: I believe that something must have happened after the *Treatise* formulations were completed.

Samuelson: And I should mention the Macmillan Committee hearings, which I think were very important and where there was at least one forceful statement of the Say's-Law view for Keynes to go against. I wouldn't want to disagree with Cliff Lloyd's amended version of 'gradual', but I think there is one part that I would suggest he purge of it, namely, that Keynes knew it all along, because that's the great illusion. This is what drives Don Patinkin mad: if I sit down and say, now what was it I believed as a young student at the University of Chicago about classical monetary theory – and then I write it out. In having to write it out, you already are changing it.[2]

There's many a person who thinks he has it, but he doesn't have it. That's why proof is not something superfluous to a mathematician. He does not really understand the theorem until he understands the proof. A conjecture usually is a conjecture of how the proof is going to go. They are not distinguishable. So it's very easy to say that we knew that all along; that's what we always believed – particularly, if you have something amorphous to alibi with, namely an oral tradition.

Patinkin: I don't think it's a question of anybody here saying that one day Keynes awoke and suddenly saw everything. Actually what I feel we're doing here is to exemplify a famous mathematical theorem, I'm sure that Paul can give us its name, that if you have an infinitely long road and if at time t_0 you observe a chicken on one side of the road and at time t_1 it's on the other side of the road, that at some point between t_0 and t_1 the chicken has crossed the road.

Samuelson: Rolle's Theorem.

Patinkin: And I feel that this is essentially what we're doing. That is, I don't think people really get this bright idea and before it there was nothing and then suddenly there is everything. In fact, my whole feeling is exactly the opposite: that it takes time for an individual to develop a new idea. And what I think that we have narrowed down — or at least what I have narrowed down to my satisfaction on the basis of the evidence that I have presented, and you have to decide if it is also to your satisfaction — is that in the case of Keynes the crossing of the road occurred sometime between his lectures in the fall of 1932 and those in the fall of 1933. So it's a very slow process. I think that Paul's reference to autobiographical is really very important. We're all projecting ourselves, especially when we discuss historical events. And who has not had the experience of getting an insight and not at first seeing its full implications: it's a time consuming process. I very much sort of generalise from my own experiences and I think we all do.

Walter Salant: I just wanted to say one thing *à propos* this effort to find a date. As Paul's observation implies, the process that we're examining is one in which Robert Merton would be very much interested because it has everything that he has pointed out in connection with the sociology of science. It is simply a case of the creative process. That really could be the subtitle of this conference. Now, in that process I think that there is not likely to be, or at least is not necessarily, a day on which it all happens. The process may be one of gradual recognition of deficiencies in old explanations and of new insights into individual parts of the whole, and then at some moment you may realise that they all go together. If that realisation happens in some blinding flash, you may then be able to identify one day or moment when you think you made the discovery or you may recall one day which is an important or memorable stage of that process and thus date the discovery retrospectively. That may give you a distinguishable day. But generally it marks only one stage of a longer process. Particular problems with the old theory may have been bothering you for some time and building up a dissatisfaction with it, perhaps subconsciously. That building up of dissatisfaction is part of the whole process and it may have been going on for some time. In that case, the date or short period you pick retrospectively as the time when you got an insight into one of the building blocks or when you saw consciously how those you already had really fit together is a date that may not mean much. I suppose that there are also cases in which a great insight really does occur all at once without much preceding build-up, so I suspect that no generalisation about the dating of the creative process is possible. In the case of the *General Theory* it looks as if there was no date or very short period that can be pinpointed.

Samuelson: I would want to elaborate just a little bit. If any of us has ever watched a film from a Polaroid camera develop, it's a gradual process and something like this must often be involved in the changing of a person's ideas. I would say that if you observed a friend in life becoming conservative, you do not generally find that he went to bed a citizen in the army of humanity and got up a misanthrope. It's a very gradual process. But, when it comes to mathematical theorems, there are *gestalts* that are suddenly seen. And if you go into psychology – looking at an optical illusion, you see something which is just ink blots, and suddenly you see the face of Christ. Every psychologist reports that that is a very quick thing and you can't lose it, once you've seen it. So I would say that to the degree that we're not talking about Keynes's *weltanschauung* with respect to policy, and the need to face up to the fact that in a great depression previous neo-classical certitudes are not enough, and departing from them in an unsystematic way is not enough; what you need is a fancy theory of why you are departing from them. There is hope that you'll find a point when you cross something in the road which is discontinuity. And Joan Robinson's 1933 article on 'The Theory of Money and Output' (which I now look at in a different way, both as a creative force in its own right, but also as simply a reflecting signaling device) – whatever the date when this article was actually written, I thought of it in my 1946 obituary of Keynes, as showing that they had by then arrived at the theory of output. It now looks as if what was arrived at was a realisation that therein lies the variable for which you must find the equation, and the actual formulation of a theory of output was a little bit later. I'm assuming she was in close touch throughout with Keynes.

Robinson: Can we distinguish between finding the questions and finding the answers? I think we had by then found the question, but we hadn't found the completely formulated answer.

Samuelson: Yes, I think that is an important consideration. So that there can't be an exactitude in determining the date of formulation, and attempts to do so reach a point of diminishing returns. Now, I would like to put one minor codicil on what Austin has said about the *Treatise*. It's very relevant, and we apply it to other writers and to oneself, that I must not have known about this on such and such a date because I then wrote what's clearly a reflection of a previous epoch. I accept that because the *Treatise* was a tremendous thing done over a long period; it covered an awful lot of territory. You would have at least sneaked in, if only for priority, a hint of the new idea. On the other hand, you'd have to have made it sometime just before the final proofs went in or something like that.

But the amendment that I want to make, and this is a very minor addition to Tom Kuhn (1962), is that he doesn't prove that we think about only one paradigm at a time. That is an oversharp distinction. Scientists are opportunistic: on Monday, Wednesday and Friday, I can be a Say's Law person working with a Ramsey-Solow model with no problem of effective demand, while on Tuesday and Thursday I can work with another paradigm. I can do it within the same problem. And so, I must not place too much weight on the argument that the fact that he didn't mention it in this context shows that he had never yet arrived at it, even though I do accept that the difference between the *Treatise* and the *General Theory* suggests that anybody who tries to find a theory of effective demand in any 1920s writing would have to assume that things were lost.

May I mention two instances in the history of science, of a sudden *gestalt*. Darwin claims that he got his theory of natural selection from economics. He was climbing a stile or something and he suddenly thought of Malthus. This is interesting because Wallace, fever-ridden in a tent in Malaysia, couldn't go to sleep and he thought of Malthus and it came to him. Now what's interesting is that scientists have done research on that and they show that part of that is an illusion in Darwin: that he did have an awful lot of the puzzle before that. He has the feeling that he got the whole thing in a flash, the essence of it, in walking over that stile, but it's like the misleading notion that you dream in the last five minutes, because you hear a bell, and you wake up and you've had an elaborate dream. I always knew that was untrue and that modern science would catch up with my understanding the matter, because I can dream of theorems in mathematics and the proof of them takes place in real time and the notion that in my sleep I can do it a hundred times as fast as I can do consciously, the detailed steps of a proof in the last seconds, needs more than ringing bells to support it. We now know from sleep research, from eye movements and so forth, that it's a much more intermittent process. So you can't even take the moment of announcement by Archimedes – 'eureka, I have it!' – as more than one bit of evidence. It's not conclusive evidence that he had it after that and didn't have it before that.

Eric Davis (Carleton University, Ottawa): One event occurring between the *Treatise* and the *General Theory* that has not been mentioned thus far is the collapse of the international monetary system in the summer of 1931. I have been struck by Keynes's later writings on expectations where he writes in a style of shifts and shocks to the state of expectations, when one might expect he would write in terms of pessimistic expectations being validated by an unfortunate world. I wondered if anyone has seen indications that those events had any impact on Keynes's change in thinking?

Winch: I am pleased that the role of 'external' events has been raised by Eric Davis. There are so many crude 'environmentalist' or 'externalist' accounts of the Keynesian revolution in the earlier literature that some of the virtues of this approach, when carefully conducted, have perhaps been overlooked in our discussion so far. Now that we appear to have achieved a considerable degree of agreement – absent in the earlier literature – on the 'internal' logic of the shift from the *Treatise* to the *General Theory*, I think we may be in a better position to assess the part played by 'external' events, and more especially by those connected with Keynes's involvement in contemporary policy-making.

At the time that Keynes was putting the final touches to the *Treatise*, and during the year after its publication in 1930, he was deeply involved – as a member of the Macmillan Committee, as Chairman of the Committee of Economists set up by the Economic Advisory Council, and as adviser to the Prime Minister and the Treasury – in the dramatic events which led to the downfall of the Labour Government and Britain's departure from the gold standard in September 1931. Susan Howson and I have just completed a book on the Economic Advisory Council which, among other things, deals with Keynes's part in the policy deliberations which surrounded these events. I would like to mention one or two related matters that could have a distinct bearing on the shift from the *Treatise* to the *General Theory*.

In the course of expounding the policy implications of the *Treatise* analysis before the Macmillan Committee and the Committee of Economists, Keynes had to confront the opposition and incomprehension of several of his fellow-economists, notably Robbins and Pigou. This was clearly one of the factors that, together with the findings of the 'Circus', convinced him of the need for a restatement of his position – one that was primarily addressed to his fellow-economists. But external events of a less purely intellectual variety are equally important to any explanation of the change of theoretical focus in the *General Theory*, and these do not require us to have recourse to the interpretative strategy adopted by some partisan Keynesians of treating the book simply as an elaborate policy tract.

Take, for example, the two problems of interpretation posed by (a) the change in emphasis from monetary to fiscal policy in the *General Theory*, and (b) the fact that the *Treatise* deals with an 'open' economy in which the foreign balance plays a major role, whereas the *General Theory* is couched in terms of a 'closed' model. In order to explain shifts of this kind, it seems necessary to take into account the change in British economic circumstances after September 1931, when two of the policies which Keynes had been pressing for in the latter half of the 1920s had been implemented, namely reduction in the long term rate of interest and management of the pound on international exchange markets. As far as cheap money is concerned, it seems clear that the failure of this policy to achieve adequate levels of employment, in spite of recovery on some fronts, must be introduced as a reason for Keynes's new emphasis on fiscal policy in the *General Theory*, as well as his pessimism concerning the effectiveness of monetary policy in the face of volatile private investment expectations. Although management of the pound fell far short of the kind of international monetary order which Keynes advocated in the

Treatise, the relative success of British policy on this front after 1932 should not be ignored in any attempt to account for the lack of attention paid to the foreign balance, and international economic affairs generally, in the *General Theory*.

What I really wanted to say, however, follows on from some of Paul Samuelson's remarks about the significance of the Keynesian revolution from a history of science point of view. I want to emphasise that I speak here very much as a historian of economics rather than as a practitioner of economic science: the divergent preoccupations of historians and economists is one of the new facts of life that will have increasingly to be recognised. While there is always a danger of falling into the historian's habit of over-stressing uniqueness, I would not like this occasion to pass without underlining its special character to the historian of economics. I do not have to mention the intrinsic importance of the *General Theory*, but it is perhaps worth saying that there can be no other book in the history of economics about which so much is now known concerning its composition, and the events and personalities surrounding its completion and post-publication life. As this Conference demonstrates, we are also in the unique position for an event of this magnitude of being able to bring together personal recollection and documentary evidence, as well as deploy the more usual techniques of rational and historical reconstruction. Unlike their counterparts in natural science, historians of economics do not usually command the same resources and recognition among practitioners, or indeed among other intellectual historians. On this occasion, however, we do not have to adopt the defensive posture normal in similar gatherings of practitioners.

Taken in conjunction with the publication of the Keynes edition, this Conference marks an important juncture in the history of Keynes scholarship. Borrowing the language employed by philosophers and historians of science, we appear to be passing from a phase in which the logic and context of justification or validation has been uppermost in the minds of practitioners, into a phase in which the logic and context of discovery will become the chief concern of historians and scholars. The first of these phases began with the publication of the *General Theory*; it comprises all the work of exposition, clarification, criticism, and simplification that has gone on since 1936. It includes a good deal of inter-professional polemics as well as such classic reconstructive interpretations put forward by Hicks, Harrod, and Modigliani. Leijonhufvud's book *On Keynesian Economics and the Economics of Keynes* (1968) might be taken as one of the latest examples of the practitioner's approach to interpretation. It is an influential *post hoc* rationalisation which makes use of classic historical texts to launch an argument which is basically non (if not un-) historical in character. I do not wish to adopt a superior attitude to such work; it may be essential to the process by which any community of practitioners defines and re-defines its interests. I merely wish to distinguish it from the way in which the historian of economics is likely to proceed in future, especially in the light of the scholarly standards set by the new edition.

But even if I am right in thinking that we are moving towards a period of greater interest in the logic and context of discovery, where practitioners are going to take second place to historians, it is still not clear what interpretative strategies are going to prove most fruitful. We have less experience in these matters than historians of natural science. There is, for example, no real equivalent in the economics literature to the sophisticated historiographic debate that has taken place between historians and philosophers of science in recent years – a debate which has substantially helped to clarify (if not resolve) the relative merits of the 'externalist' and 'internalist' approaches to the history of science.[3] The nearest equivalent is the attempt to apply Kuhnian perspectives to the history of economics, and speaking as one who has made gestures in this direction, I would have to admit that the economics literature is, to say the least, highly uneven (see Winch (1969), pp. 184–7, 192–3).

I am fairly certain that we shall continue to use the 'internalist' methods of rational reconstruction, though more disciplined by historical evidence and less exclusively present-oriented than has frequently been the case so far. We shall also have to find a place for 'external' factors, while eschewing the cruder kind of environmentalism, especially those approaches that place exclusive weight on ideological perspectives. I have briefly indicated earlier one way in which this might be done in the case of the shift from the *Treatise* to the *General Theory*; and Elizabeth and Harry Johnson have already begun to explore a cultural and microsociological dimension.[4] It seems unlikely that a figure of Keynes's stature will escape a psycho-history, though whether this is thought to be a threat or a promise will depend on personal taste for that genre. But I would like to close with a question which picks up Walter Salant's reference to Robert Merton's classic work on the sociology of science: why is it so difficult to think of an equivalent piece of work devoted to economics or any of the other social sciences? We can all agree, surely, that in the case of the Keynesian revolution we are faced with an event which merits experiment with a number of different approaches.

Patinkin: Insofar as Leijonhufvud is concerned, I think that he would agree with the way Donald Winch has described his work. Indeed, in one of the more recent things that Leijonhufvud has written (1972, pp. 1–2), he has stated that the doctrinal aspects of his work should be considered as secondary, and that his main purpose is instead further to develop existing macroeconomic theory.

Let me now make some general observations about the basic question that we have been discussing: namely, how one should approach the problem of understanding and following the development of an idea?

One principle that I follow – I'm giving my credo now, that's a big word – anyway, I follow what might be called the Principle of Fallibility. And I think that you can't understand the history of the development of any idea unless you start out with such a principle. I don't only mean fallibility in the sense that a writer's ideas are not always consistent; for clearly, if we try to interpret a man's work, and even more so the development of his work, from the viewpoint that everything that he said is necessarily consistent with everything else that he ever said, or even necessarily consistent with everything that he said at roughly the same time in other contexts – and that is the basic, if implicit, assumption (and consequently weakness) of the frequently referred to Talmudic method – then we'll obtain a distorted picture of how the man actually thought and worked.

But in addition to this there is fallibility in the broad sense of lack of completeness: the individual frequently does not see the full implications of his argument at a given point of time. Now, I said 'he does not see,' and I immediately add 'we don't see,' for we are all in the same position. How many times have we said to ourselves, why didn't I see that before? – which means that we didn't see it before. So the procedure of taking a text and saying: he said A; now, logically A implies B; obviously then he understood B – that procedure is a very dangerous one to apply to the history of ideas. In particular, I think that part of the difference between Paul and myself is that I'm more hesitant about saying, 'therefore he saw B' than Paul is. I also think that at least in part this reflects the fact that Paul can always see B much faster than I can, and so finds it more difficult to believe that someone else did not do so.

All this has essentially come up already in our earlier discussions here about the role that should be assigned to Kahn's 1931 multiplier article. But I would like now to provide an additional and most illuminating example of this principle – one that I have used on an earlier occasion[5] – from a somewhat different field. It's a very convenient example, in the sense that it is an example that many of us have personally experienced. I am referring to Milton Friedman's permanent-income hypothesis, which to my mind is his greatest scientific contribution. When Friedman presents this hypothesis in the first chapter of his *Theory of the Consumption Function* (1957), he says it's all in Irving Fisher, and cites Fisher's analysis in his *Rate of Interest* (1907) and *Theory of Interest* (1930) of an individual maximising the utility of consumption over two periods subject to a budget restraint which is the present value of his income stream over the two periods. And since this present value is identical with the individual's wealth, Fisher's analysis implies that consumption is a function, not of current income, but of total wealth, for which permanent income is a proxy.

Not only does Friedman say, look, it's in Fisher, but he also refers in this context to one of the least-read chapters in Hicks' *Value and Capital*

(1939): the technical, seemingly academic and pedantic chapter 14 on the definition of income in which Hicks provides four different definitions of this concept and goes on to explain why, in non-stationary economy 'we should not regard the whole of [an individual's] current receipts as income' (Hicks (1939), p. 172). And Hicks' reasons are exactly the same as those involved in the permanent-income hypothesis: windfalls are not part of income, the question of permanency, and so forth.

Now, everybody in the 1940s had the works of Fisher and Hicks before them. But at the same time people continued to fit econometric consumption functions with consumption as a function of current income, and nobody, including Hicks, said, 'Gentlemen, you are using the wrong variable.' Because in one compartment of our mind we had Fisher and Hicks; and in another compartment we were fitting empirical consumption functions. We never put the two together. And the great accomplishment of Milton Friedman was seeing the implications of the theoretical analysis of consumption for the corresponding empirical studies. And consumption has never been the same since.

Then you ask, when was the permanent-income hypothesis formulated? When did it appear on the scene of economic analysis? And I think we would be misrepresenting things if we said that Irving Fisher did it. Instead I think we should date its appearance to that 'moment of truth' when Milton Friedman saw certain implications that were not seen before. I think anyone who has worked creatively has had the experience of achieving such moments of truth – though, as I have already indicated, I think (and of course I am again projecting from myself) it generally occurs only after one has struggled with the problem for a while: you see an implication that you did not see before; you haven't learned any new facts, you haven't added any additional assumptions, but you suddenly see an implication that you didn't see before. That's part of the human condition and, as Walter Salant has so rightly said, that's what we are studying here at this Conference. Indeed, that's what a good part of the study of the history of ideas is about. Well, that's one of my guidelines whenever I look at texts and try to determine how people have developed their ideas: that we are all human beings, we're all fallible.

A second thing that we all know we have to be very careful about in tracing the development of an idea is to read things in their context: a sentence in the context of the article or chapter in which it appears; a chapter in the context of the whole book; and perhaps even a book in the context of a man's life's-work.

Thus let me take the specific example of the paragraph in the Harris lecture which I discussed yesterday and which Paul referred to in his 1946 essay on Keynes. In this passage, as you will recall, there is a reference to 'a sufficiently low level of output which represents a kind of spurious equilibrium' (*JMK* XIII, pp. 355–6). And you are immediately tempted to say, here is the beginning of the *General Theory*! But if we read this sentence in the context of the whole discussion there – and this is what I pointed out in my paper yesterday – we see that it is not the *General Theory* at all.

But I would also like to go on and say that what made me suspicious in the first place about interpreting that sentence as an adumbration of the *General Theory* is the context of the 1931 Harris lecture in the work of Keynes as a whole. For this lecture is first and foremost a song of praise to his *Treatise*: thus as I noted yesterday, it was the fundamental equations of the *Treatise* that Keynes had in mind in this lecture which he proclaimed 'That is my secret, the clue to the scientific explanation of booms and slumps (and of much else as I should claim) which I offer you' (*JMK* XIII, p. 354). Which brings me to observe that though Keynes alluded to the Bible on more than one occasion in his writings (e.g., the 'widow's cruse'), the verse in the Book of Proverbs (27:2), 'Let another man praise thee, and not thine own mouth' was apparently not one of his favorites.

In any event, the Harris lecture is essentially a non-technical presentation of the argument of the *Treatise*, and the only thing that is sort of outside the conceptual framework of the *Treatise* is that sentence about the 'low level output ... of spurious equilibrium'. So then I asked myself, well maybe it doesn't quite mean what it at first sight seems to? And this is what brought me to the closer examination of the immediate context of that sentence and to the resulting conclusion that I have already noted.

My third general observation is that the study of the history of doctrine should be looked upon as an empirical study, with the universe from which the relevant empirical evidence is drawn consisting of the writings and teachings of the economists in question. When I first made that observation a few years ago,[6] all I meant was that economists who wanted to write about the history of doctrine had an obligation to support their interpretations with evidence from the relevant texts – and there was a reason for saying that at the time. But now, from the further work that I have been doing, especially on the work of Keynes, I see it as an empirical science in the broader sense that as historians of thought we are like econometricians fitting a multivariate regression equation to a man's writings: we're trying to pass a regression line through them that will best explain them. Now, one thing about a regression line is that there are always points off of it, and then the question is whether they are random departures from the line, or whether they reflect a systematic influence that you have not taken account of. And the same is true when you pass a regression line through a man's writings: there will generally be some passages in his writings that you have not explained. And then you have to decide what is the true meaning of the man, what is his regression line and what is a chance phrase, a chance formulation, or perhaps even a mistake, whose departure from the regression line shouldn't make us change our view about the nature of the line.

I think this approach is particularly important in the case of Keynes. First, because of the tremendous quantity and variety of the man's writings on economic questions. Second, because these writings reveal Keynes as a man who was not primarily interested in rigor and precision, or at least as a man for whom the quality of internal logical consistency was not of the highest priority.

I think I can best make my point by comparing Keynes's *General Theory* with another book written at roughly the same time, John Hicks' *Value and Capital* (1939). A regression line through that book would have a correlation of almost 1.00: practically all points in the book will be on the line because Hicks is a man with a major concern with logical consistency. There was one thing that somebody picked up – the fact that the substitution effect is defined in two different ways, in the text of *Value and Capital* and in the mathematical appendix –

Samuelson: Actually, in the limit these two ways are the same.

Patinkin: That's even better. Anyway, these are only minor deviations like that one from the regression line. And then you have the *General Theory*, which is written in a completely different way by a completely different kind of man.

And so when I try to interpret Keynes's writings, I view each individual passage as a single observation in a multitude of observations through which I am trying to draw a regression line to explain what the man meant. Correspondingly, I do not find it automatically necessary to change the whole conception of what I think Keynes said on the basis of a single isolated quotation. Instead, I want to read it in the context of everything that Keynes was writing during the period and see how it fits in with his general view, with his general regression line. But all this clearly calls for a lot more development and discussion than I can provide here.

NOTES

1. [We regret to note the death of Cliff Lloyd in January 1977. – Eds.]
2. [See Samuelson (1968) and Patinkin (1972). – Eds.]
3. As an indication of the kind of debate I have in mind see Roger H. Stuewer (ed.), *Historical and Philosophical Perspectives of Science* (1970).
4. In addition to their respective papers given to this Conference, see Elizabeth S. Johnson and Harry G. Johnson, 'The Social and Intellectual Origins of the *General Theory*' (1974).
5. See Patinkin (1974), pp. 8–9.
6. See Patinkin (1969), p. 93.

Appendix I Robert B. Bryce's 1935 lecture at the London School of Economics, and related correspondence with Keynes

From R. B. Bryce to J. M. Keynes.[1]

St. John's College, Cambridge, July 3, 1935

Dear Mr. Keynes,

I am sending you herewith a copy of a paper I prepared for Dr. Hayek's seminar at the London School of Economics and which I discussed there at four of the meetings. I might add their chief difficulties were with the definitions of income and investment, with the concept of the propensity to spend, and with the way in which equilibrium would establish itself again after, say, an increase in the quantity of money. On the whole, however, they seemed able to understand it and were quite interested.

There is probably nothing new in this paper to you, but I thought it might interest you to see how your ideas are taken up and then put down in slightly different form by Research Students here.

Before leaving this country for a couple of years, I should like to thank you for the considerable interest and pleasure which I have derived from being a member of your Political Economy Club, and also for your kindness in other ways.

Yours sincerely,
[Signed] R. B. Bryce

From J. M. Keynes to R. B. Bryce.[2]

July 10th, 1935

My dear Bryce,

Many thanks for sending me a copy of your essay. I think it is excellently done, and I am astonished that you have been able to give so comparatively complete a story within so short a space. I am not surprised that your hearers found it a bit difficult. For a theory which is unfamiliar anyhow does not become easier through compression. All the same, you have got into it the main elements in my theory.

I am interested to hear that some of their chief difficulties were with definitions. I am not at all surprised, though it is extraordinarily tiresome and boring that it should be so. In my book I have deemed it necessary to go into these matters at disproportionate length, whilst feeling that this was in a sense a great pity and might divert the readers' minds from the real issues. It is, I think, a further illustration of the appalling state of scholasticism into which the minds of so many economists have got which allow them to take leave of their intuitions altogether. Yet in writing economics one is not writing either a mathematical proof or a legal document. One is trying to arouse and appeal to the reader's intuitions; and, if he has worked himself into a state when he has none, one is helpless.

Yours sincerely,
[initialled] JMK

NOTES

1. [Handwritten letter in Keynes Papers. – Eds.]
2. [Carbon of typewritten letter in Keynes Papers. – Eds.]

An introduction to a Monetary Theory of Employment

R. B. BRYCE

This paper is an attempt to give an example of the type of monetary theory held by Research Students in Cambridge. It represents only my own views on the matter. These have been very largely influenced by Mr Keynes' lectures and subsequent discussion in Cambridge, but they cannot be taken in any way as a statement of even what I believe Mr Keynes' views to be. I have not seen nor heard any part of his forthcoming book on the subject, except what may have been in his lectures or other publications. The present paper does not attempt to go deeply into all the points involved, nor can it in so short a compass clear up all the difficulties, but it aims at setting forth the general principles as clearly and concisely as possible.

I

The general purpose of the theory is to explain the determination of, and thereby changes in, total employment and production, and to trace its relation to the amount of investment (capital formation), the rate of interest and the quantity of money. In doing so a new theory of the determination of interest rates is involved, and a new approach to price level problems is opened up – though not explored. The method is such as to be of some use in analysing the process of change as well as the requirements of equilibrium.

The basic divergence of this theory from orthodox equilibrium theory is that while it retains the primary postulate that the self-interest of entrepreneurs maintains the marginal productivity of labour in all its uses equal to the wage rate (or to marginal labour cost), nevertheless it rejects the assumption that the action of labour maintains the marginal disutility of labour equal to the wage (or, to the marginal income). For the theory is interested in a world where unemployment may be present, and unemployment we understand to mean the existence of labour not employed but willing to work for a money wage worth in real goods as much as or less than the present money wage. When such unemployment is present the marginal disutility of labour in all uses cannot be equal to the wage. The present theory assumes usually, though it can deal with all cases, that unemployment can exist without causing money wages to fall; and it denies that a general fall in money wages leads to a fall in real wages except indirectly through its effects on investment and the distribution of income.

That unemployment as above defined often exists in the real world without causing significant reductions in money wages let alone real wages, is only too obvious. It includes of course those unemployed because their Trade Union holds out for a given money wage but not for a given real wage. Incidentally it is worth noting the fundamental difficulty involved in trying to use orthodox equilibrium theory to explain the amount and causation of unemployment when one of its fundamental postulates denies the possibility of unemployment.

The present theory holds that money is of considerable significance in determining employment. On reflection I think it only has this importance because labour so often sets its supply price in money rather than real terms – or else custom or policy prevents reductions in money wage rates.

In this paper I shall assume until section (v) that the general level of money wages remains unchanged and that the supply of labour at this wage is elastic up to the point where it is all employed. Differences in value of labour will be considered rather as differences in amount, e.g., a skilled workman getting £6 a week is considered as twice as much labour as an unskilled man at £3. Because the men to be had for the going wages are likely to be in the most productive situations, an increase in employment will reduce the efficiency and therefore the marginal productivity of labour, and the real wage – but not the money wage – that will be offered and accepted. I shall also assume a closed system for simplicity of exposition, until section (vi) is reached.

The definitions now used in Cambridge are much more in accord with the ordinary usage of terms than formerly but a clear understanding of them is essential to the argument. So far as possible only those terms have been used whose quantitative character is clearly observable, though the actual delimitations may have to be somewhat arbitrary.

Employment we have defined above, as the number of men working multiplied by their time and made commensurable one with another by considering one man to be providing more labour per unit time than another if he gets a greater wage per unit of time. Thus if W be the rate of money wages for a given kind of labour (for example, common road labour) chosen as standard then the total employment is equal to total wage bill divided by W. N is used as the symbol for total employment.

Income is defined as the money receipts of all individuals in the community in the given period of time (or as a rate at a point of time) accruing to them for their productive services or rights *used* during that period (or at that point of time). These receipts are considered to include those not actually paid over – for example wages earned but not paid till the end of the week, or profits earned but not paid till the end of the year and so forth. Some difficulty may be found in the exact delimitation of

Appendix I

income, especially the residual income of the entrepreneurs but as long as any reasonable limit is taken and used consistently it will not affect the validity of the argument. Changes in the value of existing assets due to changes in expectations of future value, to changes in the rate of interest, or to events not caused by the process of production should be excluded from income in any case.

It is perhaps worth while to notice that income has two aspects. First it is received by individuals, either in money, in kind or in equities for their services, and they must dispose of it between saving and expenditure on consumption. Secondly it is paid out by entrepreneurs (including of course their own profits which may be in a real form) in the production of goods and services for present consumption and future use. What the entrepreneurs 'pay out' including profits must be exactly equal to what they 'receive' from the sale of what has been produced or the retention of assets at their market value, losses being of course negative income 'paid' to themselves.

The next essential term is expenditure. This is defined as the amount spent by individuals for consumption goods, that is, for goods which they intend to use themselves, during the given period (or as a rate at the given point of time). As in the case of income the exact boundaries of what is to be considered expenditure must be arbitrary, but only a consistent usage is required for this argument.

Both investment and savings are defined as the difference between income and expenditure, when both relate to the same period or point of time. Strange as this may appear at first sight it is quite in accord with common sense. From the point of view of individuals as receivers of income their savings at any time are what they receive as income less what they spend on consumption. From the point of view of production that amount of money is being invested which is being paid out in production (including any profits being drawn, normal or abnormal, positive or negative) but which is not balanced by current receipts from the sale of consumption goods. We should recall in this connection that the net income earned and paid out in producing consumption goods in any period is no more and no less than the receipts from the sale of consumption goods in that period, that is, expenditure. Consumption goods produced in excess of current sales are part of investment. And of course in real terms a society can only save what it is creating over and above consumption, and must be 'investing' (whether voluntarily or accidentally) those of its efforts which are not being used to satisfy present consumption.

Of course by these definitions, savings and investment, being just different aspects of the same thing must be equal at all times and under any conditions. Their equality is 'guaranteed' so to speak by the definition of income and effectuated by the variation in income. For example, if part of the community is 'saving' more than total investment, the other part must be 'dissaving' to the extent of the difference, selling assets to the first part to finance their own expenditure, so that net saving remains equal to investment and total income is still the sum of investment and expenditure.[1]

The next and very important term is the propensity to spend (or its converse the propensity to save). This refers to the desire of the community to divide its income between saving and expenditure on consumption goods. It is defined as the function relating the amount that the community will spend to the amount of their income, i.e., if Y is income and C expenditure, $C = F(Y)$ where F is the propensity to spend. The propensity to save can be deduced from this – since savings must always equal income minus expenditure.

The propensity to spend will depend upon the preferences of individuals as between saving and spending, i.e., their time preference; on the amount of real income represented by the money income, i.e., the level of prices; particularly upon the distribution of income as between individuals and classes with different preferences; on expectations of future conditions, and on the rate of interest. In turn, as we shall see the propensity to spend itself influences these other factors.

It is necessary to make one fundamental assumption about the propensity to spend but it seems very likely to be true of the real world. This is, that if incomes increase, savings must also increase, not necessarily as a proportion of income but absolutely. Therefore if incomes increase expenditure on consumption may increase but it cannot increase by as much as incomes, as long as the propensity to spend remains the same.

It will be convenient too, to have a term which we shall call the supply curve, or supply function of consumption goods, although it actually will only represent an aggregation of many supply curves for individual firms. This function will relate the quantity of labour which will be employed in making consumption goods, N_1, to the expenditure on consumption goods C. It is possible of course that actual employment and expenditure may diverge from those associated values given by this curve in so far as entrepreneurs make mistakes in estimating the future expenditure. However we will assume that the curve is the short period equilibrium curve so that any deviation of expenditure off this curve will lead to an adjustment of employment to that amount required by this equilibrium condition. The curve will be determined by all the technical and cost conditions, and demand conditions for each firm as well. A similar curve may be conceived for employment on investment goods – relating the number employed there, N_2, to the money volume of investment. These two curves will be interrelated, and the distinction between what labour belongs on one and what on the other is one of type only and the dividing line arbitrary. We shall assume in each case – and it seems quite reasonable – that higher quantities of employment are associated with higher expenditure or investment (i.e., that the 'elasticity of supply' is not less than 1).

II

We come now with a fairly complete set of terms to the first step in the analysis of how employment is determined. Now in truth all our quantities, – employment, income, investment, expenditure and our functions – the propensity to spend and the supply curves of consumption and investment as well as others that will be later introduced, are interrelated and hence the actual determination of the quantities must come as the working out of these interrelationships. We *could* only find what they would be by solving a number of simultaneous equations, and could only observe the effect of a change by noting how it worked through or changes these equations. In this respect the problem is like that of the general equilibrium theory of value. But just as the general theory of value can be broken up to observe the working of, and conditions of equilibrium within, one part of it, so this general theory of employment can be taken apart to see how it works, and the conditions of equilibrium found within certain regions of analysis. It is only by doing so that we shall ever be able to know what happens in the whole.

Therefore let us begin by assuming that the amount of investment, the supply functions of consumption and investment goods, and the propensity to spend are given. Then we can show that income, expenditure and employment are determined by these data. For the amount of investment being given, income must be such as to yield that amount of saving, with the given propensity to save and spend. Any other income would be incompatible with one or other of the two conditions, and as we shall show in a moment, any attempt to change this income – as by mistakes on the part of the entrepreneurs – will produce forces that will lead back to this equilibrium value. Income and the propensity to spend being then determined and given, expenditure must be determined. Expenditure being determined and the supply function of consumable goods, the employment in producing consumable goods is determined. Because investment and the supply function of investment goods are known, employment in investment is easily determined. Therefore total employment is determined.

None but this unique value of employment will satisfy all the conditions. If employment in consumption industry were different while the propensity to spend remained the same, income from producing consumption goods would be no larger – the reduction in income of the entrepreneurs offsetting the increase in wage income, in the case where employment was greater than the equilibrium level. Expenditure would not be greater than the equilibrium value, and therefore entrepreneurs would reduce employment toward the equilibrium value. Similarly if employment were less than the determined value, income and net savings would be the same – the reduced income of others being balanced by increased entrepreneurial income. Expenditure would be no less than before, so that competition between entrepreneurs would expand employment toward the equilibrium level. It can now be seen why our fundamental assumption about the propensity to spend (on p. 132) is necessary – for if when income increased expenditure increased equally then the output of consumption goods would be in neutral equilibrium, for an increase in employment could generate sufficient expenditure to maintain itself. It is because this is not the case that unemployment can persist in a state of at least short period equilibrium, and that the actual amount of employment is a function of investment.

While it is true that employment cannot increase without a change in some one of these five things, a change in any one of them will cause a change in employment. Thus an increase in the propensity to spend will increase expenditure, incomes and employment in consumption. Therefore anything which increases the propensity to spend may increase employment, and similarly for a decrease. Therefore in so far as chance variations, mistakes perhaps of entrepreneurs, increase employment beyond equilibrium and in doing so change the distribution of income, they may change the propensity to spend and thus total incomes, while saving remains the same. Hence for a stable equilibrium we need to stipulate that temporary variations in employment shall not permanently increase the propensity to spend and particularly that an increase in employment beyond the equilibrium value shall not cause enough redistribution of income to increase the propensity to spend sufficiently to increase expenditure to that value which will hold employment at its new level. It seems hardly likely that a change in employment will produce such a change in the distribution of income if it is a movement to another point on the supply curve of output; but if it is a movement off the supply curve – so that entrepreneurs are making unexpected profits or losses, the distribution itself will only be temporary so that the change in the propensity to spend will also be temporary, and equilibrium will be stable.

The supply functions of consumption and investment goods are determined largely by technical conditions and relative demands. When labour is in elastic supply changes in wage rates will not be arising to influence it – although the varying efficiency of the labour available will do so. The propensity to spend, though dependent to some extent on expectations and the rate of interest will be largely determined by personal and technical considerations and customs, and will be affected by the supply functions through their influence on the distribution of incomes. All these factors, though subject to change from time to time are relatively stable, except perhaps in so far as the propensity to spend is upset by changes in expectations and 'mass psychology'. It is investment, the remaining determinant of employment, whose changes are more important in real life and it is to the determination of investment we now turn.

III

There is probably less new in the present theory regarding the determination of investment than on other matters, so it will be dealt with more briefly. However it must be stressed that up to the state of full employment of labour and other productive resources, an increase in investment, as was shown in the last section need not be accompanied by a reduction of consumption – as orthodox theory assumes – but rather it will usually be accompanied by an increase in consumption.

Now, some of the excess of income over expenditure, that is investment, may be created by entrepreneurs unwillingly – as for example when unsold stocks accumulate. But in general investment is only undertaken when the demand for the investment goods or services (investment can be made in such intangible things as 'goodwill' by means of advertising) is sufficient to induce their voluntary production. This demand is derived from the expected future yield of these investment goods – whether they be stocks of wheat, machinery or houses. And this applies not only to that investment which is new capital – if such can be separated from the total – but to any replacement or maintenance expenditure which is only made because it is expected to yield a future return.[2]

Because investment goods are demanded only for their future return, the demand price will depend not only upon the more or less uncertain expectation of this future return but also on the rate of interest at which this return must be discounted in order to arrive at its present value, which will be the demand price. This rate of interest used in discounting must be equal to the market rate of interest for loans for the same period of time. Otherwise there will be either a clear profit to be made simply in borrowing to create the investment and repaying the loan from the anticipated future return,[3] or, if the rate of interest is higher it would pay to lend money rather than use it in the purchase of the investment.

Thus the demand for investment goods depends upon two things, – their expected future returns, or as Mr Keynes has called it, the expectation of quasi rents, and the rate of interest. Given then the supply function of investment goods, and the rate of interest. Given then the supply function of investment goods (discussed in section I) their output is margin where the cost of production of the good in question is equal to the sum of the future incomes it yields discounted at the market rates of interest for the appropriate periods. Keynes has summed it up by defining that rate of interest which equates the present value of the expected quasi-rents of a possible bit of investment to its cost of production as the efficiency of capital in that use, and then states that investment will be pushed to the point where the marginal efficiency of capital equals the rate of interest. Because the most profitable investments will be made rather than others, the marginal efficiency of capital must decline as the amount of investment in a given period increases, for example, if 400 million £ a year can be profitably invested at 4%, then in order that 600 million £ can be invested the rate will have to fall – perhaps to 3 or $2\frac{1}{2}$%.

Thus investment on a given period is determined by the estimated marginal efficiency of capital and the rate of interest. Other things will influence it only through their influence on one of these – as in the case of the ordinary determination of price by demand and supply. The actual amount of present incomes – as well as the state of business confidence – may of course influence the expectation of quasi-rents and hence the amount of investment by way of the marginal efficiency of capital. Changes in working capital are of course part of investment and they depend very largely on present and immediate future incomes. The volume of employment in producing consumption goods will also affect investment through affecting the cost of production of capital and thus its marginal efficiency. Of course in a condition of full employment, or when wage rates are not assumed fixed but can vary with employment, this latter consideration is most important.

The fact that much investment is made in the expectation of returns in the distant future, of which our knowledge must be very small, means that the amount of investment will be quite sensitive to changes in 'business confidence' and uncertainty in regard to the general economic outlook. Therefore, and because of the importance of investment in determining employment and income, the whole employment situation is quite sensitive to all the caprices of 'market psychology' and the political and other factors influencing it.

IV

We come now to the determination of the interest rate and here we may pause to examine the inadequacy of the orthodox interest rate theory (as presented, say, by Fisher) in an economy where unemployment is present. This classical theory says, in brief, that the interest rate is determined by the supply and demand for new savings or 'free capital'. The amounts the public and corporations would save at various interest rates are said to give one a supply curve (its actual shape need not detain us here), while the amount of investment, which forms the demand for savings in terms of the interest rate it will yield, is said to give the demand curve. Assuming a perfect market the interest rate will settle at that figure which equates this supply and demand.

However we have seen that savings and investment must always be equal at any rate of interest simply because both of them are the surplus of income over consumption expenditure, and that any tendency for them to diverge is checked by changes in income or its distribution. Now it is true that both the time preference of the consumer and the marginal productivity (or efficiency) of capital must always equal the rate of interest. But this is not enough to determine it, though as we shall see it sets a lower limit to the rate that can be maintained without serious inflation.

What does happen is that the time preference adjusts itself to the rate of interest by a variation in income and the proportion of it saved, while the marginal productivity (or efficiency) of capital adjusts itself to the rate of interest by variations in the amount of investment.[4] It is only because the orthodox theory always assumes a condition of full employment that it can explain the rate of interest in this simple manner. But as we have observed these assumptions are not only unreal but absurd since they rule out the very things that are of most interest.

Searching then for the actual determinants of the interest rate it is not surprising to find them much closer to the money market in the supply of and demand for money stocks. Interest is not the reward for all saving or 'not spending' but rather and more directly important, it is the reward for 'investing' or not hoarding savings. Hence it is the price paid by an individual (or corporation) for holding his wealth in the form of money rather than as income bearing assets. An individual, either consumer or entrepreneur, derives utility of some kind from holding money, the nature of which we will examine in a moment. In order that he should be in equilibrium the marginal utility of holding money must be equal to the marginal return he can get by investing it, which is the market rate of interest. Therefore we can draw up a schedule or demand curve showing the amount of money that any individual or market will hold at various rates of interest, under given conditions including of course the whole complex of present and expected future prices. If now there is a given supply of money, or supply curve of money in terms of the rate of interest, then the equilibrium rate is determined by the intersection of these two curves.

Should the rate of interest be greater than this equilibrium level people will attempt to buy income-yielding assets, bonds and equities, in order to get the rate of interest. But if their demand curve for money remains fixed the money and capital market will only be in equilibrium when the price of bonds and shares (and short term bills etc.) has been driven up by this competition to buy them to the point where the yield on them is equal to this marginal utility of the given quantity of money. In so far as the fall in the interest rate through its effects on investment, employment and incomes increases the marginal utility of the given quantity of money, it reduces the distance the interest rate must fall. Similarly if the rate of interest were less than the marginal utility of holding money stocks the market will attempt to sell income-yielding assets until their yield has increased to equal this marginal utility, which now may be reduced by the effects of the rising interest rate. Thus the rate of interest is not the price balancing saving and investment but rather that balancing the supply and demand for money stocks; it must be such as to bring equilibrium between the desire to hold wealth in the form of money and in the form of income yielding assets. The speed of business on the capital market enables this equilibrium to be quickly adapted to rapidly changing circumstances.

This demand for money stocks in terms of the rate of interest has been called by Mr Keynes 'Liquidity Preference'[5]. This follows from the fact that the utility yielded by these money stocks is what is rather vaguely known as 'liquidity'. This consists of the convenience and certainty of having a store of value in the form of means of payment to make purchases or to meet debts. The desire for this liquidity, in conjunction with many objective conditions and estimates of the future, gives rise to the demand for money stocks. These other factors conditioning the demand include expectations and uncertainty in regard to interest rates, prices and obligations in the future, the present levels of wages prices and employment, the methods and costs of making payments and capital transacting and other factors influencing 'market psychology'.[6]

It is through its effect on the rate of interest that the quantity of money actually affects investment, incomes, employment and prices. The relationship of the quantity of money to any of these latter elements is rather complex so that it is no wonder that the simple directness of the quantity theory of money could shed little light on what actually happens.

Changes in the quantity of money, in so far as they affect expectations and 'market psychology' may in themselves alter liquidity preference and the demand for money, so that actually the rate of interest may be unchanged, or even perversely changed; but the cases where this would happen seem likely to be rare, even if perhaps important in times of crises. We will show later that the marginal efficiency of capital and the consumers time-preference as expressed through the propensity to save, set a lower limit to the rate of interest if inflation is to be avoided. We may note too that changes in time preference and the marginal efficiency of capital will affect incomes and prices and thereby the demand for money and the rate of interest. If the marginal efficiency of capital increases and people prepare to increase the amount of investment there will be an increased demand for funds through the sale of new investment securities. This will usually mean an increase in the demand for money stocks of the group carrying on new investment before the increased incomes are actually created from which the increased saving equal to the new investment will come. This will tend to depress the price level of securities and increase the rate of interest, perhaps even above the level that will be in equilibrium when the demand for money returns to what is normal at the higher level of investment and incomes. In other words, the demand for money stocks is apt to be unusually high while investment is increasing.

If we relax our simplifying assumption of an unchanging level of money wages, we may observe that the demand for money will be a function of the level of money wages; both directly in so far as much money is held against wage payments, and also because the price level is a function of the wage level. A general fall in money wage rates in a depression will likely lead to less requirements for money and hence a fall in the rate of interest if the money supply is not decreased, and hence more investment and employment. It may be checked by other factors, such as for example, an expectation of further wage reductions which would tend to defer investment. But we should note that this beneficial effect of the wage reduction could be lead simply by increasing the quantity of money with none of the great difficulties of wage deflation.

V

We have now covered the main essentials of the theory and can pause to review it a little by tracing the effects of changes, before we go on to consider some special cases and to remove the assumptions made to simplify the argument. For our first example consider the probable effects of an increase in the quantity of money, other things remaining the same except as they are affected by the changed money supply. The banks will increase the quantity of money through the extension of their advances and the purchase of securities. Both of these tend to decrease the rate of interest directly. But more important, the receivers of money in the community will find their money stocks increasing and will try to buy securities and to some extent consumption goods as well, thus decreasing the rate of interest and perhaps increasing the propensity to spend. The fall in the rate of interest will increase investment, which with given, or possibly increased, propensity to spend will increase incomes and expenditure and therefore the employment in producing consumption goods as well as in investment goods. In so far as the fall in the rate of interest also affects the propensity to spend it may either add to or detract from the increase in expenditure and employment. The fall in the interest rate will finally be checked by an increasing demand for money with increasing incomes and employment so that a new position of equilibrium will be established with greater employment and real income than the first.

As another example suppose that the propensity to spend should increase. This will increase expenditure and incomes, investment being still the same. The increased expenditure will increase the output of consumption goods, and employment. In addition the greater present demand for consumption will likely increase the expectation of future quasi-rents and therefore increase investment. However the rise in incomes will increase the demand for money and thereby tend to increase the rate of interest and tend to check, or even reduce investment. Again the new equilibrium will be established with more employment.

Finally take the case where there is a fall in expectations of quasi-rents, and therefore in the marginal efficiency of capital other things again being supposed to remain the same except as they are influenced by this change. The fall in the marginal efficiency of capital will reduce investment and therefore incomes and expenditure. The first effect of this will be a fall in profits and then a contraction of output and employment will follow both in consumption and investment production. This fall will be checked by a fall in the demand for money and a consequent reduction in the rate of interest which in turn will check the decrease in investment and bring equilibrium at a lower level of investment, employment and incomes.

We should notice that the accumulation of capital in modern economies tends to reduce the opportunities for profitable new investment and therefore reduce the marginal efficiency of capital, except in so far as this is offset by invention. At the same time the increase in real income tends to increase the amount saved at any given level of employment. Consequently we should expect a chronic tendency to underemployment except in so far as the rate of interest falls to offset these two tendencies. If money wages are not reduced this fall in the interest rate will require a steady increase in the quantity of money since the demand for money is likely to increase with real income, though we cannot say in what proportion.

VI

Relaxing now our simplifying assumption of a closed system we look to see how foreign trade and foreign investment fit into this theory. It becomes evident that the excess of exports over imports (including 'invisible' items) is equivalent to investment in its effect on incomes and employment. For the production and sale of exports creates incomes available for spending and saving in our country while the buying of imports reduces the amount of income available for investment or expenditure on home produced goods. Now this surplus of exports over imports, which we shall call the foreign balance, must be balanced on the exchange market by an equivalent amount of foreign lending (long or short term) or imports of gold.[7] Both the foreign lending and the imports of gold appear as saving to the home country, which saving is exactly equal to the investment comprised in the foreign balance. Therefore not only is total saving necessarily equal to total investment but 'foreign' saving is always equal to 'foreign' investment, and 'home' saving equal to 'home' investment.

The foreign balance is determined in a different way to the rest of investment and one must analyse it separately. It depends on all the multitude of factors which determine foreign trade, foreign lending and gold movements. It will require the willingness of people to lend abroad (or import gold) in order to exist at all, and its magnitude will depend on their readiness to do so, since that will affect the exchange rate. It will depend upon the level of costs and prices at home and abroad and the rates of exchange. More important in these days it will depend upon tarriffs, quotas and exchange restrictions. The rate of interest will influence

Appendix I

through affecting peoples' willingness to lend abroad, and also by affecting home investment and thereby incomes and costs, which in turn will influence the demand for imports and the supply conditions of exports. Finally it depends on conditions and events abroad, in fact it is hard to think of anything which does not influence it.

Because the foreign balance is equivalent to investment it is important in its influence on total income and is the principal means by which depression or propensity is passed from country to country. To some countries its changes are more important than those in home investment in their effects on incomes and employment. And in such countries even when the foreign balance does not alter a considerable change in exports and imports may have serious effects on the supply conditions of investment and consumption goods and on the propensity to spend, and for both reasons on employment and production.

The foreign balance is not so closely related to changes in the amount of money and the rate of interest as is home investment. Interest rates will affect (and be affected by) international capital movements, i.e., foreign lending, and thereby the exchange rate or gold movements. Thus, for example, an attempt to increase home investment by increasing the quantity of money and the rate of interest will increase the readiness of owners of wealth to lend abroad. This will reduce the exchange rate, increasing exports and diminishing imports therefore increasing the foreign balance. In so far as the country attempts to maintain the parity of its foreign exchanges it will have to export (or reduce its imports of) gold or reduce its other foreign lending (or borrow from abroad). In this case the foreign balance will have no tendency to increase, and the rise in costs and incomes at home will probably decrease it.

It may be noted that the technique of managing the foreign balances has been greatly developed in recent years and far more attention has been paid to it than to maintaining home investment. A positive foreign balance for one country must of course be equalized somewhere else by negative foreign balances. Therefore a gain in employment in one country due to it increasing its foreign balance is apt to be offset in part at least by a reduction somewhere else where the opposite change occurs in the balance. Differences in the propensity to spend, as well as in more indirect effects, will mean differences in the size of the changes at home and abroad following from equal but opposite changes in the foreign balance so that changes in foreign trade can bring about net increases or decreases in world employment.

When the foreign balance is considered, changes in the general level of money wages may have considerable influence on investment and income when exchanges are stable. Thus a reduction in money wages will reduce the cost of exporting and reduce the ability to buy imports and hence increase the foreign balance and employment. But just as no more advantage in employment could be obtained in a closed system by cutting wages than by increasing the quantity of money, so little more is to be gained in an open economy by cutting money wages than by depreciating the exchange rate. We may notice also that both actions are likely to lead to similar action abroad.

VII

A few remarks about what happens when there is no unemployment will show how this monetary theory fits in with the classical theory. Under this condition of full employment the wage is equal both to the marginal productivity of labour and its marginal disutility, in all employments.[8] The supply of labour will now be somewhat elastic in terms of real wages but not in terms of money wages alone. However an increase in output by increasing employment could only yield a smaller real wage, so that it is not possible.

Even in this condition all we have said holds good about income depending upon investment and the propensity to spend – but we must remember that they are defined in money terms, and that real income cannot now be increased. However a decrease in investment will still lead to a reduction of income and, therefore, of expenditure on consumption goods, and as a consequence a decrease of output and employment in both investment and consumption goods. Thus to a movement in this direction the general remarks apply.

However it is the effects of a possible increase in investment that are now interesting. Suppose that a new discovery enables capital to be made more productive and this increases its marginal efficiency, and therefore investment begins to increase. This will increase incomes, expenditure and savings in terms of money. But now the money demand for both investment and consumption goods has increased while employment cannot increase. Entrepreneurs faced with this increased demand, and probably getting abnormally high profits, will compete for the available labour supply by bidding up money wage rates; but while these wage rates rise, prices rise as well and real wages are unchanged.[9] The increase in wages and prices will increase the demand for money and hence the rate of interest unless the quantity of money is increased to offset the increased demand.

In so far as employment has now increased in the production of investment goods it must have decreased in producing consumption goods. This means people must be saving a larger fraction of their unchanged real income. To some extent the rise in the rate of interest may induce them to do this and increased real investment will be possible with equilibrium. But if investment is greater than this possible equilibrium level then the increase in the amount saved will be due to unexpected changes or to an unstable distribution of incomes; for it seems unreasonable that an increase in the money value of the same real income should induce people permanently to save more of it. Therefore because real investment is more than people will save in equilibrium, people will be attempting to spend more on consumption than is necessary to maintain its output, and hence the consumption industries will be attempting to expand and bidding up the level of wages in trying to draw labour from investment industries. Prices and wages will be driven higher, increasing further the demand for money.

If now the supply of money is limited the rate of interest will rise until investment is checked and reduced to the amount that will be in equilibrium with the stable propensity to save, which in turn may be greater at the higher rate of interest. Equilibrium will now be possible at a higher level of wages and prices and a higher rate of interest. The increase in the marginal efficiency of capital will have increased the equilibrium level of the rate of interest and probably the amount of real income going into savings and investment.

If however the supply of money is not limited but increases so rapidly that the rate of interest remains below the new equilibrium level, then investment will continue to exceed the amount that would be in equilibrium with a stable propensity to save, and expenditure will always remain in excess of that needed to keep consumption industries in equilibrium. Hence wages and prices will increase rapidly and without limit and we will have a cumulative inflation which can only be stopped by limiting the supply of money.

Hence it can be said that the marginal efficiency of capital and the propensity to spend determine the lowest limit of the rate of interest at which equilibrium is possible. If the rate should fall below this, prices and wage rates rise until it returns, while if the rate is held below this prices and wages keep rising, at a rate dependent, in part at least, upon the divergence between the market rate and this lowest limit of the equilibrium rate. This limit we can see to be just a special case of the generalization that the marginal efficiency of capital and the propensity to spend (that is, capital productivity and time preference) determine that rate of interest which will give any particular volume of employment up to full employment.

VIII

We may return now to clear up a few minor points ruled out by our assumption that the supply of labour was perfectly elastic. We assumed that employment could increase without an increase in the general level of money efficiency wages, – that the unemployed would come back to work at a money wage per unit of product no higher than the prevailing money wage. But obviously this may be quite untrue of the real world, and either convention or the action of labourers individually or collectively may require that the general rate of wages rises if employment increases, i.e., that the money wage supply curve of labour is rising. In this case whatever increased employment by our former argument will increase it now but in addition will increase wage rates, and similarly for decreases. The changing money wages will show themselves on steeper supply curves of employment in terms of money investment and expenditure. That is, investment and expenditure will have to increase more in order to increase employment a given amount, while the increase in wage rates and therefore prices will make the demand for money increase more rapidly with increasing employment than otherwise. However employment and output will still be determined in the same way as under our assumption of a perfectly elastic labour supply.

One further point remains. When the amount of unemployment is small in a modern progressive economy, those unemployed (in our technical sense) will consist largely of those who have been fairly recently thrown out of work by shifts in demand or changes in technique. In order to find new employment these people will probably have to accept a lower real wage for some time – as their relative efficiency will be less in the new than the old job. However it seems reasonable to expect that they will resist this for a while and spend some time in looking for work paying a money wage equal to what they used to get, and that they will gradually reduce the money wage which they would be willing to accept until they find a job. Now it will be seen that if money wage rates generally are rising those technologically unemployed will find work at a satisfying money wage sooner than if wage rates were stable and therefore they will spend less time unemployed and hence total employment will be greater with rising than with constant wage rates. The more rapidly wages are rising under these conditions the less time men will spend looking for work and therefore the greater will be total employment, until we approach completely full employment as a theoretical limit attainable only with rapidly rising wages.

In order that wage rates should be permanently rising in this manner and the economy be in equilibrium the money value of investment, income and expenditure must be also rising, and the rate of interest somewhat lower than that rate which would give maximum employment with constant money wages. The amount of money would have to increase steadily. Price levels might be either falling or rising, depending on whether or not technical advances and the accumulation of capital were lowering marginal real labour costs more rapidly than the wage rates were increasing. Indeed it would appear that the stabilisation of a representative price-level of consumption goods with fairly full employment in modern times would require this steady rise in money wages. However I can see no reason to believe that such a condition of employment with slowly but steadily rising wage rates is any more unstable than any other condition, providing only that the amount of money is being increased at the appropriate rate. It can form a consistent and desirable structure of expectations in which the need to reduce money wage rates, the notoriously sticky elements in modern economies, is reduced as near to the minimum as is practicable.

NOTES

1. Investment as here used is essentially the same as used in the *Treatise on Money* but Saving is different – being equal to the sum of 'Savings' and 'Profits' as there defined.
2. The exact line drawn between consumption production and investment production must of course be arbitrary and is a practical and statistical rather than theoretical problem. It is related of course to the distinction between expenditure and saving.
3. Due allowance must be made here both for risk, that is, the mathematical expectation of the return must be used, and also for uncertainty and the cost of bearing it.
4. These adjustments will very likely affect liquidity preference and hence the rate of interest as well.
5. I prefer to use the term 'demand for money', as the actual demand may be regarded as the result of the subjective preferences of individuals together with all the objective conditions such as income, prices, costs of transactions, uncertainties etc. On the other hand must be set the fact that the interest rate must under all these conditions be equal to the amount of preference.
6. Expectations of changes in prices will be rather complex in their effects, in so far as they do not directly influence the relative desiredness of holding stocks of money and money-credits. They do influence the profitability of holding any form of fixed money asset, but only in so far as the present prices of future goods are not altered in accordance with the changed expectation of future prices.
7. Gifts and reparations may be treated as invisible imports if they are made from what would otherwise be expenditure, or as part of foreign lending if they are financed from savings.
8. Due allowance of course being made for rent elements in wages, for imperfection in the labour market, for the divergence of long and short period productivity and transfer costs, and for uneconomic behaviour.
9. The new invention will probably enable some increase in real wages to be paid, but this can be neglected, especially if we suppose the invention to be one increasing the future productivity of capital.

Appendix II Correspondence between Richard F. Kahn and Don Patinkin on the 1931 multiplier article and the Cambridge 'Circus'

From Don Patinkin to Richard F. Kahn

Jerusalem, February 25, 1974

Dear Richard,

... may I bother you with some further questions about Keynes, and about your relations with him in particular:
(a) In Moggridge's interesting article on Keynes[1] in the Spring 1973 issue of *History of Political Economy*, he refers (p. 74, footnote 7) to your belief that the importance of your 1931 article 'does not lie principally in [the] estimate of the multiplier.' This naturally raises the question of in what you do see the primary importance to lie – and I would greatly appreciate having your views on this.

. . . .

(c) Would you describe the members of the 'Cambridge Circus' – yourself, James Meade, Piero Sraffa, Joan and Austin Robinson (according to *JMK* XIII, p. 338) as having been 'students' of Keynes? Did you all study with him in one form or another at Cambridge? Were you all lecturers there at the time (i.e., the early 1930s)? What about R. F. Harrod? Was his absence from the 'Circus' due to his being at Oxford?

From my reading of Harrod's *Life of Keynes*, I have a rough idea of the answers to these questions – but I would nevertheless greatly appreciate hearing your views on them.

(d) In Keynes's 'Preface' to the *Treatise on Money*, he thanks you for having helped him 'in the avoidance of errors.' Do you recollect to what in particular Keynes was referring?

I hope you'll forgive my bothering you with all these questions – but the subject is fascinating! And thanks beforehand for whatever help you can give me.

Sincerely yours,
[signed] Don

Appendix II 147

From Richard F. Kahn to Don Patinkin.[2]

Cambridge, England, 19th March, 1974.

Dear Don,

. . . .

(a) I regard the main importance of my 1931 article as: (1) finally disposing of the 'Treasury view' that at a time of unemployment, an increase in one kind of investment will be at the expense of another kind. I demonstrated how the whole of the necessary finance is provided in the form of an increase in saving. The point is that in *Can Lloyd George Do It?*, Keynes and Hubert Henderson seem to imply that only part of the additional finance would be provided as a result of the investment. I did not actually express the identity between saving and investment until in a later number of the *Journal* I replied[3] to a comment on my article by Warming, a Danish economist. In my article, the identity appears in the rather clumsy form of 'Mr. Meade's Relation'. (James Meade was spending a year in Cambridge while I was completing my article, and I had a lot of talk with him.) (2) Finally disposing of the idea that the price level is determined by the quantity of money. I never had been able to understand the quantity theory. What I explained in my article is that the price level is determined by the conditions of demand and supply in much the same way as the price of an individual commodity. I took it for granted that the supply curve of consumption goods as a whole was, in the short period, a rising one. Later statistical work by Dunlop and Tarshis[4] threw doubt on this assumption and seemed to indicate perfectly elastic supply under conditions of heavy unemployment. In his comment on Dunlop and Tarshis, Keynes [1939] pointed out that this assumption gave *a fortiori* force to his arguments. (3) I had not altogether escaped from Keynes's *Treatise*, and I thought it necessary to translate my ideas into terms of the *Treatise*. Although I was not conscious of that at the time, the effect was to demonstrate how unsuitable the terminology and assumptions of the *Treatise* were.

. . . .

(c) At the time of the 'Circus', neither Joan Robinson nor I had yet been made University Lecturers, though I think that we both were giving some lectures – I on a subject having no relation to Keynes's work, but possibly Joan was giving some lectures about Keynes's ideas. Austin Robinson was a university lecturer. I rather think that Piero Sraffa had already resigned his university lectureship, but I cannot remember whether he had yet been made an Assistant Director of Research to take charge of all our research students, who in those days were very few. James Meade was an Oxford economist who was spending a year as a visitor in Cambridge. Roy Harrod had had his year in Cambridge many years earlier, and was fully established in Oxford. I have no doubt that had he been in Cambridge, he would have been a member of the 'Circus'.

I was the only one who had actually been a pupil of Keynes as an undergraduate. As I have said, there were very few research students in those days, and none of us were post-graduate students. We all of us were members of Keynes's Political Economy Club – which met fortnightly, and was mainly intended for the most promising undergraduates, but was also attended by a number of Dons. Piero Sraffa had been brought over to Cambridge from Italy, and was a close friend of Keynes, but Piero was never very successful in discussing Keynes's ideas with him. Although Austin Robinson knew Keynes very well – partly because Austin was Secretary of the Faculty Board – the only member of the Circus who at that time was actively discussing Keynes's ideas with him was myself. As Moggridge brings out,[5] I was the link between the 'Circus' and Keynes. I was a Fellow of King's and Austin Robinson was a Fellow of Sidney Sussex College. Sraffa was a Member of the King's High Table. Meade was attached to Trinity.

(d) I did not complete my Fellowship dissertation on *The Economics of the Short Period*, which had nothing to do with Keynes's ideas until December 1929, having started on it in the Autumn of 1928. Keynes did not want to divert me from writing my dissertation, and it was only after December 1929 that he started giving me for comments the proofs of the *Treatise*. As the *Treatise* was finished in September 1930, I did not really have much opportunity for exercising an influence on it. I may have persuaded Keynes to alter a few passages, and no doubt I discovered a number of misprints. Before I had finished the index, I went away for a holiday in the Alps and left Joan Robinson to finish it.

. . . .

Yours sincerely,
[signed] Richard

NOTES

1. ['From the *Treatise* to the *General Theory*: An Exercise in Chronology'. D.P.]
2. [Reprinted with the kind permission of Richard F. Kahn. – Eds.]
3. ['The Financing of Public Works: A Note' (1932). – Eds.]
4. [See Dunlop (1938) and Tarshis (1939). – Eds.]
5. [*JMK* XIII, pp. 338–9. – Eds.]

Appendix III Some Comments on Keynesianism and the Swedish Theory of Expansion Before 1935

BERTIL OHLIN

This report of the Conference proceedings adds considerably to our knowledge about the conditions under which the remarkable *General Theory* was created. It is a privilege to be invited to make some comments.

1. WICKSELL

In my opinion there can be no doubt whatsoever about the considerable influence which Wicksell's theory about the relation between the normal rate of interest and the market rate, exercised on Keynes's thinking. I refer to Volume I of the *Treatise* (pp. 167, 170–1, 176–8; pp. 186, 190, 196–8, respectively, of the original edition). When I met Keynes in 1935 and he told me about his forthcoming *General Theory* he had evidently almost forgotten the inspiration and knowledge he had obtained from Wicksell[1]. This may have been due to the fact that for a couple of years he had been making an effort to get out of his mind certain essential ideas from the *Treatise*. Otherwise these ideas might interfere with his new thinking.

In the Swedish edition of his *Lectures on Political Economy*, published in 1906 (English edition 1935), Wicksell emphasised the possibility of a lack of balance between aggregate supply and aggregate demand more strongly than he had done eight years earlier in *Geldzins und Güterpreise* (*Interest and Prices*). But already in the latter volume he made it quite clear that as a change in the price of one commodity is due to a change in the relation of supply to demand, the same must be true of a change in the average of all commodity prices.

On 9 April, 1929 I wrote to Keynes about a possible rejoinder by me to his March 1929 paper on German reparation payments in the *Economic Journal*. My letter also contains the following passage: Professor Gregory told me that you had found Wicksell's old book *Geldzins und Güterpreise* very valuable, and that there was a chance of its being translated into English. If that is so, I venture to suggest that you include some of Wicksell's papers on monetary theory, which have so far only appeared in Swedish.

In a letter of 16 May, 1929, Keynes – in continuation of an early preliminary letter – wrote as follows about an English edition of Wicksell's contribution to monetary theory. It 'has been further considered to-day by the Council of the Royal Economic Society. I told them about my correspondence with you, and upon this they authorised me to invite you to undertake the editorship of the English edition, including the writing of an introduction summarising the general nature of Wicksell's contribution to Monetary Theory.'

In the autumn of 1930 I wrote Keynes that I had started working on the 'Introduction' but that from January 1931 I had to go to Geneva to make an investigation about the world economic depression and felt that I had to put the matter off for 9 months. Keynes replied in January 1931: 'I am rather horrified to contemplate such a long further delay.'

In September 1931 he returned to the matter: 'The translator of the Wicksell volume [Richard Kahn] is getting on quite well, but we have not yet sent any manuscript to the printer. I will let you have galley proof of the translation as soon as it is ready. Meanwhile I shall look forward to getting your introduction some time in October.' He then went on to say: 'Could you kindly send me the translation of Wicksell's last paper on monetary theory[2] as soon as possible. . . .' Four days later – on 28 September – I replied: 'I hasten to send you the translation of the Wicksell article, which I hope you will find as interesting as I do'. In his letter of 31 October, 1931, Keynes then answered: 'The translation of the Wicksell paper reached me safely.'

Unfortunately I caught an eye disease in September and could not do any work during more than 7 months. On 15 April, 1933 I finally sent the 'Introduction' to Keynes. Kahn had been even more delayed than I was. But he was then almost ready with his skilful translation of Wicksell's book.

In view of Keynes's lively interest in the whole matter, I suppose one can assume that he read my 'Introduction' in 1933. Unfortunately there was some further delay with Kahn's translation of the book. In a letter of 16 August, 1935, he told me that he had just finished it. It did not appear on the market until early in 1936.

Permit me two long quotations from my 'Introduction' to *Interest and Prices* which describe some of Wicksell's most important innovations:

> Already in his *Geldzins*, Wicksell had stressed the idea that as a change in the price of one commodity is due to a change in the relation of supply to demand, the same must be true of a change in the general commodity price level. This constituted a new approach to monetary

theory. Until then, as a matter of fact for long afterwards, it was regarded as self-evident that, since commodities are exchanged for commodities, a change in the general price level must be due to entirely different circumstances from a change in individual prices. Hence, the analysis of variations in the general price level, contained in economic text-books in the chapters on money, started with a discussion of the monetary mechanism and was not brought into any organic connection with the theory of pricing and distribution.

Wicksell's most fruitful innovation in his analysis is, I am inclined to think, the important step which he took in bridging the gap between price theory and monetary theory. Following up the idea that a rise in the general price level is due to a rise in total demand in relation to total supply, Wicksell intuitively realised that it would be profitable to divide each of these two categories into two classes: the supply of consumers' goods and the supply of capital goods, on the one hand, the income to be spent and the income to be saved, on the other hand. A study of the relations between these four factors gave him a deeper insight into the character of price movements than that obtained as a result of the analysis of changes in price levels by means of the old quantity theory, which ignored those changes in relative commodity prices which are so characteristic of price movements. Furthermore, by Wicksell's line of approach the analysis of the construction of the monetary mechanism – the organisation of the monetary and banking system – is given a secondary place. This seems to me to carry with it many advantages, for example that the foundations of monetary theory can be made more general than when they are expressed in terms of a monetary system of a special construction. Through his brilliant assumption of a pure credit economy, Wicksell successfully escaped from the tyranny which the concept 'quantity of money' has until recently exercised on monetary theory. (pp. xiii–xiv).

Briefly expressed, Wicksell's doctrine – which on this point coincided on the whole with Cassel's – amounted to this: if more money is lent to investors, and used by them for real investment, than is saved, then total purchasing power is increased, and prices rise. But if equilibrium is maintained between savings and investment, purchasing power is kept constant and prices cannot rise, at least not more than in proportion to any reduction in the available volume of commodities (pp. xix–xx).

In the paper of 1925 he had begun to doubt the validity of his own theory.

Discussing the influence of war-time scarcity of commodities, Wicksell observed that in this kind of reasoning is reflected a 'lack of a clear conception of the term *purchasing power*. It is only *money* purchasing power which here comes into question. It therefore stands to reason that a general rise in the market prices of both goods and services *itself* creates the purchasing power required for meeting the higher prices.' In addition is needed only '*an increase in volume of the medium of exchange*. If all payments were made on a cheque basis this increase would, of course, take place quite automatically.' The velocity of means of payments of every kind would increase, for most people are more conservative in regard to their habits of consumption than in regard to their habits of making payments. Besides, a new demand for credit would arise from people who wanted to increase their holdings of cash. It cannot be regarded as certain that credit restrictions will keep down such a demand for credit. 'A rise in the rate of interest is certainly an almost infallible means of restricting the demand for credit on the part of all *producers*, but it can hardly have a similar effect on those who merely desire to strengthen their cash position in view of the increase in the volume of exchange' (p. xx).[3]

It follows from my account above that Keynes received my 'Introduction' about a month *after* the writing of his articles in *The Times* on 13–16 March, 1933, which soon afterwards were printed as a pamphlet under the title *The Means to Prosperity*. The English translation of Wicksell's last paper he had received 17 months earlier.

I refrain from speculations about the possibility that Keynes's thinking – without his being aware of it – might have been influenced in a general way by his reading these two documents in 1931 and 1933 – if he did read them. At that time his ideas were probably not yet quite fixed about the approach and construction, which he was to use in the *General Theory*.

2. EARLY SWEDISH PUBLICATIONS

As pointed out by Landgren (1960) and Steiger (1971),[4] I published in 1927 a pamphlet in Danish about a policy to increase employment in Denmark, where the sudden rise of the external value of the Danish krona by about 40 per cent had caused a large unemployment. Apart from recommending stable nominal wage rates in most industries, I suggested a *temporary* wage reduction in the building trades *for a fixed period*, which would make an increase in real investment e.g. in industry profitable. This would set in motion a development towards larger employment. The idea of a cumulative process was quite clear. Apart from Wicksell's early theory about the movement of price levels it had been discussed in newspaper articles by two Danish engineers in connection with a debate about tariff policy.

Wicksell and later Lindahl – the latter in his important book *Penningpolitikens medel* (The Means of Monetary Policy) published in 1930 – were interested in the determination of price movements and monetary stabilisation – not the volume of output. But the same type of reasoning can be used if there are unused resources and if, therefore, an increased demand leads to a growth of output. Lindahl gave a brief account of this kind of possible development to explain how price level changes come about during periods of essential unemployment. However, his interest was concentrated on price development.

If I should go into the discussion in Stockholm – in a way similar to the one referred to in the Conference proceedings about Cambridge contacts and the dawn of a new approach – I should mention that output as *a central variable* was not introduced into the core of the theory of money until the latter part of 1932 and the whole of 1933.[5] I wrote a paper which was circulated among some economists in the autumn of 1932 and printed in practically identical form in 1933.[6] There and in Myrdal's appendix to the government budget, which was presented in January 1933, variations in the volume of output and employment were given attention. Both Myrdal and I were at that time preparing reports for the public committee working on the causes of unemployment and means against it. Myrdal (1934) dealt with financial policy. I wrote (1934) about monetary policy, public works, subsidies and tariffs. He discussed many different aspects of a 'sound' financial policy, including the influences on the business cycle movements, where changes in output and employment were tacitly assumed to move with the variation of the cycle. Variations in output and employment were dealt with more critically in my study.

What I want to stress is that in a process of expansion the upward movement of the price level and the upward movement of the volume of output are parts of the same mechanism: What we called 'the economics of unused resources' would at the same time throw light on the development of the gross output and the movement of the price level. Am I right in saying that when reading British and American theoretical discussions later in the 1930s – after the *General Theory* – about variations in output as an essential 'equilibrating' variable, one often got the impression that this analysis was considered separately from the analysis of price level variations? Yet the same concepts – total output and aggregate expenditure as well as savings and investment – had to be used in both cases. Often the quantity of output and price levels vary at the same time. They determine the changes in total income and both play what one can call an 'equilibrating' role.

3. TOTAL DEMAND AND THE MECHANISM
OF INTERNATIONAL CAPITAL MOVEMENTS

I come now to a few observations on certain aspects of a possible influence on the development of Keynes's theory from 1930 to 1936.

It has several times been pointed out that Keynes in his analysis of German reparation payments in 1929 refused to take into account the increased aggregate demand aspect of the mechanism. It was not that he insisted on a certain monetary policy as a condition for this increase in demand; instead, he denied the existence or relevance of total demand changes in more general terms. This led him to negative conclusions about indemnity payments. In the letters which we exchanged in the summer of 1929 he declared himself unable to follow what seemed to me to be a very simple reasoning. The total demand in the receiving country would rise more than its national income. But as I have indicated in my paper about 'The Slow Development of the Total Demand Idea' (1974) I received a brief letter from Keynes in January 1931, where he accepted the idea that reparation payments 'caused a shift in the demand curve of the receiving country irrespective of any rise in the price level of that country'.

I have never given any thought to the question whether this discussion between Keynes, Rueff and myself in the 1929 *Economic Journal* and the letters Keynes and I exchanged may have helped to bring him into a more consistent attitude to the relation between aggregate demand and aggregate supply, which is fundamental in *General Theory*. But, I confess that after reading the Conference discussion I feel a certain curiosity about the following aspects: Did any member of the brilliant Cambridge 'Circus' point out the importance of this relation during the discussions in the early 1930s? Did perhaps Mr. Kahn observe the new approach when he read and translated Wicksell's book and later – in the spring of 1933 – my 'Introduction' with its summary of some of Wicksell's essential points?[7] Did no one notice the stimulating paper by Myrdal (1933) in a volume on monetary theory, edited by Hayek?

4. THE DISTINCTION BETWEEN LOOKING FORWARDS AND BACKWARDS

Myrdal's 1933 paper, building on his Swedish doctoral thesis (1927), made clear the necessity of a sharp distinction between 'looking backwards' and 'looking forwards'. He discussed the differences between expectations and the realised development. Book-keeping is chiefly – apart from depreciation – concerned with *a past period* and, therefore, quite different from an analysis of plans and more or less uncertain expectations for a coming period. Lindahl (1930) had recommended declarations of public goals for the future price level as a method to influence the otherwise more destabilising expectations about an uncertain future. There are also my own publications in 1933 and 1934 and Keynes's comments on my papers in the *Economic Journal* (1937a).[8]

It seemed to me obvious that Keynes's reasoning would have been

Appendix III   155

clearer, if he had consistently used the ex-post versus ex-ante distinction. Sometimes the reader has to guess whether the author is looking forwards or backwards (see, e.g., *General Theory*, p. 115). The same is true of Wicksell's earlier writings. Evidently Myrdal's concepts contributed to clarity of thinking and presentation, although perhaps less for his own equilibrium technique than for the types of period analysis Lindahl and I used. In the English translation of his 1933 paper, published in 1939 as *Monetary Equilibrium*, Myrdal revised and rewrote his presentation in a way which brought the section on sequence analysis closer to the methods I used in my report of 1934 and *Economic Journal* paper of March 1937.

As one can see from the latter paper, I emphasised the ex-post concepts of income, saving and investment. In terms of money the latter two would always be equal during a past period. The most natural terminology seemed to be saying that *actual savings always equals investment*.[9] The increase in investment would have some owner: it was a part of the national income, which evidently had not been consumed. Hence, it had been saved. I also stressed the importance of a theory of interest as the price of credit in the explanation of a process of expansion – a matter my Swedish colleagues had given rather scanty attention. The interest level which is compatible with a stable price level for goods depends on the disposition to save and to invest.

The 'forward looking' concepts – expected income, planned consumption, planned saving and planned investment – have a different role to play in an explanation of economic actions. In this ex-ante analysis Myrdal and Lindahl stressed saving and investment, while from 1933 I emphasised the relation of total income and expenditure for consumption and investment versus total output and prices, i.e. output in monetary terms.[10]

I do not deny that it can bring some advantages to use an equilibrium construction. Alternatively one can present a reasoning in the form of a period analysis, which explains the connections between expectations, decisions about consumption and investment, the outcome with regard to quantity and value of output and income when the period is finished. The differences between expectations and results are important for the following expectations and actions. These types of demand and supply are functions of income ideas, profitability calculus, quantities of cash available, credit conditions etc. In my opinion such analysis might lead to a more realistic picture than a comparative statics analysis by means of curves of aggregate supply and aggregates of consumption demand – and of investment demand – similar to the Marshall curves for individual commodities.

My 1933 paper, which contained the sequence type of approach, was accepted by Professor Davidson – editor of the *Ekonomisk Tidskrift* – in a letter on 26 February, 1933. The paper was evidently written before the publication of Keynes's articles in *The Times* in March 1933 and their appearance as a booklet entitled *The Means to Prosperity* soon afterwards. Davidson's delay in printing the next issue of his journal has in one respect misled Landgren – and several economic historians, who have followed him. The 'time table' is important for the whole discussion about Keynes's influence on the Stockholm theory. Landgren indicates that reading Keynes's pamphlet I found a foundation for the development of a theoretical analysis about which he makes very generous observations: for example 'a preliminary Keynesian theory before Keynes himself'.[11]

To the extent that the Stockholm theory in the version which I presented in 1933 contains some ideas similar to those in Keynes' pamphlet and the *General Theory*, the two types of analysis must have been developed independently of one another.

5. A MODIFICATION OF THE UNDEREMPLOYMENT EQUILIBRIUM

Naturally, as I explained in the *Economic Journal* (1937) and in earlier Swedish publications, the relevant flow concepts have one ex-ante form and one ex-post form.

I must pass over some aspects of my discussions about depreciation and reinvestment demand. Neither can I comment on the importance of changes in relative commodity prices and the time structure of commodities from the point of view of production changes or the important question of the order of events and the speed of reactions. The period analysis is well suited for an analysis of the latter question.

Professor Ingerman said at the Conference: 'What is the mainspring determining output – and I understand Keynes to say it's investment' (see p. 79). Of course this is not to be taken literally. The consumers' decisions to alter their purchases can have as much influence as the decisions of investors. Often, but not always, the latter may be less difficult to lead and control through economic policy.

Public works financed through borrowing in such a way that credit to business is not reduced will lead to larger aggregate demand than in the preceding period. Sales and profits during the second period will be found to have exceeded expectations. Stocks may have been reduced. Some consumers have had larger incomes than they expected, for example through longer working hours which the producers planned but the workers did not know in advance. For all these reasons the expectations for the third period and the decisions concerning that period will be affected.

Thus the volume of savings – it must agree with the volume of investment expressed in money – will be increased through *unintentional* savings of *unexpected* incomes. In the following periods the *expected* incomes will be rising and planned savings will grow. There will also be unintentional savings from profits of which the businessmen were unaware until after the end of the period concerned. Keynes's theory of employment does not, in my opinion, sufficiently stress the fact that not only the intentional savings but also the unintentional type of savings will affect the possibility of a certain volume of investment, which implies a certain expansion of total demand. The volume of output and employment will differ from Keynes's 'equilibrium position' as a result of uncertainty and mistakes about the real development, when expectations and plans are formed. In this respect the theory I have indicated is more 'Keynesian' than the *General Theory* itself.

6. OTHER SIMILARITIES

There are some further similarities between the Stockholm theory (my own version) and Keynes's *General Theory* – in spite of his 'equilibrium method' and our 'sequence analysis with time periods'. (In the latter the possible equilibrium of planned savings and planned investment did not play any major role. It did not exclude cost inflation through general wage increase.)

First, there is the relation of aggregate demand variations to aggregate supply variations. My own reasoning, based on Wicksell, but with output changes included, seems to me to be almost the same as that which is usually regarded as 'Keynesianism'. The *General Theory*, particularly page 23 about 'effective demand', has a complicated reasoning which seems to lead to the same thing. The cost calculations are, however, different.

Second, we both emphasised the importance of consumers reactions and investment reactions in a process of expansion or contraction. Consumption and savings decisions are functions of the expected income for some future periods. Available and expected cash and credit also affect consumers' actions. So do various exogenous factors.

Third, we were both aware that in a situation of unused resources investment can be increased without necessarily any decisions to increase savings. The fact that nevertheless savings may grow as a result of increased incomes was emphasised already in the British publications of 1928–9 (for example, the 'Yellow Book' (1928)) although at that time it was overlooked by many people. The same conclusion inevitably follows from the Swedish analysis. But as this reasoning was worked out in 1930–2 it is quite possible that a stimulus may have come from reading the British publications. However, when you have once decided to regard saving and investment ex-post as equal, it is hard to see how you can avoid the conclusion.

Fourth, while from the point of view of methodology there is the above-mentioned fundamental difference, the knowledge conveyed seems to me to be similar on the points indicated. There is less simplification in the 'disposition to save' which is the other side of the consumption function, as described in my report in 1934, but there is unavoidably less precision than in Keynes's simplified equilibrium, or rather succession of disequilibria.[12]

Axel Leijonhufvud (1968) also emphasised that an essential part of Keynes's theory is that his model is used to describe a process, which has 'income restraints'. Why does a process of expansion and inflation not go on indefinitely with great speed?

Wicksell pointed out that price increases make the value of output in monetary terms higher and thereby create corresponding incomes and enough purchasing power to buy the products at those higher prices.[13] One has to answer the question why an inflationary movement once started does not 'run amok'. As an answer to this question I followed up Wicksell in arguing that from a certain given state of conditions the consumption demand is governed largely by income expectations of the consumers.[14] Investment demand is governed by cost and profit calculations. Besides, the liquidity position – in other words the supply of cash and the streams of means of payments and the expectations of future cash in the hands of each individual and the expected possibilities of obtaining new credit – will influence consumption and above all investment. Interest rates and credit policy come in as parts of this process. Obviously one may call this an 'income-constrained model'. Keynes uses a more simplified model which concentrates attention on available income or income expectations, the marginal productivity of capital, and interest rates but later on brings in other considerations. In this matter one can find a fifth similarity.

Another characteristic of Keynes's theory, which is rightly stressed by Leijonhufvud, is his alteration of the usual assumptions about the relative velocity of changes in prices of commodities and in wage rates, as well as changes in the quantity of output and employment. The first effect of an increase in demand in a state of depression will be a rise in the quantity of output and employment. Later on, when the position approaches full use of resources prices will, of course, rise but wage rates rise less. Real wages fall, he maintains.

In the study of the effect of expansionist policies, which were made by the Swedish economists in the early 1930s the usual assumption was that wages and costs per unit of output are rather 'sticky' or 'slow-moving'. So are prices sticky upwards in a depression, with some exceptions, but most prices change more easily than nominal wages. Hence an increased total demand will lead to greater output and employment and not to much price increases. Later on when capacity is better used, prices will go up. In many cases, however, the stocks of raw materials are limited and raw material prices will rise at an early date as a result of speculation. This brings *some* price increase for finished products at an early stage. Profits will rise first as a result of larger output and later on because prices often go up more than unit costs. Such increases in profits and – earlier still – the more optimistic profit expectations will lead to increased investment. Furthermore, the increased output will raise the sums of wages and the demand for consumers goods. In the Stockholm reasoning built on Wicksell it was self evident that one had to consider investment reactions as well as consumers' reaction. In the Cambridge theory there was in the early 1930's a tendency to emphasise consumers' reactions more than investment reactions. It was tempting to use the beautiful theory of the employment multiplier, built on consumers' reactions, which Kahn had presented in his famous paper (1931). We naturally considered the fact that the speed with which a quantitative expansion is possible – and the speed of the price movements – depends also on the stocks of raw materials and semi-manufactured goods. (Ohlin, 1934).

As far as I can see there is a great deal of affinity between the picture drawn by the Stockholm analysis above and the one which is to be found in the Cambridge theory, particularly since the latter had absorbed Harrod's 'accelerator' analysis of investment (Harrod, 1936). If I am right, we here have similarity number six. It is true that Keynes uses a more formal equilibrium model and therefore, can describe a number of successive stages of underemployment equilibrium. But one has to remember that this precision is partly due to some simplifications and the lack of consideration of essential circumstances, like the part of unexpected national income and savings and unintentional investment in increased commodity stocks. In other words the difference between ex-ante and ex-post.

As mentioned above, Keynes sometimes failed to make the distinction between 'looking backward' and 'looking forward'. It would be interesting to know at which time some other Cambridge economists pointed this out to him.

It is quite interesting that a first rate economist like Lerner (1940) expressed the view – as Paul Samuelson mentions in the discussion (see p. 77 – that there was nothing important in Myrdal's German paper of 1933 and book of 1939.[15] This indicates how alien Myrdal's important distinction was at that time to many economists. All the greater is the merit of having presented it.

7. THE INFLUENCE OF 'UNCERTAINTY' – AN
   IMPORTANT INNOVATION

I now turn to other important aspects of Keynes's theory. In the *General*

Theory he emphasises *the uncertainty of the future* and the importance of opinions about the future as a basis for action by businessmen and consumers. When he came to Stockholm in the autumn of 1936 and gave a lecture to our little Political Economy Club he – to our surprise – emphasised the analysis of this aspect as more of an innovation than any other aspect of the *General Theory*. His opinion was that its vital importance had been underestimated.

Early in the century Wicksell, Cassel and Davidson had discussed the importance for an economic process of more or less accurate prediction. Myrdal had gone further into the subject – following Knight's (1921) example – in his thesis (1927). Lindahl stressed the importance of expectations e.g. about future price developments in his book in 1930, and emphasised its importance for Wicksell's cumulative process.

It must be added, however, that Keynes's analysis of the forward market and some other aspects went much further and contained a realistic analysis of markets to which there was no counterpart in Swedish writings. He had written about this subject already in the 1920s.

8. POLICY PROBLEMS

I now come to some questions that are more typically concerned with policy. Neither in Stockholm nor Cambridge was there any assumption that it would be reasonable to assume that, in a state of depression, there would be a greater flexibility of wages than of prices and that this would in normal cases automatically bring about an upward movement of output and employment to the neighbourhood of full employment. Wage reductions would in many situations cause quick reductions of commodity prices or would be preceded by the latter. There might be no increase in the demand for labour. The result may even be increased unemployment as a result of pessimistic expectations of further deflation. All this belonged to the current doctrine among the younger economists in Stockholm.[16] On the other hand, changes in relative prices, interest rates, liquidity and expectations might possibly lead to an end of deflation and a growth in employment. This possibility under special assumptions is exemplified in business cycle theory.[17]

In Stockholm from 1930 a great deal of emphasis was put on supplementing credit policy, including open market operations by the central bank, with budget deficits and increased public works. I refer to Lindahl's 1930 book. Also, in the summer of 1931 I gave a lecture to the Nordic Economic Meeting in Stockholm where I proposed very large deficits to keep up 'purchasing powers' *and employment* during the depression. To emphasise the need of very forceful action I jokingly suggested that the minister of finance would hand out to the tax payers the sums of money indicated on their tax bills instead of asking them to pay the same amount to the treasury (Ohlin 1931). The possibility of the liquidity trap was pointed out in this lecture and in my report of 1934 mentioned above. As to the best policy to stimulate aggregate demand, the emphasis was on a combination of interest policy and general availability of credit, 'monetary goal' declarations to influence expectations and on public finance policies, including public works. But relatively little attention was given to the importance of variations in the value of assets. About tariff policy as a means against unemployment, see Ohlin (1934).

My impression is that most of the practical conclusions about economic policy under periods of unemployment, which were the outcome of the *General Theory* in 1936 and partly of Keynes's earlier (1932–3) writings, were put forward in Stockholm in the early thirties as a result of theoretical analysis in the years 1930–4, under some stimulus from earlier British publications, as indicated above.

9. PERSONAL CONTACTS

During the Conference some questions were asked about my visit to Cambridge in the inter-wars period. Austin Robinson (see p. 33) kindly referred to visits by Margit Cassel and myself in the 1920s. The facts are as follows. I spent the summer of 1922 – on my way to Harvard – and the time from middle September 1923 to the end of November, at Cambridge, England. Margit Cassel arrived early in December in the latter year and stayed a couple of months. We were both writing our doctor's theses. Mine was nearing its completion in September 1923. Neither of us were members of any college, and neither took part in any seminars or had organised contacts with research. I was not a student 'intra muros' but just a foreign visitor to Cambridge who got permission to follow some lectures but no seminars. Besides, I was put to bed for four weeks owing to an eye disease from the end of October. I paid a brief visit to Pigou and another to D. H. Robertson, whose lectures I followed in October 1923. I do not remember their theme, but it was not money or international trade. The only economist I got into some real contact with was Austin Robinson, whom I had met already in the summer of 1922. With him I had a number of friendly and stimulating talks. I did not meet Keynes, as far as I remember. Perhaps I could add that at Cassel's suggestion I sent a summary of a central part of my doctor's thesis – the equilibrium of the price system of two countries including the factor proportion theorem – to Edgeworth as editor of the *Economic Journal*. He sent it on to his coeditor Keynes, who on a piece of paper wrote: 'This amounts to nothing and should be refused, J.M.K.' Probably by mistake it was included in the package, when I got my manuscript back. I still have the note, and regard it as a valuable document. The paper Keynes rejected was never published. It was similar to the essence of Chapters 1–3 and Appendix I of my subsequent *Interregional and International Trade* (1933).

About my meetings with Keynes in 1929–1930 and 1932 – all in London but the latter also at Cambridge – my memory tells me the following. The first two were dinner parties where there was a lively general discussion. At the first one some leading city people dominated. I had a private talk in the corner of the room with Keynes about the mechanism of international capital movements. I tried to convince him that if people in Scotland borrowed money in England and spent it on housebuilding, their ability to buy commodities would be increased through their borrowing, while that of the British lenders would be reduced, given a normal credit policy. The same thing would happen if borrowers and lenders lived in different countries although the monetary mechanism would then be somewhat different and more dependent on the credit policy of the central banks. We did not agree.

In 1930 there was a general economists' dinner where Robbins, Hayek, Keynes, Gregory and half a dozen others were present after some lecture I had given. The discussion was lively but I cannot recall what we talked about.

In 1932 I lectured about anti-depression policy, including international aspects,[18] in the University College (the Newmarch Lectures). Keynes invited me to lunch. We discussed chiefly the economic situation and the policy of the Bank of England, but not as far as I can remember any basic question of monetary theory. As far as I know, he had not at that time found a basic construction of monetary theory different from the one he used in his *Treatise on Money* in 1930. Keynes also suggested that I should visit Cambridge one afternoon to talk to one or two economists and to attend a meeting of his Political Economy Club, which I did. I do not recall the subject under discussion. At that time I was just beginning my serious writing on monetary theory. I am not sure whom I met in the late afternoon before the Club meeting. My next visit to Cambridge was in 1936 (Marshall lectures); it gave me a chance of stimulating talks with D. H. Robertson, Joan Robinson, Kahn and other leading economists. Keynes was not at Cambridge, but I may have met him briefly in London.

Some central questions on monetary theory we did, however, discuss when we met in Brussels in 1935 at an economic conference. A long boat trip gave me this opportunity. He summarised some essential traits of his forthcoming *General Theory* and explained why he did not think it useful at the present state of opinion to discuss further with Henderson and Robertson. I explained briefly that post-Wicksell theory in Sweden was based on a very similar idea as the one he indicated in his oral account. Wicksell's refutation of Say's law was our basis. The planned investment during one period had no fixed relation to the sums which other people planned to save in that same period.

The existence of an old common sense opinion that public works may increase employment and, on the other hand, the late development of a consistent theory of the effects of changes in total demand seem to me to be a strange matter. The minority report of the two Webbs around 1908 emphasised the usefulness of public works because of their effect on employment. They were probably the pioneers. This was repeated in England and preached also in Sweden. Not only the Swedish labour party advocated this policy. A municipal committee in the city of Lund, which had a conservative majority, was very explicit in a resolution in the year 1913.

In the middle of the 1920s Professor Gösta Bagge advocated increased public investment in depressions and reduction in boom periods to keep a higher average level of employment. Many people writing about business cycles based their conclusions on a similar common sense reasoning before and after the First World War. This raises the question why Keynes maintained that only the monetary cranks had had some such idea and that orthodox economics was quite wrong. One could say that there was no connection between the section about business cycles and the section about price and distribution in leading text books. But one could not say that the former section left out of account the possibility of expansion through increased investment. The connection between investment changes, business cycles and unemployment was not overlooked.

10. CONCLUDING OBSERVATIONS

To sum up, it seems quite clear that apart from the very considerable influence of Wicksell on Keynes, any other influence of the Swedish work on Keynes's development from 1930 to 1936 is very uncertain. The possible but unconscious influence of Wicksell's last paper, which Keynes received in October 1931 in translated form, cannot be corroborated. Keynes's debate with me in 1929 on changes in aggregate demand may have left some trace in his mind. So could perhaps the summary of Wicksell's monetary innovations in my 'Introduction' to the English edition of Wicksell's *Interest and Prices*, which I sent to Keynes in the spring of 1933.[19] But I have seen no indication in this direction from economists who were in close contact with him in the following two years.

My emphasis in these comments is, therefore, not so much on 'influences' as on the parallel development of several essential aspects of theory and policy in Cambridge and Stockholm in the first half of the 1930s.

NOTES

1. As I report later, however, in the early 1930s Keynes was eager to learn about Wicksell's theory. My conversation with Keynes in 1935 is also noted, as well as in my paper 'On the Slow Development of the "Total Demand" Idea in Economic Theory' (1974).
2. 'The Monetary Problem of the Scandinavian Countries', originally published in Swedish in *Ekonomisk Tidskrift*, 1925. The translation was ultimately published as an appendix to the English edition of *Interest and Prices*.
3. Quotes of Wicksell are from 'The Monetary Problem of the Scandinavian Countries', published as the appendix to *Interest and Prices* (pp. 201, 202 and 203). Italics in original.
4. Both these books are very stimulating and provide a penetrating analysis. On some points I disagree with Landgren. Steiger, who wrote his book a decade later, has presented a very careful history survey and analytical comment which he has followed up in a recent paper (1976), to which I return below. I am grateful to both these colleagues for much illumination. The discussion between them is also interesting.
5. In the early thirties discussion proceeded along the new lines in the Economic Club. In addition to Lindahl, Myrdal and myself, active participants were chiefly Dag Hammarskjöld, Alf Johansson, Karin Kock, Erik Lundberg, Tord Palander, and Ingvar Svennilson. The older economists were critical towards the new approach and its results. So was Johan Åkerman.
6. 'Till frågan om penningteorins uppläggning' (On the Question of the Method and Structure in Monetary Theory) (1933).
7. I do not know whether Keynes sent the English translation of Wicksell's paper to Kahn towards the end of 1931. Otto Steiger has referred to Paul Samuelson's observation that Mrs. Joan Robinson, who was a member of the 'Circus', published a paper in *Economica* in February 1933 which was still 'within the framework of *A Treatise on Money* . . . while she in another article in the *Review of Economic Studies* in October 1933 anticipated the essential parts of the *General Theory*' (Steiger (1976), p. 345, footnote 6). See also L. R. Klein (1947).
8. A further hitherto unpublished comment by me which was also discussed by Keynes is partly included in *JMK* XIV (pp. 186–201) (Ohlin, 1937b).
9. This construction I used from the autumn of 1932, when writing my paper that was circulated and later printed in the 1933 *Ekonomisk Tidskrift*, and in my Dublin lectures in 1934, which I later used as a basis for my first paper in the 1937 *Economic Journal*.
10. It would carry me too far if I were to comment on the methodological differences between Myrdal, Lindahl and myself, nor can I take up Lundberg's (1937) original and skilful use of quantitative simplified dynamic models with an inherent tendency to cyclical variations ('rocking horses'), which to some extent followed other lines than the Swedish publications in 1930–4.
11. Landgren (1960, p. 166). See my March 1937 *Economic Journal* paper about my inspiration from Wicksell, Lindahl and Myrdal and – as far as the expansionist attitude is concerned – from Keynes in the late twenties. Lindahl concentrated his interest on the price level development.

Appendix III 165

12. See Leijonhufvud (1968). pp. 333–4. He maintains that Keynes concentrates his attention in the *General Theory* on the problems of macroeconomic adjustment processes in the short run. In other words, he studies 'macrodisequilibrium' as an instrument of 'dynamic' analysis.

13. See Wicksell's 'The Monetary Problem of the Scandinavian Countries' (1925). In particular, see my quotation from this paper in Section 1 above.

14. See my 1934 report for the public committee on the causes of unemployment and means against it.

15. Myrdal, who originally was an 'equilibrium lover' with attention concentrated on price development, revised this paper in the direction of sequence analysis before the publication of the English translation in 1939. Lindahl also added some essential improvements before publishing his volume in English the same year.

16. I refer, for example, to Alf Johansson's report for the public committee on the causes of unemployment (1934). I made some critical comments on Keynes's wage policy analysis which have been reproduced in *JMK* XIV, pp. 196–9.

17. See Haberler, *Prosperity and Depression* (second ed. 1939). This revised edition gave a good account of some aspects of the Stockholm theory. In 1934 or 1935, when I presented a survey of the Swedish concepts and analysis in the Political Economy Club in Geneva, Haberler's comment was: 'There is one thing which economists like even less than to use each other's toothbrushes. It is to use each other's concepts'. He was very sceptical about the definition of savings as equal to investment.

18. Cf. my paper 'Ungelöste Probleme der gegenwärtigen Krisis' (Unsolved problems of the contemporary crisis') (1932).

19. Compare the above excerpts from my 'Introduction' with Keynes's views as reproduced in *JMK* XIV, pp. 85 and 119–23.

Bibliography

Brown, D. V. et al. *The Economics of the Recovery Program*. New York and London: Whittlesey House, McGraw-Hill, 1934.
Cannan, Edwin. *A Review of Economic Theory*. London: 1929. As reprinted A. M. Kelley, New York.
Clark, J. M. 'Business Acceleration and the Law of Demand: A Technical Factor in Economic Cycles.' *Journal of Political Economy* Vol. 25 (March 1917), pp. 217–35.
Dunlop, John T. 'The Movement of Real and Money Wage Rates.' *Economic Journal* Vol. 48 (September 1938), pp. 413–34.
Eshag, Eprime. *From Marshall to Keynes: An Essay on the Monetary Theory of the Cambridge School*. Oxford: Blackwell, 1963.
Fisher, Irving. *The Rate of Interest*. New York: Macmillan, 1907.
———. *The Purchasing Power of Money: Its Determination and Relation to Credit Interest and Crisis*. New York: Macmillan, 1911.
———. *The Theory of Interest*. New York: Macmillan, 1930.
Forster, E. M. *Maurice: a Novel*. London: Edward Arnold, 1971.
Friedman, Milton. *A Theory of the Consumption Function*. Princeton: Princeton University Press, 1957.
Frisch, Ragnar. 'Circulation Planning: Proposal for a National Organization of a Commodity and Service Exchange.' Parts I–II, *Econometrica* Vol. 2. (July–October 1934), pp. 258–336, 422–35.
Garvy, George. 'Keynes and the Economic Activists of Pre-Hitler Germany.' *Journal of Political Economy* Vol. 83 (March–April 1975), pp. 391–405.
Gustaffson, Bo. 'A Perennial of Doctrinal History: Keynes and the Stockholm School.' *Economy and History* Vol. 16 (1973), pp. 114–28.
Haberler, G. *Prosperity and Depression. A Theoretical Analysis of Cyclical Movements*, 2nd Edition, Geneva: League of Nations, 1939.
Harrod, R. F. *The Trade Cycle. An Essay*, Oxford: Clarendon Press, 1936.
———. *The Life of John Maynard Keynes*. London: Macmillan, 1951.
Hawtrey, R. G. 'Public Expenditure and the Demand for Labour.' *Economica* Vol. 5 (March 1925), pp. 38–48.
Hayek, F. A. von. 'Reflections on the Pure Theory of Money of Mr. J. M. Keynes.' *Economica* Vol. 11 (Aug. 1931), pp. 270–95; Vol. 12 (Feb. 1932), pp. 22–44.
Hicks, J. R. 'Mr. Keynes' Theory of Employment.' *Economic Journal* Vol. 46 (June 1936), pp. 238–53.
———. *Value and Capital: An Inquiry into Some Fundamental Principles of Economic Theory*. Oxford: Oxford University Press, 1939.
Howson, Susan and Donald Winch. *The Economic Advisory Council 1930–1939: A Study in Economic Advice During Depression and Recovery*. Cambridge University Press, 1977.
Johansson, A. *Löneutvecklingen och arbetslösheten* (The Development of Wages and Unemployment), Stockholm: Kungl. Boktryckeriet, 1934.

Bibliography

Johnson, Elizabeth. 'The Collected Writings of John Maynard Keynes: Some Visceral Reactions.' In *Essays in Modern Economics*, Proceedings of the Association of University Teachers of Economics, Aberystwyth: 1972.

———. 'John Maynard Keynes: Scientist or Politician?' *Journal of Political Economy* Vol. 82 (Jan./Feb. 1974), pp. 99–111.

——— and Harry G. Johnson. 'The Social and Intellectual Origins of the *General Theory*.' *History of Political Economy* Vol. 5 (Fall 1974), pp. 261–77.

Johnson, Harry G. 'An Error in Ricardo's Exposition of His Theory of Rent.' *Quarterly Journal of Economics* Vol. 62 (Nov. 1948), pp. 792–3.

———. 'The General Theory After Twenty-Five Years.' *American Economic Review* Vol. 51 (May 1961), pp. 1–17.

———. 'The Keynesian Revolution and the Monetarist Counter-Revolution.' *American Economic Review* Vol. 6 (May 1971), pp. 1–14.

———. 'Keynes and British Economics' in Milo Keynes ed., *Essays on John Maynard Keynes*. Cambridge: Cambridge University Press, 1975.

Kahn, Richard F. 'The Relation of Home Investment to Unemployment.' *Economic Journal* Vol. 41 (June 1931), pp. 173–98. As reprinted in Kahn (1972), pp. 1–27.

———. 'The Financing of Public Works: A Note.' *Economic Journal* Vol. 42 (September 1932), pp. 492–5.

———. *Selected Essays on Employment and Growth*. Cambridge: Cambridge University Press, 1972.

Keynes, John M. *The Economic Consequences of the Peace*. 1919. As reprinted in Keynes's *Collected Writings*, Vol. II.

———. *A Revision of the Treaty*. 1922. As reprinted in Keynes's *Collected Writings*, Vol. III.

———. *A Tract on Monetary Reform*. 1923. As reprinted in Keynes's *Collected Writings*, Vol. IV.

———. 'The German Transfer Problem.' *Economic Journal* Vol. 39 (March 1929), pp. 1–7; 'A Rejoinder' (June 1929), pp. 179–82.

———. *A Treatise on Money, Vol. I: The Pure Theory of Money*. 1930. As reprinted in Keynes's *Collected Writings*, Vol. V.

———. *A Treatise on Money, Vol. II: The Applied Theory of Money*. 1930. As reprinted in Keynes's *Collected Writings*, Vol. VI.

———. *Essays in Persuasion*. 1931. As reprinted with additions in Keynes's *Collected Writings*, Vol. IX.

———. 'An Economic Analysis of Unemployment.' In *Unemployment as a World Problem*, Harris Foundation Lectures, editor Quincy Wright. Chicago: University of Chicago Press, 1931, pp. 1–42. As reprinted in Keynes's *Collected Writings*, Vol. XIII, pp. 343–67.

———. 'The Pure Theory of Money: A Reply to Dr. Hayek.' *Economica* Vol. 11 (Nov. 1931), pp. 387–97. As reprinted in Keynes's *Collected Writings* Vol. XIII, pp. 219–36.

———. *Essays in Biography*. 1933. As reprinted with additions in Keynes's *Collected Writings*, Vol. X.

———. *The Means to Prosperity*. 1933. As reprinted with additions in Keynes's *Collected Writings*, Vol. IX, pp. 335–66.

———. *The General Theory of Employment, Interest and Money*. 1936. As reprinted in Keynes's *Collected Writings*, Vol. VII.

———. 'Alternative Theories of the Rate of Interest', *Economic Journal* Vol. 47 (June 1937), pp. 241–52. As reprinted in Keynes's *Collected Writings*, Vol. XIV, pp. 201–15.

———. 'Relative Movements of Real Wages and Output.' *Economic Journal* Vol. 49 (March 1939), pp. 34–51. As reprinted in Keynes's *Collected Writings*, Vol. VII, pp. 394–412.

———. *The General Theory and After, Part I: Preparation*. Edited by Donald Moggridge. Vol. XIII of Keynes's *Collected Writings*, 1973.

———. *The General Theory and After, Part II: Defense and Development*. Edited by Donald Moggridge. Vol. XIV of Keynes's *Collected Writings*, 1973.

———. *Activities 1906–1914, India and Cambridge*. Edited by Elizabeth Johnson. Vol. XV of Keynes's *Collected Writings*, 1971.

———. *Activities 1914–1919, The Treasury and Versailles*. Edited by Elizabeth Johnson. Vol. XVI of Keynes's *Collected Writings*, 1971.

———. *Activities 1920–1922, Treaty Revision and Reconstruction*. Edited by Elizabeth Johnson. Vol. XVII of Keynes's *Collected Writings*, 1977.

———. *Activities 1931–1939, World Crises and Policies in Britain and America*. Edited by Donald Moggridge. Vol. XXI of Keynes's *Collected Writings* (forthcoming).

———. *Collected Writings*. London: Macmillan for the Royal Economic Society, 1971–7.

——— and J. R. Ackerley. 'A Delicate Question of Payment.' *Encounter* Vol. 43 (Nov. 1974), pp. 24–8.

——— and Hubert Henderson. *Can Lloyd George Do It?: An Examination of the Liberal Pledge*. 1929. As reprinted in Keynes's *Collected Writings*, Vol. IX, pp. 86–125.

Klein, Lawrence R. *The Keynesian Revolution*. New York: Macmillan, 1947.

Knight, Frank H. *Risk, Uncertainty and Profit*. New York: Houghton Mifflin, 1921.

Kuhn, Thomas S. *The Structure of Scientific Revolutions*. Chicago: University of Chicago Press, 1962.

Landgren, Karl-Gustav. *Den 'nya ekonomien' i Sverige: J. M. Keynes, E. Wigforss, B. Ohlin och utvecklingen 1927–1939 (The 'New Economics' in Sweden: J. M. Keynes, E. Wigforss, B. Ohlin and the Development 1927–1939)*. Stockholm: Almqvist & Wiksell, 1960.

Leijonhufvud, Axel. *On Keynesian Economics and the Economics of Keynes*. New York: Oxford University Press, 1968.

———. 'Effective Demand Failures.' Department of Economics, University of California, Los Angeles: Discussion Paper Number 27, November 1972.

Lekachman Robert, ed. *Keynes' General Theory: Reports of Three Decades*. New York: St. Martin's Press, 1964.

Lerner, Abba. 'Some Swedish Stepping Stones in Economic Theory'. *Canadian Journal of Economics and Political Science* Vol. 6 (Nov. 1940), pp. 574–91.

Liberal Party. *Britain's Industrial Future. Being the Report of the Liberal Industrial Inquiry*. London: Ernest Benn, 1928. (The 'Yellow Book').

Lindahl, E. *Penningpolitikens medel* (The Means of Monetary Policy), Förlagsaktiebolagets i Malmö Boktryckeri, 1930.

———. *Studies in the Theory of Money and Capital*, London, 1939.

Lundberg, E. *Studies in The Theory of Economic Expansion*, Stockholm Economic Studies, No. 6, Stockholm: Kungl. Boktryckeriet, 1937.

Marget, Arthur W. *The Theory of Prices: A Re-Examination of the Central Problems of Monetary Theory.* Vol. I and II. 1938. Reprinted New York: Augustus M. Kelley, 1966.

Marris, Robin L. *The Economic Theory of Managerial Capitalism.* New York: Free Press, 1964.

Marshall, Alfred. *Principles of Economics.* 8th edition. London: Macmillan, 1920; 9th edition (with annotations by C. W. Guillebaud). London: Macmillan for the Royal Economic Society, 1961.

Marx, Karl. *Capital: A Critique of Political Economy*, 3 volumes (1867–1879). Chicago: Charles H. Kerr, 1906.

Moggridge, D. E. 'From the *Treatise* to the *General Theory:* An Exercise in Chronology.' *History of Political Economy* Vol. 5 (Spring 1973), pp. 72–88.

———. 'Keynes: The Economist.' In Moggridge (1974), pp. 53–74.

———. editor, *Keynes: Aspects of the Man and his Work.* London: Macmillan, 1974.

———. *Keynes.* London: Fontana and Macmillan, 1976 (published in the U.S. as a Penguin under the title *John Maynard Keynes*).

——— and Susan Howson. 'Keynes on Monetary Policy, 1910–1946.' *Oxford Economic Papers* Vol. 26 (July 1974), pp. 226–47.

Myrdal, G. *Prisbildningsproblemet och föränderligheten* (Pricing and the Change Factor), Uppsala: Almqvist & Wiksell, 1927.

———. 'Der Gleichgewichtsbegrift als Instrument der geldtheoretischen Analyse' in F. A. von Hayek, ed., *Beiträge zur Geldtheorie.* Vienna, 1933. [Revision and enlargement of the original Swedish version of 1931; see also Myrdal (1939)].

———. *Finanspolitikens ekonomiska verkningar* (The Economic Effects of Fiscal Policy), Arbetslöshetsutredningens betänkande II, bilagor, band 2, Statens offentliga utredningar 1934: 1, Stockholm: Kungl. Boktryckeriet, 1934.

———. *Monetary Equilibrium.* London: W. Hodge, 1939 [translation of Myrdal (1933), with some changes].

Ohlin, B. *Saet Produktionen I Gang* (Start Up Production Again) Copenhagen: H. Ascheboug & Co., 1927.

———. 'Transfer Difficulties, Real and Imagined.' *Economic Journal* Vol. 39 (June 1929), pp. 172–8.

———. 'Den internationella penningpolitiken och dess inverkan på konjunkturutvecklingen' (International Monetary Policy and its Influence on Business Activities and Development), Nordiska Nationalekonomiska Mötet, Stockholm, June 15–17, 1931, Haeggströms Boktryckeri, 1931.

———. 'Ungelöste Probleme der gegenwärtigen Krisis', *Weltwirtschaftliches Archiv*, 36. Band (1932 II), pp. 1–23.

———. 'Till frågan om penningteoriens uppläggning', (On the Question of the Method and Structure in Monetary Theory), *Ekonomisk Tidskrift*, XXXV, häft 2 (1933), pp. 45–81. (a)

———. *Interregional and International Trade*, Cambridge, Mass.: Harvard University Press, 1933. (b)

———. *Penningpolitik, offentliga arbeten, subventioner och tullar som medel mot arbetslöshet* (Monetary Policy, Public Works, Subsidies and Tariffs as Remedies for Unemployment), Arbetslöshetsutredningens betänkande, II, bilagor, band 4, Statens offentliga utredningar 1934:12, Stockholm: Kungl.

Boktryckeriet, 1934.
———. 'Introduction' to English translation of Knut Wicksell's *Interest and Prices* (1936), pp. vii–xxi.
———. 'Some Notes on the Stockholm Theory of Saving and Investment', *Economic Journal* Vol. 47, I (March 1937), pp. 53–69; II (June 1937) pp. 221–40. (a)
———. 'Some Notes on the Stockholm Theory of Saving and Investment' III (unpublished, 1937). Reproduced in part in Keynes's *Collected Writings*, Vol. XIV, pp. 191–200.(b)
———. 'Alternative Theories of the Rate of Interest: A Rejoinder' *Economic Journal* Vol. 47 (September 1937), pp. 423–7. (c)
———. *The Problem of Employment Stabilization.* New York: Columbia University Press, 1949.
———. 'On the Slow Development of the "Total Demand" Idea in Economic Theory: Reflections in Connection with Dr. Oppenheimer's Note.' *Journal of Economic Literature* Vol. 12 (September 1974), pp. 888–96.
Okun, Arthur. 'Inflation: Its Mechanics and Welfare Costs.' *Brookings Papers on Economic Activity* No. 2 (1975), pp. 351–90.
Patinkin, Don. 'The Chicago Tradition, the Quantity Theory, and Friedman.' *Journal of Money, Credit and Banking* Vol. 1 (Feb. 1969), pp. 46–70. As reprinted in *Studies in Monetary Economics* by Don Patinkin, New York: Harper and Row, 1972, pp. 92–117.
———. 'Samuelson on the Neoclassical Dichotomy: A Comment.' *Canadian Journal of Economics* Vol. 5 (May 1972), pp. 279–83.
———. 'Keynesian Monetary Theory and the Cambridge School.' in *Issues in Monetary Economics*, edited by H. G. Johnson and A. R. Nobay. Oxford: Oxford University Press, 1974, pp. 3–30.
———. 'The Collected Writings of John Maynard Keynes: From the *Tract* to the *General Theory*.' *Economic Journal* Vol. 85 (June 1975), pp. 249–70.
———. *Keynes' Monetary Thought. A Study of Its Development.* Durham: Duke University Press, 1976(a).
———. 'Keynes and Econometrics: On the Interaction Between the Macroeconomic Revolutions of the Interwar Period.' *Econometrica* Vol. 44 (Nov. 1976) pp. 1091–1123. (b)
Pigou, A. C. 'The Value of Money.' *Quarterly Journal of Economics* Vol. 32 (1917–1918), pp. 38–65.
———. *The Economics of Welfare.* London: Macmillan, 1920.
———. *Industrial Fluctuations.* 1st edition, 1927. 2nd edition. London: Macmillan, 1929.
———. *The Theory of Unemployment.* London: Macmillan, 1933.
———. *The Economics of Stationary States.* London: Macmillan, 1935.
———. *Employment and Equilibrium.* London: Macmillan, 1941.
———. '[Keynes:] The Economist.' In *John Maynard Keynes 1883–1946, Fellow and Bursar.* A Memoir prepared by direction of the Council of King's College Cambridge. Cambridge: University Press, 1949, pp. 21–3.
Proctor, P. D. '[Keynes:] At the Treasury, 1940–1946.' In *John Maynard Keynes 1883–1946, Fellow and Bursar.* Cambridge: University Press, 1949, pp. ·24–9.
Robertson, D. H. *Banking Policy and the Price Level.* London: P. S. King and Co., 1926. Reprinted with a new introduction. New York: Kelley, 1969.

———. 'Increasing Returns and the Representative Firm.' *Economic Journal* Vol. 40 (March 1930), pp. 80–9.
———. 'Industrial Fluctuations and the Natural Rate of Interest.' *Economic Journal* Vol. 44 (Dec. 1934), pp. 650–6.
Robinson, E. A. G. *The Structure of Competitive Industry*. London: Nisbet, 1931.
———. 'John Maynard Keynes 1883–1946.' *Economic Journal* Vol. 57 (March 1947): pp. 1–68. As reprinted in Lekachman (1964), pp. 13–86.
———. 'Could there have been General Theory without Keynes?' In Lekachman (1964), pp. 87–95.
———. 'John Maynard Keynes: Economist, Author, Statesman.' *Economic Journal* Vol. 82 (June 1972), pp. 531–46.
———. 'A Personal View.' In Milo Keynes (ed.) *Essays on John Maynard Keynes*, Cambridge: Cambridge University Press, 1975, pp. 9–23.
Robinson, Joan. 'A Parable on Savings and Investment.' *Economica* Vol. 13 (Feb. 1933), pp. 75–84.
———. 'The Theory of Money and the Analysis of Output.' *Review of Economic Studies* Vol. 1 (Oct. 1933), pp. 22–26. As reprinted in J. Robinson (1951), pp. 52–8.
———. *The Economics of Imperfect Competition*. London: Macmillan, 1933.
———. *Collected Economic Papers*, Vol. 1. Oxford: Blackwell, 1951.
———. 'What Has Become of the Keynesian Revolution?' In *After Keynes*, edited by Joan Robinson. Oxford: Blackwell, 1973, pp. 1–11.
Rueff, J. 'Mr. Keynes' Views on the Transfer Problem: A Criticism.' *Economic Journal* Vol. 39 (September 1929), pp. 388–99.
Salant, Walter S. 'A Note on the Effects of a Changing Deficit.' *Quarterly Journal of Economics* Vol. 53 (Feb. 1939), pp. 298–304.
———. 'The Demand for Money and the Concept of Income Velocity.' *Journal of Political Economy* Vol. 49 (June 1941), pp. 395–421.
———. 'Introduction to William A. Salant's "Taxes, the Multiplier and the Inflationary Gap."' In a symposium on 'Origins of the Balanced-Budget-Multiplier Theorem.' *History of Political Economy* Vol. 7, No. 1 (Spring 1975), pp. 3–18.
Samuelson, Paul A. 'Interactions between the Multiplier Analysis and the Principle of Acceleration.' *The Review of Economics and Statistics* Vol. 21 (May 1939), pp. 75–8.
———. 'Appendix: A Statistical Analysis of the Consumption Function.' In A. H. Hansen, *Fiscal Policy and Business Cycles*. New York: W. W. Norton, 1941, pp. 250–60.
———. 'Lord Keynes and the General Theory.' *Econometrica* Vol. 14, (1946), pp. 187–200. As reprinted in Lekachman (1964), pp. 315–31.
———. *Foundations of Economic Analysis*. Cambridge, Mass.: Harvard University Press, 1947.
———. 'The Simple Mathematics of Income Determination.' In L. A. Metzler et al., *Income, Employment and Public Policy: Essays in Honor of Alvin Hansen* New York: Norton, 1948, pp. 133–55.
———. 'A Brief Survey of Post-Keynesian Developments' (1963). In Lekachman (1964), pp. 331–47.
———. 'What Classical and Neoclassical Theory Really Was', *Canadian Journal of Economics* Vol. 1 (Feb. 1968), pp. 1–15.

——. 'The Balanced-Budget Multiplier: a Case Study in the Sociology and Psychology of Scientific Discovery.' In a symposium on 'Origins of the Balanced-Budget-Multiplier Theorem', *History of Political Economy* Vol. 7, No. 1 (Spring 1975), pp. 43–55.
Schumpeter, Joseph A. *The Theory of Economic Development*, trans. Redvers Opie. Cambridge, Mass.: Harvard University Press, 1934.
——. *Ten Great Economists: From Marx to Keynes*. London: George, Allen and Unwin, 1952.
——. *A History of Economic Analysis*. New York: Oxford University Press, 1954.
——. *Das Wesen des Geldes*, ed. Fritz Karl Mann. Göttingen: Vandenhoeck & Ruprecht, 1970.
Shove, Gerald. 'The Representative Firm and Increasing Returns.' *Economic Journal* Vol. 40 (March 1930), pp. 94–116.
Smith, Adam. *The Wealth of Nations* (1776), ed. E. Cannan. New York: The Modern Library, 1937.
Sraffa, Piero. 'The Law of Returns under Competitive Conditions.' *Economic Journal* Vol. 36 (Dec. 1926), pp. 535–50.
——. 'Increasing Returns and the Representative Firm: a Criticism.' *Economic Journal* Vol. 40 (March 1930), pp. 89–92.
Steiger, Otto. *Studien zur Entstehung der Neuen Wirtschaftslehre in Schweden: Eine Anti-Kritik*. Berlin: Duncker & Humblot, 1971.
——. 'Bertil Ohlin and the Origins of the Keynesian Revolution.' *History of Political Economy* Vol. 8, No. 3 (Feb. 1976), pp. 341–66.
Stein, Herbert. *The Fiscal Revolution in America*. Chicago: University of Chicago Press, 1969.
Strachey, John. *The Coming Struggle for Power*. London: V. Golancz, 1932.
Stuewer, Roger H. (ed.). *Historical and Philosophical Perspectives of Science*. Minnesota Studies in the Philosophy of Science, Vol. V, 1970.
Tarshis, Lorie. 'Changes in Real and Money Wages.' *Economic Journal* Vol. 49 (March 1939), pp. 150–4.
——. 'An Exposition of Keynesian Economics.' *American Economic Review* Vol. 38 (May 1948), pp. 261–72.
——. 'The Elasticity of the Marginal Efficiency Function.' *American Economic Review* Vol. 51 (December 1961), pp. 958–85.
Theiss, Edward. 'A Quantitative Theory of Industrial Fluctuations Caused by the Capitalistic Technique of Production.' *Journal of Political Economy* Vol. 41, 1933, pp. 334–49.
——. 'Dynamics of Saving and Investment.' *Econometrica* Vol. 3, 1935, pp. 213–24.
Uhr, Carl G. 'The Emergence of the "New Economics" in Sweden: A Review of a Study by Otto Steiger.' *History of Political Economy* Vol. 5 (Spring 1973), pp. 243–60.
Viner, Jacob. *Studies in the Theory of International Trade*. New York: Harper, 1937.
Wicksell, Knut. *Interest and Prices: A Study of the Causes Regulating the Value of Money* (1898). Translated by R. F. Kahn. London: Macmillan, 1936.
——. *Lectures on Political Economy*, translated by E. Claassen, and edited with an introduction by L. Robbins, Vol. 1, *General Theory* (1901) Vol. 2, *Money* (1906). London: Routledge, 1935.
——. 'The Monetary Problem of the Scandinavian Countries,' *Ekonomisk Tid-*

skrift (1925). English translation by Mrs. H. Norberg published as Appendix to Wicksell's *Interest and Prices* (1936).

Winch, Donald. 'The Keynesian Revolution in Sweden.' *Journal of Political Economy* Vol. 74 (April 1966), pp. 168–76.

———. *Economics and Policy: A Historical Study*. London: Hodder and Stoughton, 1969.

GOVERNMENT PUBLICATIONS

Committee on Finance and Industry (Macmillan Committee). *Hearings*. London: HMSO, 1931.

Memoranda on Certain Proposals Relating to Unemployment. Cmd. 3331, London: HMSO, 1929.

UNPUBLISHED MATERIALS

Bryce, Robert B. Notes on Keynes's Lectures at Cambridge, Autumn term 1932, 1933 and 1934. Handwritten notes deposited at Carleton University, Ottawa. Unchecked typewritten version of these notes filed in Keynes's Papers.

———. 'An Introduction to a Monetary Theory of Employment.' 1935 (published for first time in Appendix I to this volume).

Salant, Walter. Notes on Keynes's Lectures at Cambridge, Autumn term, 1934. Handwritten notes in Salant's possession.

Tarshis, Lorie. Notes on Keynes's Lectures at Cambridge, Autumn term, 1932, 1933, 1934 and 1935. Handwritten notes in Tarshis's possession.

Index of names

This index does not include an explicit entry for Keynes, for the vast majority of the entries in this index can effectively be read as 'Keynes and . . .'. Neither does it include references of programme-participants to one another in the course of Conference discussions. References to specific publications of an individual are listed chronologically by short-titles at the end of his entry.

Åkerman, Johan, 164n
Alexander, Sidney, 73
Alps, 30, 148
Alston, Leonard, 25
Anderson, John, 82
Apostles, Society of, 104, 113
Applied Economics, Department of, 33, 100–1, 107
Austrian Economics, 5

Baedeker, 79
Bagehot, Walter, 85
Baker, Philip Noel, 30
Bensusan-Butt, D. M., *see* Butt, David
Bladen, Vincent, 49
Bloomsbury Group, 28
Böhm-Bawerk, E. von, 5
Bowley, Arthur, 84
Britain's Industrial Future (1928), *see* 'Yellow Book'
Brown, Douglass, 44
Brown, John, 92
Bryce, Robert B., 33
  evangelist of K., 40, 68
  notes on K.'s lectures, 14–16, 24n, 47
  translates Myrdal, 75–6
Burn, Duncan L., 25
Butt, David, 33

Cairncross, Alec, 33, 50
Cambridge, 37, 71n
  academic arrangements at, 65, 100–6
  double revolution at, 27, 69
  isolation of faculty members, 65, 106
  K.'s half-week at, 32
  physical arrangements of, 65, 106–7
  research students at, 33, 68, 75, 129
  teaching style at, 111–12
  see also Department of Applied Economics; Faculty Board; King's College; Trinity College

Cambridge 'Circus', 20, 43, 62, 70n, 109
  criticisms of *TM*, 21, 33–6, 120
  information on, 64
  and Kahn as link to K., 33, 35, 67, 80, 148
  members of, 6, 28, 146–7, 164n
  period of activity, 6, 9, 25, 65
  and Schumpeter, 88
  and Swedish economics, 154
  too much claimed for, 6, 17, 80
  and 'widow's cruse fallacy', 6, 66
Cannan, Edwin, 106
Carnegie Foundation, 85
Cassel, Gustav, 151, 160
Cassel, Margit, 33, 161
Chamberlin, Edward, 44
Champernowne, David, 33
Chicago, University of, 50, 100
China, 78, 91
Christie, Agatha, 30
Churchill, Winston, 30
Clark, Colin, 37n, 50, 52, 68
Clark, J. M., 84–5
Clissold, 91, 96n
Cohen, Ruth, 107
Committee of Economists, 65, 120
Committee on Finance and Industry, *see* Macmillan Committee
Conant, James, 46

Darwin, Charles, 119
Davidson, David, 155, 156, 160
Davis, Eric, 119
Democratic Party, 100
Dennison, Stanley, 33
Department of Applied Economics, 33, 100–1, 107
Dobb, Maurice, 26, 27, 37n, 101, 105, 106
  as communist, 27, 101
Douglas, Paul H., 50
Dunlop, John T., 53, 147

175

Index of names

Eccles, Marriner, 46
Economic Advisory Council, 8, 26, 65, 71n, 120
Economic Journal
  K. as editor of, 31, 32, 161
Economics of the Recovery Program (1934), 44–5
Eisner, Robert, 78
England, *see* Great Britain
Eshag, Eprime, 70n
Eton, 32
Evans, Leslie, 25

Faculty Board, 29, 30, 103
Federal Reserve Board, 46
Fisher, Irving, 136
  and marginal efficiency of capital, 10, 87, 89n
  Rate of Interest (1907), 123–4
  Purchasing Power of Money (1911), 23n
  Theory of Interest (1930), 89n, 123–4
Food and Agricultural Organization (FAO), 109
Forster, E. M., 104
Foxwell, H. S., 98
France, 93
Friedman, Milton, 123–4
Frisch, Ragnar, 78

Garvy, George, 23n, 46, 84
Germany, 91, 92
  see also Index of subjects, German reparation payments
Gifford, Charles, 27
Girton, 26, 27
Great Britain
  unemployment of the 1920s, 42, 45, 66
Gregory, T. E., 149, 162
Guillebaud, Claude, 26, 28, 37n, 89, 89n, 104
Gustaffson, Bo, 76, 89n

Haberler, Gottfried, 165n
Halm, George, 76
Hammarskjöld, Dag, 164n
Hansen, Alvin H., 46
Harris Foundation, 4, 17, 48, 67, 124, 125
Harris, Seymour, 44
Harrod, Roy F., 89n, 111, 121
  as critic of *GT*, 10, 20–2, 24n, 36, 68
  Trade Cycle (1936), 159
  Life of Keynes (1951), 8, 63n, 146
Harvard, 44–5, 47, 73, 100
  Bryce at, 40–1
  Ohlin at, 161
  Salant at, 44

Schumpeter at, 44–5, 79, 88
Hawtrey, Ralph, 9, 68, 70n
  as critic of *TM*, 6–8, 49, 66
  as critic of *GT*, 5, 20–2, 36, 60
  and 'Treasury View', 84
Hayek, Friedrich von, 112, 154, 162
  as critic of *TM*, 5–6, 9, 66–7, 70n
  as critic of *GT*, 7, 21
  at LSE, 40–1, 74, 127
Heisenberg, Werner, 85
Henderson, Hubert, 26, 50, 69, 70, 162
  Can Lloyd George Do It? (1929), 9, 19, 77, 147
Hicks, J. R., 37n, 111, 121
  Value and Capital (1939), 123–4, 126
Higgins, Ben, 74, 88
Hollond, Marjorie, 26, 27, 37n
Hoover, Herbert, 48
Hopkins, Richard, 84
Hotson, J. H., 78
Howitt, Peter, 23n
Howson, Susan
  (and Moggridge) 'Keynes on Monetary Policy' (1974), 67
  (and Winch) *Economic Advisory Council* (1977), 8, 120
Hutchison, T. W., 33

Ickes, Harold L., 46
India, 90, 91
  East India Company, 50, 73
  Royal Commission on (1913), 90
Ingerman, S. H., 79
Innis, Harold, 49
International Monetary Fund, 43

Japan, 91
Joad, C. E. M., 113
Johansson, Alf, 164n, 165n
Johnson, Elizabeth, 23n
  (with H. G. Johnson) 'Social Origins *GT*' (1974), 122, 126n
Johnson, Harry
  (with E. Johnson) 'Social Origins *GT*' (1974), 122, 126n

Kahn, Richard, 37n, 115
  as 'angel messenger', 33, 36, 80
  and Cambridge 'Circus', 6, 33–6, 49
  contribution to *GT*, 79–81, 86–7
  and discussions related to *TM*, 66–8, 71n, 146, 148
  and discussions leading to *GT*, 13, 17, 21, 29, 33–6, 38n, 70, 79–81, 86–7
  fellowship dissertation, 148

Index of names

and imperfect competition, 27
at King's College in 1950s, 101–2, 107–8
lectures on 'The Short Period', 26, 53, 62, 148
and marginal efficiency of capital, 89n
and multiplier, 18–20, 24n, 67, 69, 81–4, 123, 146–7, 159
and Ohlin, 162
and Opie, 89n
and Political Economy Club, 50
and Schumpeter, 79
translator of Wicksell, 75–6, 150, 154, 164n
'Relation of Home Investment to Unemployment' (1931), see 'and multiplier' above
Kaldor, Nicholas, 103, 107, 108, 111
King's College
  and Cambridge 'Circus', 34
  High Table, 109, 148
  and homosexuality, 104
  and Kahn, 26, 102
  K. as bursar of, 32, 113
  K.'s supervisees at, 32, 72, 111
  and Pigou, 30, 110
  and Sraffa, 29, 148
Klein, Lawrence R., 81, 164n
Knight, Frank H., 160
Kock, Karin, 164n
Kuhn, T. S., 118, 122

Laidler, David, 23n
Landgren, Karl-Gustav, 76, 77, 152, 156, 164n
Lavington, Frederick, 26
Layton, Walter, 26
Leijonhufvud, Axel, 54, 121, 122, 158, 165n
Lenin, Vladimir, 41
Leontief, Wassily, 44
Lerner, Abba, 77, 85, 159
Lindahl, E., 74, 153, 155, 160, 164n, 165n
  Means of Monetary Policy (1930), 152, 154, 160
Lloyd, Cliff, 114
Lloyd George, D., 26, 93
London, K.'s half-week at, 32
London and Cambridge Economic Service, 44
London, Ontario, 1
London School of Economics, 5, 40, 71n, 74, 98, 127
Low, David, 50
Lundberg, Erik, 76, 77, 164n

Macmillan Committee, 4, 7–8, 65, 71n, 116, 120

Malthus, Robert, 37, 119
Manchester Guardian, 4, 90, 91, 110
Marget, Arthur W., 47
Marris, Robin L., 114
Marshall, Alfred, 112
  and Guillebaud, 28, 104
  influence on Cambridge, 27, 30, 37, 112
  interest theory, 53
  K.'s memoir on, 35, 94, 97n
  and Pigou, 98
  and value theory, 28, 50, 54, 155
  Principles, 28, 29, 49–50, 53
Marshall, Mary Paley, 89
Marshall Lectures, 162
Marshall Library, 29, 101, 107
Marshall Society, 50
Marx, Karl, 27, 41, 51, 52, 88
Mason, Edward, 44
Matthews, Robin, 105
Meade, James, 68, 112
  and Cambridge 'Circus', 6, 33–6, 66, 146, 147–8
Means, Gardiner, 47
Menken, Jules, 82
Merton, Robert, 122
Mill, J. S., 37, 53
MIT, 100
Modigliani, Franco, 121
Moggridge, Donald E., 23n
  account of Cambridge 'Circus', 6, 34
  'From *Treatise* to *GT*' (1973), 23n, 64, 146, 148n
  (and Howson) 'Keynes on Monetary Policy' (1974), 67
Moulton, Harold G., 46
Mynors, Humphrey, 26, 27, 37n
Myrdal, Gunnar, 74–7, 153, 160, 164n, 165n
  Monetary Equilibrium (1933), 75–6, 154–5, 159
  Economic Effects of Fiscal Policy (1934), 153

Napoleon, 88
Newmarch Lectures, 162
Newton, Isaac, 35, 37

Ohlin, Bertil
  and anticipations of *GT*, 76–7, 89n, 149–65
  at Cambridge, 33, 161–2
  and German reparations debate, 4, 113, 149
  paper rejected by K., 161–2
  and Stockholm School, 74–6
  'Start up Production Again' (1927), 152

Index of names

'International Monetary Policy' (1931), 161
'Unsolved Problems' (1932), 165n
Interregional and International Trade (1933), 162
'Monetary Policy . . .' (1934), 154, 159, 161
'Some Notes on the Stockholm Theory' (1937), 154–5, 164n
'Slow Development . . .' (1974), 154
Okun, Arthur, 47, 63n
Opie, R., 87, 89n
Oxford, 71n, 79, 113
  Harrod at, 20, 33, 146
  Meade at, 6, 33, 112
  Opie at, 87, 89n
  teaching style at, 111–12
  and *The Times*, 110
Oxford–Cambridge–LSE seminar, 71n

Palander, Tord, 164n
Patinkin, Don, 62
  'Chicago Tradition and Friedman' (1969), 126n
  'Samuelson on the Neoclassical Dichotomy' (1972), 126n
  'Keynesian Monetary Thought and the Cambridge School' (1974), 126n
  Keynes' Monetary Thought (1976), 23n, 24n, 35, 71n, 89n
Pigou, A. C.
  as Cambridge professor, 25–31 *passim*, 37, 98, 105, 110
  and Committee of Economists, 120
  critic of *TM*, 66, 70n
  and dates, 86–7
  and Keynes, 31, 95–6
  and Ohlin, 161
  and Political Economy Club, 50
  writes books to digest ideas, 30, 37n
  'The Value of Money' (1917–18), 23n
  Economics of Welfare (1920), 30
  Industrial Fluctuations (1927), 85
  Theory of Unemployment (1933), 37n
  Economics of Stationary States (1935), 37n
  Employment and Equilibrium (1941), 37n
  'Keynes: the Economist' (1949), 97n
Plumptre, A. F. W. (Wynn), 33
Political Economy Club, 52
  Bryce at, 39, 127
  discussions at, 43, 48–9, 73–4
  and Kahn, 49, 148
  K. at, 41, 50, 52, 68
  Ohlin at, 162
  participants in, 44, 50

Political Economy Club (Geneva), 165n
Political Economy Club (Stockholm), 160
Proctor, P. Dennis, 92, 95, 96n
PWA, 46

Ramsey, Frank, 113
Rao, V. K. R. V., 33
Reddaway, Brian, 33, 102
Republican Party, 100
Ricardo, David, 37, 87, 106
Robbins, Lionel, 98, 120, 162
Robertson, D. H., 26, 28, 29
  and Cambridge 'Circus', 36
  as Cambridge teacher, 25, 31–2, 37n, 39, 98
  discussions of *TM*, 8, 9, 66–7, 70n, 113
  discussions leading to *GT*, 6, 20–2, 36, 47–8, 68, 70
  and K., 31–2, 67, 69
  and Ohlin, 161–2
  and Pigou, 105
  and Political Economy Club, 50, 103–4
  Banking Policy and the Price Level (1926), 31, 42, 69
  'Symposium' (1930), 26
Robinson, Austin
  attends K.'s lectures, 67
  and Cambridge 'Circus', 6, 33–6, 66, 146–8
  as Cambridge teacher, 39, 146–8
  as co-editor *EJ*, 31, 32, 107
  and Faculty Board, 29, 148
  and Ohlin, 161
  and Political Economy Club, 50
  and Royal Economic Society, 107
  Structure of Competitive Industry (1931), 27
  'John Maynard Keynes 1883–1946' (1947), 8, 9
  'A Personal View' (1975), 69
Robinson, Joan, 29, 106
  and aggregate supply function, 62
  attends K.'s lectures, 24n, 67
  and Cambridge 'Circus', 6, 33–4, 66, 146–7
  as Cambridge teacher, 26, 37n, 39, 101–3, 146–7
  claims K. failed to perceive his revolution, 6
  correspondence with K., 24n, 64
  discussions of *TM*, 33–4, 148
  discussions leading to *GT*, 17, 21, 67–8
  and imperfect competition, 27, 79
  and index of *TM*, 148
  and Ohlin, 162
  and Political Economy Club, 50

'The Theory of Money and Output' (1933), 15, 65, 118, 164n
Economics of Imperfect Competition (1933), 27, 53, 79
'What Has Become of the Keynesian Revolution?' (1973), 6
Rolle's theorem, 116
Roosevelt, Franklin Delano, 46
Rowe, J. W. F., 37n, 50
Roy, Andrew, 104
Royal Economic Society, 107, 150
Rueff, J., 154
Russia, 85, 94, 96n, 97n
Rutherford, E. R., 37
Rymes, T. K., 24n

Salant, Walter, 33
notes on K.'s lectures, 24n
Samuelson, Paul A., 164n
'K. and the General Theory' (1946), 78
Foundations of Economic Analysis (1947), 109
'What Neoclassical Theory Really Was' (1968), 126n
Say's Law, 53, 84, 116, 118, 162
Schrödinger, E., 85
Schultz, Henry, 50
Schumpeter, Joseph, 106
on Kahn's role in writing *GT*, 70, 80
and marginal efficiency of capital, 87–8, 89n
rivalry with K., 87–8, 89n
visits to Cambridge, 79, 88
Wesen des Geldes, 89n
Theory of Economic Development (1934), 87
History of Economic Analysis (1954), 70, 87
Scitovsky, Tibor, 63n
Shakespeare, William, 86, 90
Shaw, Bernard, 88
Shove, Fredegond, 28
Shove, Gerald, 26, 28, 37n, 39, 67, 101
as conscientious objector, 28, 101
Sidney Sussex College, 148
Smith, Adam, 49
Snowden, Philip, 96n
Social Democrats (Sweden), 76
Sraffa, Piero, 37, 106
and Cambridge 'Circus', 6, 33–4, 66, 146–8
as Cambridge teacher, 26–7, 29, 37n
and discussions of *TM*, 69, 70n, 71n
and King's College, 29, 148
and Marxian economics, 52, 88
and Political Economy Club, 50, 52
and Schumpeter, 79

and Trinity, 29
Steiger, Otto, 77, 89n, 152, 164n
Stein, Herbert, 46
Stockholm School, 74–6, 149–61
simultaneous development of *GT*, 156
see also Ohlin; Wicksell
see also under Index of subjects
Stolper, Wolfgang (Wolfie), 75, 76, 88
Stone, Richard, 33, 107
Strachey, John, 51, 52
Stuewer, Robert H., 126n
Svennilson, Ingvar, 164n
Sweden, 76, 163
'Symposium', 26, 79

Tarshis, Lorie, 33, 147
notes on K.'s lectures, 14, 16, 24n, 47
Taussig, Frank W., 73
Taylor, Overton, 45
Thatcher, William S., 29
Theiss, Edward, 78
Thompson, J. J., 37
Tilton, 65, 70n
The Times, 110, 152
'Treasury View', 84, 147
Trinity College, 6, 29, 148
Truman, Harry, 46

Uhr, Carl G., 89n
United Kingdom, *see* Great Britain
United States, 84, 97n, 108
audience for K., 91
employment policy, 46

Versailles, Treaty of, 92, 95
Viner, Jacob, 22, 24n

Walker, Ronald, 50
Walras, Leon, 37
Warming, Jens, 147
Webb, Beatrice, 163
Webb, Sidney, 163
Weintraub, Sidney, 78
Wells, H. G., 91
Wicksell, Knut, 5, 162
and Cambridge 'Circus', 154
and cumulative process, 77, 152, 160
English translation of, 75–6, 149–50, 164n
and ex-post/ex-ante distinction, 155
influence on K., 77, 149, 154, 163
monetary theory of, 150–2, 158–9, 165n
and *TM*, 77
Interest and Prices (1898), 23n, 76, 77, 149, 163, 164n

Lectures on Political Economy (1906), 149
'Monetary Problem of the Scandinavian Countries' (1925), 150, 165n
Wilde, Oscar, 78
Wilson, Woodrow, 93
Winch, Donald
 Economics and Policy (1969), 89n, 122
 (and Howson) *Economic Advisory Council* (1972), 8, 120
Woolf, Virginia, 94
Wootton, Barbara, 30, 37n
World War I, 85, 163

Yale, 100
'Yellow Book', 82, 89n, 157
Yntema, Theodore, O., 27

Index of subjects

Aggregate demand (function), 11, 72
  in Stockholm theory, 154–7 *passim*
  see also effective demand, theory of; marginal propensity to consume; propensity to spend
Aggregate supply (function), 53, 56–63, 78, 132
  in Stockholm theory, 154–7 *passim*
  see also supply function
Austrian economics, 5

Capital accumulation, 140, 144
Closed economy, 82, 120, 140
Communists, 101
Creative process, nature of, 115–19, 122–4
Cumulative process, 77, 153, 160

Definitions
  in *TM*, 5, 42
  in *GT*, 40, 96, 128
Degrees, 'classes' of, 103
Diagrams and K., 11, 22, 72

Editor, K. as, 31, 32
  rejects Ohlin's paper, 161
Effective demand, theory of, 6, 11, 15, 119
Equilibrating mechanism, 11–18, 40, 48, 133–4
Ex-ante/ex-post, 154–5, 156, 159
Expectations, 79, 119, 135–6, 154–7

Foreign trade, 82, 140–1
Fundamental equations, 4–5, 125

General equilibrium, 21
Geography of economics, 98–9, 106
German reparations debate, 4, 113, 149, 154
Gestalt, 118–19
Gold standard, international, 119–20

Homosexuality, 104

Imperfect competition, 27, 62, 69, 79, 80
Index of *TM*, 148
Interest rate, 22, 135–9
International capital movements, 162

International trade, 82, 140–1
Isomorphism, 85–6

Journalism
  K.'s activities in, 3–4, 8, 90–1

Lecture notes, K.'s, 14, 24n, 39, 64
Lectures
  formal nature of at Cambridge, 105
  K.'s at Cambridge, 17, 39, 49–50, 63n, 67–8, 72–3, 129
Liquidity preference, 10, 137–8

Marginal analysis, not in *TM*, 7
Marginal efficiency of capital, 10, 87, 89n, 135–8, 142–3
Marginal propensity to consume, 11, 132–3
Marxian economics, 27, 51–2, 88
Monetary theory
  narrow view of in *TM*, 7
Morality play, 8–9, 33
Mountain climbing, 30
Multiplier, 18–20, 34–5, 81–6, 159

Open economy, 82, 120, 140
Output as equilibrating variable, 11, 76–7, 153

Pacifists, 28, 101
Paradigm, 78, 118
Period analysis, 154–7
Permanent-income hypothesis, 123–4
Polaroid camera, 117
Postal service, 20, 105–7
Propensity to spend (consume), 131–2
Public works, 82, 84–5
  distinct from *GT*, 9–10, 46, 48
  in Swedish economics, 77, 153–63 *passim*

Quantity theory, 147, 151

Rate of interest, 22, 135–9
Regression line, 125–6
Reparations payments, German, 4, 113, 149, 154
Revolution, double one at Cambridge, 27, 69
Rigor, not in K., 126

Rolle's theorem, 116

Simultaneous discovery, 77, 163
Sociology of science, 122
Spurious equilibrium 17, 67, 125
Sterling, 1931 devaluation of, 119–20
Stockholm School, 74–6, 149–61
    simultaneous development of *GT*, 156
    see also Index of names: Ohlin, Wicksell
Students, Commonwealth, 103
Substitution effect, 126
Supply function, 132–4
    see also aggregate supply function

Time-pressures on K., 7–8, 69–70, 71n

Transfer payments, *see* international capital movements; reparations payments, German
'Treasury view', 84, 147
Tripos, 26, 101, 103, 111

Uncertainty
    emphasised by K., 159–60
Unemployment, 3, 42, 45, 66, 153

Wage rate, 52–3, 129–30, 138–9, 143–4
Wicksellian economics, 5, 162
    see also Index of names: Wicksell
'Widow's Cruse', 6, 125